APOCRYPHAL GOSPELS

AN INTRODUCTION

HANS-JOSEF KLAUCK

Translated by
Brian McNeil

T & T CLARK INTERNATIONAL
A Continuum imprint
LONDON • NEW YORK

T&T CLARK LTD
A Continuum imprint

The Tower Building
11 York Road
London SE1 7NX, UK

15 East 26th Street
New York 10010
USA

www.continuumbooks.com

British Library Cataloguing-in-Publication Data
A catalogue record for this book is available from the British Library

ISBN 0 567 08390 X (Paperback)
ISBN 0 567 08918 5 (Hardback)

Typeset by Fakenham Photosetting Limited, Fakenham, Norfolk
Printed and bound in Great Britain by The Cromwell Press, Trowbridge, Wiltshire

CONTENTS

Introduction   1

1 Agrapha ('Scattered Words of Jesus')   6
  (a) Definition of the concept   6
  (b) Textual examples   8
  (c) Summary   19

2 Fragments   22
  (a) Papyrus Egerton 2   23
  (b) Papyrus Oxyrhynchos 840   26
  (c) The Strasbourg Coptic papyrus   27
  (d) The 'Unknown Berlin Gospel'   28
  (e) The 'Secret Gospel of Mark'   32

3 Jewish-Christian Gospels   36
  (a) The Gospel of the Hebrews   38
  (b) The Gospel of the Nazaraeans (?)   43
  (c) The Gospel of the Ebionites   51

4 Two Gospels of the Egyptians   55
  (a) The Greek text in Clement of Alexandria   55
  (b) The Coptic text from Nag Hammadi   59

5 Infancy Gospels   64
  (a) The Protevangelium of James   65
  (b) The Infancy Gospel of Thomas   73
  (c) The Gospel of Pseudo-Matthew   78

6 Gospels about Jesus' Death and Resurrection   82
  (a) The Gospel of Peter   82
  (b) The Gospel of Nicodemus (Acts of Pilate)   88
  (c) The Gospel of Bartholomew   99

7 Gospels from Nag Hammadi   105
  (a) The Gospel of Thomas   107
  (b) The Gospel of Philip   123
  (c) The Gospel of Truth   135

8 Dialogues with the Risen Jesus   145
  (a) The Sophia Jesu Christi   147
  (b) Epistula Apostolorum   152
  (c) The Gospel of Mary   160
  (d) The Apocryphon of John   169

9 Non-Localized Dialogues with Jesus   176
  (a) The Book of Thomas   176
  (b) The Dialogue of the Saviour   185

10 Legends about the Death of Mary   192
    (a) Typology and topology   192
    (b) A textual example   194

11 Lost Gospels   205

12 An Anti-Gospel: The Toledoth Yeshu   211

Conclusion   221

General Bibliography   226

Index of Selected Texts   229

Index of Matters and Persons   233

Index of Modern Scholars   235

INTRODUCTION

It is no easy matter to give a precise definition of 'apocryphal gospels', or indeed of apocryphal writings as a whole. One could simplify things by merely stating that the adjective 'apocryphal' covers all the texts collected in the *New Testament Apocrypha* (NTApo, cf. General Bibliography), which was first edited by Edgar Hennecke and has been brought up to date by Wilhelm Schneemelcher, but such a definition of our concept would be a circular fallacy, since the choice of texts included in this collection depends on a specific prior understanding of what 'apocryphal' means. Besides this, the contents of this work have varied considerably in its successive editions. For example, the first edition (1904) and the second (1924) included the 'apostolic fathers', viz. the first and second Letters of Clement, the Letters of Ignatius, the Letter of Polycarp, the Letter of Barnabas, the Didache, and the *Shepherd* of Hermas; and this group in its turn is an artificially assembled corpus which owes the name of 'apostolic fathers' to an edition of the texts in 1672.

From the third edition (1959) onwards, greater attention was paid in the *New Testament Apocrypha* to the Nag Hammadi texts (see ch. 7 below). Some new texts were added but later removed, e.g. the Letter to Diognetus and the Sentences of Sextus (both included only in the second edition), and the Odes of Solomon (included only in the second and third editions).

Christoph Markschies, who is preparing a new edition of this valuable collection of texts, has recently proposed that we should speak of 'ancient Christian apocrypha'. The term 'ancient' indicates a chronological restriction to the period of the early church; this is important, because apocrypha continued to be composed in the middle ages and in the modern period. 'Christian' is intended to detach the concept from its fixation with the New Testament. It is, however, an open question whether this disposes of all the terminological problems. It is also intended to remove the Nag Hammadi documents – including the Gospel of Thomas, the object of so much scholarly attention – from the collection and to publish a new complete translation of these works.

The word 'apocryphal' comes from the Greek (*apokruphos*) and means literally 'hidden, concealed, secret'. When it is applied to early Christian writings, it can have two meanings, which are antithetical and yet inter-related.

(1) The term 'apocryphal' is applied to *secret revelations* which are not included in the generally acknowledged corpus of revelatory documents, but are much more relevant – in the eyes of particular groups – than those doctrines which are professed and accepted in the public life of the church. In this case, the term 'apocryphal' has an

unreservedly positive meaning, and it is used in this sense, for example, in the writings of Clement of Alexandria.

(2) The adherents of orthodoxy in the *Grosskirche*, who defend a scriptural canon with clear boundaries, react by equating 'apocryphal' with *'falsified, unreliable'*. In the Gelasian Decree, a sixth-century list of the scriptural canon, 'apocryphal' appears in stereotypical manner alongside a large number of writings and means 'heretical'. The intention is to make it clear that such writings possess no kind of authority whatsoever.

Both these uses of the adjective 'apocryphal' define a relationship between these documents and the New Testament canon, which was basically defined towards the end of the third century. In regard to some of the so-called apocrypha, especially those composed at a later date, this correctly describes one factor which led to their production: the New Testament writings served as a criterion. The authors intended to complete these, to develop them, and to fill in supposed gaps; sometimes the intention was also to promote the author's own theological views, where these differed from the New Testament. This is why the great genres of the New Testament were adopted – Gospels, Letters, Acts of the Apostles and Apocalypses.

This perspective, however, fails to do justice to one important aspect. This is why Walter Rebell's definition of the apocrypha as 'rival texts to the New Testament' is applicable only to some of these writings, not by any means to their totality. Some of the texts which we call 'apocryphal' are from the early period, and became 'apocryphal' only at a later date, as Dieter Lührmann points out in his title: 'Fragments of gospels which became apocryphal'. This means that their genuine *Sitz-im-Leben* is the wide current of early Christian literature antecedent to the process of the formation of a scriptural canon. There was no such canon which could have provided a criterion for the authors or for the evaluation of their writings.

There is a recent tendency, prominent in North American scholarship (cf., e.g. Helmut Koester) though not found exclusively there, to argue that some 'apocryphal' texts are not only just as ancient as the New Testament, but in fact even older than the writings collected in the canon. Taken to its extreme consequences, this position holds that the 'apocrypha' were used as sources by the New Testament authors, and that they are accordingly of central significance for the recon- struction of the historical origins of Christianity. It is exceedingly difficult to maintain such an un-nuanced position, and one must be rather cautious about this whole line of argument, since it risks simply replacing an older ideology, which was convinced of the superiority of the canon, by a newer ideology, which favours a non-canonical, unorthodox, 'free' literature (and Christianity). (To take one example, John Dominic Crossan's blurb on the dust-jacket of the translations edited by Robert J. Miller makes promises that simply cannot be fulfilled: 'Everything you need to empower your own search for the historical Jesus.') Global judgements are out of place here. Rather, we must examine each individual case and only then construct the appropriate hypothesis; and even if our general impression tends more in the direction of the older assessment, this owes nothing to apologetic aims. On the contrary, it is the detached academic study of these texts (as far as detachment is possible) which leads to such a judgement.

Let me explicitly state one methodological option which plays a role here. When one compares gospels 'which have become apocryphal' with gospels 'which have become canonical', one must pay more attention than earlier scholars to a phenomenon brought to light in recent scholarship, viz. 'secondary orality' (on this, cf. the important work by Samuel Byrskog). In many cases, oral traditions are antecedent to the written texts, and these oral traditions continued to flow alongside the transmission of the texts. And it is very important to note that even material which had found a written form continued to be transmitted in oral form in the classical period. This is obvious in the case of the canonical gospels, when one reflects on the fact that they were regularly read aloud in worship. The narratives in the canonical gospels thus enter a phase of new, secondary orality, where these texts are exposed to a free reformulation and above all to a harmonizing assimilation of the various versions. This too may be a route which permitted the canonical gospels to exercise indirect influence on the composition of apocryphal texts.

In the selection of texts for this introduction to the apocryphal gospels, we shall have to proceed pragmatically, without letting ourselves be hampered too much by problems of definitions and the state of our available sources. The primary consequence of this approach is that we shall have to take into account the Nag Hammadi writings in several chapters of this book. The criteria guiding the treatment of a text in greater or less detail (or for omitting it altogether) are its antiquity, contents, significance, the extent to which it is known to readers, and its historical influence. I hope that the summaries, despite their brevity, and the bibliographical indications will encourage readers to set out on their own journeys of exploration in a fascinating world which is all too little known.

I conclude this Introduction with an example of a canon list – not because of the consistently negative evaluation of a whole list of theologians, but rather in order to give an idea of the quantity of apocryphal writings which were known in the sixth century. Our example is the Gelasian Decree, mentioned above (cf. NTApo I, 47–49; for further information, above all on the incriminated theologians, cf. E. von Dobschütz, TU 38,4 [1912]):

The remaining writings which have been compiled or been recognized by heretics or schismatics the catholic and apostolic Roman church does not in any way receive; of these we have thought it right to cite below some which have been handed down and which are to be avoided by catholics.

In the first place we confess that the Synod at Ariminum which was convened by the emperor Constantius, the son of Constantine, through the prefect Taurus is damned from then and now and for ever.

Itinerary (book of travels) under the name of the apostle Peter, which is called

The Nine Books of the holy Clement	apocryphal
Acts under the name of the apostle Andrew	apocryphal
Acts under the name of the apostle Thomas	apocryphal
Acts under the name of the apostle Peter	apocryphal
Acts under the name of the apostle Philip	apocryphal
Gospel under the name of Matthias	apocryphal
Gospel under the name of Barnabas	apocryphal
Gospel under the name of James the younger	apocryphal
Gospel under the name of Thomas, which the Manichaeans use	apocryphal
Gospel under the name of Bartholomew	apocryphal
Gospel under the name of Andrew	apocryphal
Gospels which Lucian has forged	apocryphal
Gospels which Hesychius has forged	apocryphal
Book about the childhood of the Redeemer	apocryphal
Book about the birth of the Redeemer and about Mary or the midwife	apocryphal
Book which is called by the name of the Shepherd	apocryphal
All books which Leucius, the disciple of the devil, has made	apocryphal
Book which is called The Foundation	apocryphal
Book which is called The Treasure	apocryphal
Book about the daughters of Adam: Leptogenesis (?)	apocryphal
Cento about Christ, put together in Virgilian lines	apocryphal
Book which is called The Acts of Thecla and of Paul	apocryphal
Book which is ascribed to Nepos	apocryphal
Books of the Sayings, compiled by heretics and denoted by the name of Sextus	apocryphal
Revelation which is ascribed to Paul	apocryphal
Revelation which is ascribed to Thomas	apocryphal
Revelation which is ascribed to Stephen	apocryphal
Book which is called The Home-going of the holy Mary	apocryphal
Book which is called The Penitence of Adam	apocryphal
Book about the giant Ogias, of whom the heretics assert that after the flood he fought with the dragon	apocryphal
Book which is called The Testament of Job	apocryphal
Book which is called The Penitence of Origen	apocryphal
Book which is called The Penitence of the holy Cyprian	apocryphal
Book which is called The Penitence of Jamnes and Mambres	apocryphal
Book which is called The Portion of the Apostles	apocryphal
Book which is called The Grave-plate (?) of the Apostles	apocryphal
Book which is called Canons of the Apostles	apocryphal
The book Physiologus, compiled by heretics and called by the name of the blessed Ambrose	apocryphal
The History of Eusebius Pamphili	apocryphal

Works of Tertullian	apocryphal
Works of Lactantius	apocryphal
(*later addition:* or of Firmianus or of the African)	
Works of Postumianus and of Gallus	apocryphal
Works of Montanus, of Priscilla and of Maximilla	apocryphal
Works of Faustus the Manichaean	apocryphal
Works of Commodianus	apocryphal
Works of the other Clement, of Alexandria	apocryphal
Works of Thascius Cyprian	apocryphal
Works of Arnobius	apocryphal
Works of Tichonius	apocryphal
Works of Cassian, a presbyter in Gaul	apocryphal
Works of Victorinus of Pettau	apocryphal
Works of Faustus of Riez in Gaul	apocryphal
Works of Frumentius Caecus	apocryphal
Epistle of Jesus to Abgar	apocryphal
Epistle of Abgar to Jesus	apocryphal
Passion (Martyr Acts) of Cyricus and of Iulitta	apocryphal
Passion of Georgius	apocryphal
Writing which is called Interdiction (Exorcism?) of Solomon	apocryphal
All amulets which have been compiled not, as those persons feign, in the name of the angels, but rather in that of the demons	apocryphal

These and the like, what Simon Magus, Nicolaus, Cerinthus, Marcion, Basilides, Ebion, Paul of Samosata, Photinus and Bonosus, who suffered from similar error, also Montanus with his detestable followers, Apollinaris, Valentinus the Manichaean, Faustus the African, Sabellius, Arius, Macedonius, Eunomius, Novatus, Sabbatius, Calistus, Donatus, Eustatius, Iovianus, Pelagius, Iulianus of Eclanum, Caelestius, Maximian, Priscillian from Spain, Nestorius of Constantinople, Maximus the Cynic, Lampetius, Dioscorus, Eutyches, Peter and the other Peter, of whom the one besmirched Alexandria and the other Antioch, Acacius of Constantinople with his associates, and what also all disciples of heresy and of the heretics or schismatics, whose names we have scarcely preserved, have taught or compiled, we acknowledge is to be not merely rejected but excluded from the whole Roman catholic and apostolic Church and with its authors and the adherents of its authors to be damned in the inextricable shackles of anathema for ever.

Bibliography

S. Byrskog, *Story as History*; H. Koester, *Ancient Christian Gospels*; D. Lührmann, *Fragmente apokryph gewordener Evangelien*; C. Markschies, '"Neutestamentliche Apokryphen". Bemerkungen zu Geschichte und Zukunft einer von Edgar Hennecke im Jahr 1904 begründeten Quellensammlung', *Apocrypha* 9 (1998) 97–132; R. J. Miller, *The Complete Gospels*; W. Rebell, *Neutestamentliche Apokryphen*, 11–20.

1

AGRAPHA ('SCATTERED WORDS OF JESUS')

(a) Definition of the concept

The Greek term *agrapha* means literally 'unwritten' words: in the present case, 'unwritten' logia of Jesus. However, such a designation is not particularly meaningful, since the utterances of Jesus which we shall study in this chapter have not been handed down to us in an oral version, but are usually found embedded in larger textual contexts. Roughly speaking, agrapha are logia of Jesus which we find outside the canonical gospels (hence the term 'extracanonical sayings'), logia which (with a few exceptions) our sources ascribe to the *earthly Jesus*. We could translate *agrapha* as 'words not recorded in the book', since they are not in the canonical 'book' of four gospels; the literal meaning, 'unwritten', would then mean that they are not contained in that part of 'Scripture' (the 'Writings') where we otherwise find the tradition about Jesus. It has also become customary to speak of 'unknown' or 'scattered' words of the Lord. Even a brief examination of the collected agrapha shows, however, that this does not resolve all the problems of definition and demarcation.

Although there were earlier attempts at a definition, this concept was first introduced to scholarship by Alfred Resch in the late nineteenth century. In his collection, which remains a fundamental work, he listed 194 agrapha, drawn mostly from the textual tradition of the New Testament and the works of the church fathers. He distinguishes these from the 'apocrypha', a term he applies principally to fragments of apocryphal gospels, as well as to extracanonical sayings of apostles and even to Old Testament quotations whose exact source cannot be verified. Unfortunately, this distinction between agrapha and apocrypha was later abandoned; the term 'agrapha' often covers material from the remains of the Jewish-Christian gospels, the fragments of apocryphal gospels on papyrus, and especially the newly discovered Gospel of Thomas. This, however, is unhelpful, since the logia of Jesus transmitted in such texts normally possess their own independent literary context, which supplies the framework in which they ought to be discussed. They should not be isolated from this context and listed among the agrapha.

After Resch's work, Michael Asín y Palacios collected a wealth of material from Muslim authors. In two fascicles of the *Patrologia Orientalis*, he offers a total of 233 Arabic texts with a Latin translation and explanation. Exegetes have paid astonishingly little attention to this collection.

Instead, German-speaking scholarship took another path. In his well-known and influential book *Unbekannte Jesusworte*, a work of great merit, Joachim Jeremias limited himself to the study of eighteen agrapha (or twenty, if we include the two logia discussed in the appendix), characteristically including also texts from the Gospel of the Hebrews, the Gospel of the Nazaraeans, the Gospel of Thomas and the gospel fragment POxy 840. Otfried Hofius, who has taken it upon himself to look after Joachim Jeremias's inheritance, again drastically reduces the number of agrapha, so that ultimately only seven are included in the sixth edition of NTApo I.

This reduction is governed by the principle that the extracanonical logia which merit discussion should be comparable to Jesus' logia in the synoptic gospels in terms of form, contents and tradition-history. For Jeremias in particular, another important factor is whether historical authenticity can at least be taken seriously as a possibility, and we should note that this question is linked with a clear evaluation of the texts at issue: 'Only here and there among the rubble and trash do we glimpse the sparkle of a precious stone' (*Unbekannte Jesusworte,* 112). It is indisputable that such questions must be discussed, but it is highly doubtful whether they should govern the initial selection of texts, especially in view of the virtual impossibility of achieving certain results: this means that subjective assessment will always play some role. Ultimately, this critical process of reduction has led agrapha-research into a cul-de-sac.

In view of this, more recent collections propose new paths. In his useful collection, William D. Stroker cites 266 texts (though these include virtually the entire Gospel of Thomas). Klaus Berger and Christiane Nord offer a total of 270 agrapha. They make use of the first fascicle of Asin y Palacios's publications of logia of Jesus in Muslim writers, but they ignore his second fascicle.

It is clear that a more precise analysis reveals the concept of 'agrapha' to be a very nebulous category. What is left – especially if we make a decided plea for separate treatment of the Jewish-Christian gospels and the Gospel of Thomas?

One can continue to employ 'agrapha' as a heuristic instrument which allows us to detect logia of Jesus which are transmitted outside the gospels and do not fall under our other categories (e.g., 'fragments of apocryphal gospels'). Alfred Resch showed that most of these are logia quoted by the church fathers, together with other material of various provenance. If it is necessary to pose the question of authenticity, this should not be done too prematurely.

The following presentation and discussion of a few selected agrapha is intended primarily as an exemplary illustration of what we have just affirmed. We present most of those logia which are found in all of the standard collections; we have also endeavoured to include examples drawn from the variety of sources in which agrapha can be found. Some examples help to show more clearly the problems of demarcation and definition. They also indicate why agrapha came into existence.

(b) Textual examples

(1) Giving and receiving

If we define agrapha as logia of Jesus found outside the canonical gospels, our earliest examples can be found in the New Testament itself. The most important instance is in Luke's Acts of the Apostles. In the farewell discourse which Paul holds in Miletus to the elders of the Ephesian community, he states:

In all things I have shown you that by so toiling one must help the weak, remembering the words of the Lord Jesus, how he said, 'It is more blessed to give than to receive.' (Acts 20:35)

The logion which Luke's Paul quotes is not found in the gospels, not even in that of Luke himself – although it would fit in very well there, given that Luke gives greater emphasis than the other evangelists to the societal motifs in the message of Jesus. Luke has even been called 'the evangelist of the poor'; we need not discuss here whether such a designation is wholly appropriate. At any rate, Paul's words and his conduct (cf. his reference at 20:33f. to his refusal to accept support from the communities, since he prefers to work with his own hands) show that, even if his circumstances are somewhat different from those of Jesus, he is a genuine disciple and follower of the Lord.

Nevertheless, this text does not attain the radical dimension of some of Jesus' logia in the gospel, which demand a complete renunciation of private property; and we are not surprised to note that non-Christian and non-Jewish ethics in antiquity likewise emphasised the priority of giving over receiving. It suffices to quote one passage from Thucydides (2.97.4): '[The Thracians] introduced a custom different from that in the realm of the Persians ..., *that one should prefer to give rather than to receive.* It was more shameful not to give, if one was asked to do so, than not to receive, if one had made a request.'

(2) The coming of the Lord

Paul himself quotes a few logia of Jesus in his letters. Since most of these have parallels in the synoptic tradition about Jesus, they cannot be considered agrapha: this applies to the prohibition of divorce (1 Cor 7:10f.), to the interpretative words in the account of the Last Supper (1 Cor 11:24f.), to Paul's remarks on the right of itinerant missionaries to receive material support (1 Cor 9:14), and to the affirmation that all foods are pure (Rom 14:14). Resch and Berger and Nord argue that the commandment that women should keep silent (1 Cor 14:34f.) should be included among the agrapha, but this is unlikely, even though the expression 'command of the Lord' is found a few verses later (v. 37). The 'word of the Lord' at 2 Cor 12:9 – 'My grace is sufficient for you' – is something that Paul himself heard said by the risen Lord. The main candidate for inclusion in a list of agrapha is 1 Thess 4:15–17:

[15] For this we declare to you by the word of the Lord, that we who are alive, who are left until the coming of the Lord, shall not precede those who have fallen asleep. [16] For the Lord himself will descend from heaven with a cry of command, with the archangel's call, and with the sound of the trumpet of God. And the dead in Christ will rise first; [17] then we who are alive, who are left, shall be caught up together with them in the clouds to meet the Lord in the air; and so we shall always be with the Lord.

No quotation marks are employed within this English translation, since it is unclear where the supposed 'word of the Lord' is to be found: in v. 15 alone (beginning with the words 'we who are alive') or perhaps rather in the substance of vv. 16–17? It is at any rate clear that we must assume that Paul has set his own imprint very deeply on any such logion: he speaks everywhere of 'the Lord' in the third person, and this scarcely accords with the perspective of a 'word of the Lord', which would surely have used the first person. It also remains unclear whether Paul intends to refer to a logion of the earthly Jesus or to a revelation of the risen Lord. Since we are not exclusively interested in the question of authenticity, it is not so important to discuss the hypothesis that this passage refers to a word uttered by an early Christian prophet, which Paul picks up and makes more authoritative by attributing it to Jesus himself.

(3) Use and abuse of freedom

A further quarry of agrapha is the manuscript transmission of the New Testament. Occasionally, gospel manuscripts contain additions which may be secondary from a text-critical perspective, but nevertheless appear to have access to a still-extant oral tradition about Jesus. Thus, for example, the Codex Bezae Cantabrigiensis (abbreviation: D) from the fifth century offers, between the pericope about the disciples who pluck ears of corn (Lk 6:1–5) and the healing of the withered hand on the sabbath (Lk 6:6–11), the following short narrative, which fits the context and is complete in itself. Like an apophthegm, it consists of a brief indication of the situation and a pointed logion of Jesus (Lk 6:5 D; the original v. 5 in Luke, 'The Son of man is lord of the sabbath', is omitted at this point by D, which inserts it only after Lk 6:10):

When on the same day he saw a man doing work on the sabbath, he said to him: 'Man! If you know what you are doing, you are blessed! But if you do not know it, you are accursed and a transgressor of the law.'

This presupposes the biblical Jewish precept governing sabbath observance, which includes a prohibition of work (cf. the story of the man who collected wood on the sabbath day and was punished by death: Num 15:32–36). The logion with which Jesus reacts to this breaking of the law consists of three parts: the address 'Man!', a conditional blessing and a conditional curse. Both times, the condition runs: 'If you know/do not know'. Hence, the emphasis lies on knowledge, though this is not to be interpreted here in a purely gnostic sense (*gnosis* means 'knowledge'), as if the logion intended to assert that the true gnostic – and he alone – is superior to every law. Nor does it seem that the primary interest of this logion is the continuing validity or obsoleteness of the Jewish law; rather, the law serves as a practical example.

It is more helpful to situate this logion within a discussion among Christians about the meaning of Christian freedom, especially when we recall the serious threat posed by a Christian libertinism (cf. 'All things are lawful', 1 Cor 10:23 – Paul at once adds, 'But not all things are helpful ... but not all things build up'). Right knowledge would then mean the awareness that freedom is not a state where one is not bound in any way at all, but rather a new state of being bound in faith and love (cf. W. Käser, 'Exegetische Erwägungen zur Seligpreisung des Sabbatarbeiters Lk 6,5 D', *ZThK* 65 [1968] 414–30; T. Nicklas, 'Das Agraphon vom "Sabbatarbeiter" und sein Kontext: Lk. 6:1–11 in der Textform des Codex Bezae Cantabrigiensis (D)', *NT* 44 [2002] 160–75).

(4) Unbelief and repentance

The gospel of Mark ends very abruptly at 16:8 with the flight of the women from the tomb they have found empty. This conclusion was felt to be unsatisfactory, as we see from a number of manuscripts which present Mk 16:9–20, a second-century compilation from the other gospels' accounts of the apparitions of the risen Jesus; there exist shorter conclusions too. This secondary longer conclusion relates in v. 14 that Jesus 'upbraided the eleven for their unbelief and hardness of heart, because they had not believed those who saw him after he had risen'. Without any transition, vv. 15–18 present a missionary address by the risen Jesus; v. 19 then relates his ascension to heaven, and v. 20 summarizes the great success of the disciples' preaching after Easter. Vv. 15–18, which have the form of direct speech, have sometimes been included among the agrapha, although these are words of the risen Jesus.

The fifth-century Freer gospel codex (abbreviation: W), which is preserved today in the Freer Library in Washington (named after its benefactor), inserts the so-called "Freer logion" between vv. 14 and 15. Jerome seems familiar with this logion, which consists of a little dialogue between Jesus and his disciples (cf. J. Frey, 'Zu Text und Sinn des Freer-Logion', *ZNW* 93 [2002] 13–34). This would entitle us to follow NTApo I and include it among the 'Conversations between Jesus and his disciples after the resurrection'. The most obvious functions of this text are to soften the abruptness of the transition between v. 14 and v. 15 and to explain how it was possible for the disciples to fall into unbelief again after Easter (Mk 16:14 W):

And they excused themselves with the words, 'This aeon of lawlessness and unbelief is under Satan, who through the unclean spirits does not allow the true power of

God to be comprehended. Therefore,' they said to Christ, 'reveal your righteousness now.' And Christ replied to them, 'The measure of the years of Satan's power is filled up. But other fearful things draw near, also (for those) for whom I, because they sinned, was delivered to death, that they might turn back to the truth and sin no more in order to inherit the spiritual and imperishable glory of righteousness (preserved) in heaven.'

In view of Satan's apparently undiminished sovereignty over this age of the world (cf. 2 Cor 4:4), the disciples ask the Lord to inaugurate the state of perfection as soon as possible. The risen Jesus confirms that the power of Satan has already been broken through his work on earth (cf. Lk 10:18) and his death on the cross (cf. Jn 12:31). Nevertheless, the events of the last days, with the terrible phenomena that will accompany them, must still be awaited, in order that as many sinful persons as possible may have the chance to do penance in time and thus come to share in eternal life (cf. 2 Pet 3:9).

(5) Variations on the golden rule

The name 'apostolic fathers' (not in itself a particularly meaningful term) is applied to a group of early Christian writings with chronological proximity to the New Testament. One of these is the first Letter of Clement, probably composed by bishop Clement of Rome and sent to Corinth between 93 and 97 CE. When he writes at 13:1, 'Especially remembering the words of the Lord Jesus which he spoke when he was teaching gentleness and long-suffering,' Clement is definitely referring to the earthly Jesus, and he continues (13:2),

> For he [Jesus] spoke thus:
> 'Be merciful, that you may obtain mercy.
> Forgive, that you may be forgiven.
> As you do, so shall it be done to you.
> As you give, so shall it be given to you.
> As you judge, so shall you be judged.
> As you are kind, so shall kindness be shown to you.
> The measure which you use to measure
> will be used to measure you.'

It is not easy to understand why this little composition, consisting of seven logia of Jesus, is not included in some collections of agrapha, since all the formal requirements for inclusion are satisfied here. Apart from the sixth logion, which exhorts the readers to be kind, we perceive everywhere echoes of the Sermon on the Mount, and all the logia are variations and concretizations of the golden rule (cf. Mt 7:12), which is explicitly formulated in the third exhortation. However, in view of the early date of this text, its author is probably still drawing directly on the oral tradition about Jesus, rather than using the Gospel of Matthew as his immediate source.

(6) Conditions of entry into the kingdom

The Letter of Barnabas, composed *c.* 130 CE, refers less clearly to logia of the Lord, but we should mention the remarkable account and interpretation of the Old Testament rite of the scapegoat (Barn 7:6–11) which concludes with an application placed on the lips of Jesus. In formal terms, this looks like a logion of Jesus (Barn 7:11):

> Those who wish to see me and attain to my kingdom must lay hold of me through tribulation and suffering.

These words formulate a condition of entry into the kingdom of God, as e.g. at Mt 5:20. In such contexts, however, which are steeped in the atmosphere of the Old Testament, we must always ask whether a word spoken by Jesus is not meant to be understood as an utterance of the pre-existent Christ, who already knows what will happen in the future and anticipates his earthly history by relating the biblical promises to his own self.

(7) Paradisal conditions

The next agraphon, which is particularly extensive, is transmitted to us only in a series of textual refractions. In the early second century, Papias, bishop of Hierapolis, undertook researches and published the logia of Jesus which he had been able to discover in a collection in several volumes entitled: *Exposition of the words of the Lord*. Irenaeus of Lyons quotes from this work, but he also appeals at the beginning of the following text to presbyters who had heard this logion from the apostle John, before he speaks, towards the end of our text, about its attestation in Papias (*Adversus Haereses* 5.33.3f.):

> The elders who saw John, the disciple of the Lord, related that they had heard from him how the Lord used to teach in regard to these times, and say: 'The days will come, in which vines shall grow, each having ten thousand branches, and in each branch ten thousand twigs, and in each true twig ten thousand shoots, and in each one of the shoots ten thousand clusters, and on every one of the clusters ten thousand grapes, and every grape when pressed will give one thousand litres of wine. And when any one of the saints shall lay hold of a cluster, another shall cry out, "I am a better cluster, take me; bless the Lord through me".' In like manner [the Lord declared] that a grain of wheat would produce ten thousand ears, and that every ear should have ten thousand grains, and every grain would yield ten pounds of clear, pure, fine flour; and that all other fruit-bearing trees, and seeds and grass, would produce in similar proportions; and that all animals feeding on the productions of the earth should become peaceful and harmonious among each other, and be in perfect subjection to human beings. And these things are borne witness to in writing by Papias, the hearer of John and a companion of Polycarp, in his fourth book; for there were five books compiled by him. And he says in addition: 'Now these things are credible to believers.' And he says that when the traitor Judas did not believe this and asked, 'How can such growth be

brought about by the Lord?', the Lord declared, 'Those who shall come to these [times] shall see.'

In this passage, Judas – the prototype of unbelief – is surely the representative of all those hearers who were sceptical about this prediction of the future, which promises that paradisal conditions will return in the messianic age, still thought of here in innerworldly terms. Contemporary Jewish apocalyptic is also familiar with the motif of the miraculous fertility of the earth as a characteristic of the messianic age; it suffices here to quote one text from the Apocalypse of Baruch (SyrBar 29:5), 'The earth also shall yield its fruit ten thousandfold; and on each vine there shall be a thousand branches, and each branch shall produce a thousand clusters, and each cluster produce a thousand grapes, and each grape produce a cor of wine.'

(8) Near and far

We shall discuss the papyrus fragments in the next chapter of this book, but we present one text as an example here, not least because the agraphon occurs – somewhat surprisingly – in a context which is otherwise familiar. This is a fragment of papyrus found at Oxyrhynchus and dated to the fourth century (POxy 1224):

> And the scribes and <Pharisees
> and priests, when they sa<w
> him, were angry <that with sin-
> ners in the midst he <reclined
> at table. But Jesus heard <it and said:
> 'The he<althy need not the physician.
> ... And pray for
> your enemies. For he who is not
> <against you> is for you.
> He who today> is far-off – tomorrow will be
> near to you>.'

We know lines 1–6 from the account of the meal with tax collectors in Mk 2:16f. Lines 7–8 contain an echo of Mt 5:44, and lines 8–9 are well known to us from Mk 9:40. The agraphon comes in lines 9f. Another reconstruction is also possible: 'Those who stood far off – their hour will be tomorrow' (cf. perhaps Is 57:19, 'Peace, peace to the far and to the near, says the Lord; and I will heal them').

(9) Divisions

This brings us to the apologists. In his *Dialogue* with the Jewish rabbi Trypho (or Tarphon), Justin quotes the following words of Jesus, which are attested in part in the synoptic gospels (*Dialogue* 35.3):

For he [Jesus] said, 'Many will come in my name [Mk 13:6], externally clothed in sheep's clothing. But inwardly they are ravenous wolves [Mt 7:15],' and: 'There will be divisions and factions,' and: 'Beware of false prophets . . .'.

When Jesus speaks in the gospels of the end of the world, he regularly predicts divisions, which will cut across even the closest family ties (e.g. Lk 12:52f.), but it is not here that we find the closest parallel to the words: 'There will be divisions and factions'. This parallel is in Paul (1 Cor 11:18f.):

In the first place, when you assemble as a church, I hear that *there are divisions* among you, and I partly believe it, for *there must be factions* among you in order that those who are genuine among you may be recognized.

The parallel led Alfred Resch to conclude that Paul is quoting here from an eschatological discourse of Jesus; but it is more probable that an affirmation by Paul has been subsequently transformed into a logion of Jesus. This logion is found in other early Christian and patristic texts, e.g. in the Pseudo-Clementine homilies (where it occurs twice), in the Syriac Didascalia, in Lactantius and Didymus.

(10) The standard employed at the judgement

In the same work, Justin quotes another logion in which Jesus as it were freezes fast the state in which the Lord at his coming finds each individual, and makes this state the criterion of judgement (*Dialogue* 47.5):

Wherefore also our Lord Jesus Christ said, 'In whatsoever things I shall take you, in these I shall judge you.'

The fourth-century Syriac *Liber Graduum* ('Book of Steps'), which indicates the various stages by which Christian perfection may be attained, has a different formulation, but makes the same point. The Lord will send out his angels at the end of the world (cf. Mt 13:41) to assemble all human beings for the imminent judgement, and we are told (*Sermo* 3.3, and frequently):

As you are found, so you will be carried off!

This affirmation occurs, not as a logion of Jesus but as a 'word of God' or a prophetic utterance, eighteen times in patristic literature, beginning with Clement of Alexandria. It may be based on Ezek 33:20, 'O house of Israel, I will judge each of you according to his ways', perhaps as mediated by the Jewish Apocryphon of Ezekiel.

(11) Praying without cease

We remain in fourth-century Syria, and turn to the church father Afrahat. In his discourse on prayer, he writes (*Demonstrationes* 4.16):

Our Lord said: 'Pray and do not become weary.'

In the introduction to the parable of the unjust judge and the widow who comes with her petition, which belongs to the special Lukan material, we read: 'And he told them a parable, to the effect that they ought always to pray and not lose heart (18:1).' Once again, we must choose between the alternatives. Resch held that Luke had taken a logion of Jesus and cast it into narrative form; but it is more likely that later writers changed the indirect speech in Luke into direct speech on the part of Jesus.

(12) Close to the fire

We come now to Origen, the greatest exegete and theologian of the early church. In his sermons on the book of Jeremiah, which survive only in Rufinus' Latin translation, he prefaces the quotation of an agraphon with words remarkable for their caution. Nevertheless, he does in fact quote it – he does not reject it out of hand (*In Jeremiam Homiliae* 3.3):

I have read somewhere as a word of the Saviour (and I wonder whether someone has taken over the role of the Saviour, or has quoted from memory, or whether what is said here is true). At any rate, the Saviour says in that place: 'The one who is close to me is close to the fire. The one who is far from me is far from the kingdom.'

The Greek version of these words is quoted by the Alexandrian theologian Didymus the Blind, who died *c.* 398. They are reminiscent of synoptic logia such as Lk 12:49, 'I came to cast fire on the earth; and would that it were already kindled!', or Mk 9:49: 'Every one will be salted with fire.' The image of fire symbolizes the intensity with which the good news of God's sovereignty wishes to take hold of human beings, purifying and transforming them; and this good news is to spread like a bush fire. We may also recall a proverb attributed to Aesop: 'One who is near Zeus is near the lightning', which, however, is a warning against drawing too close to the god.

This logion about the fire and the kingdom is nr. 82 in the Coptic Gospel of Thomas; strictly speaking, therefore, the Nag Hammadi discoveries mean that this logion no longer has the status of an agraphon. Since Origen mentions a 'Gospel of Thomas' in another text, it is certainly possible that he found this logion in a Greek version of the Gospel of Thomas which we know in Coptic.

(13) The path into the kingdom of heaven

In his treatise on baptism, Tertullian recounts the story of Jesus on the Mount of Olives and quotes Mk 14:38, 'Watch and pray that you may not enter into temptation.' He pursues the theme of the temptation of the disciples during Jesus' passion, and adds (*De baptismo* 20.2):

For this word had already been spoken: 'No one can attain the kingdom of heaven unless he passes through temptation.'

It seems that Tertullian situates this logion in the context of the Last Supper (perhaps because of Lk 22:28f.), either as a part of the discourse at table or en route to Gethsemane. The other eight patristic witnesses (including the Didascalia and the Apostolic Constitutions) do not present it as a logion of Jesus. The same theme occurs in Acts 14:22, when Paul and Barnabas tell the communities which they have founded on their pastoral journey: 'Through many tribulations we must enter the kingdom of God', and at Jas 1:12: 'Blessed is the man who endures trial, for when he has stood the test he will receive the crown of life.'

(14) Saving one's life

Clement of Alexandria made excerpts from the writings of Theodotus, a pupil of the second-century gnostic teacher Valentinus. According to Clement, Theodotus transmitted the following words as a logion of Jesus (*Excerpta ex Theodotou* 2.2):

This is why the Saviour says: 'Save yourself and your life!'

These words are startlingly reminiscent of the command issued by the angel to Lot at Gen 19:17 when he tells him to get out of Sodom: 'Flee for your life!' This scene is recalled in the eschatological discourse of Jesus (Lk 17:29,32), who also emphasizes the urgency of flight from the terrible events of the last days (cf. also Mk 13:14–16), and this means that the imperative is not necessarily: 'Save your soul!' (although that would certainly have been in accord with the gnostic perspective). It can also be understood to mean: 'Seek a safe place of refuge in good time, before the catastrophe comes.'

(15) Great and small

Clement of Alexandria supplies a further logion, which we could also quote in versions by Origen, Eusebius or Ambrose. In his great work *Stromateis* ('Carpets'), an encyclopedic collection, he writes (*Stromateis* 1.158.2):

'For if you ask for that which is great,' he [Jesus] says, 'the small too will be added to you [by God]'.

Some other patristic writers expand this by adding a second member: 'Ask for the heavenly, and you will also receive the earthly.' We can trace these ideas back to a logion in Q: 'Seek first his kingdom and his righteousness, and all these things shall be yours as well' (Mt 6:33, par. Lk 12:31).

(16) Money-changers

Clement of Alexandria is one of about 70 witnesses to what is by far the most popular agraphon among the theologians of the early church, who all considered it an authentic logion of Jesus. In its pure form, however, it is found not in Clement but in the Pseudo-Clementine Homilies (which have nothing to do with him, but are pseudepigraphical writings of Clement of Rome). In Homily 2.51.1, we read:

Our teacher has fittingly said: 'Be good money-changers!'

This short form is often quoted in combination with 1 Thess 5:21f.: 'Test everything; hold fast what is good, abstain from every form of evil'; sometimes the logion and Paul's words are conflated. This link was suggested by the adjective *dokimoi* in the logion ('good' or 'approved'), which is related to the imperative employed by Paul, *dokimazete* ('test'); besides this, 'every form of evil' in v. 22 was often understood as 'every bad coin' – a perfectly possible way to take the Greek words.

This brings us to the 'good money-changers' and helps us to understand both the meaning and perhaps the genesis of the logion. The point is not that a good money-changer is one who looks to his own profit, or one who acts as a banker who pays interest (as in Mt 25:27). He shows his true quality by recognizing false coins immediately; he examines each coin with care, so that he will not be fooled. Hence, the logion is a metaphorical summons to the discernment of spirits. It may even have developed from the exegesis and application of 1 Thess 5:21f.

(17) The disciples' lack of understanding

For our next agraphon, we turn to another genre of texts, viz. the apocryphal Acts of the Apostles. In the Acts of Peter, the Roman senator Marcellus, who has fallen away from the Christian faith, repents and asks Peter to intercede for him. Marcellus attempts to put himself in a milder light by recalling that Peter himself did not have a firm faith during Jesus' lifetime, and that he had sometimes doubted. He emphasizes this point as follows (Acts of Peter 10):

I have heard that he [Jesus] too said: 'Those who are with me have not understood me'.

The disciples' lack of understanding is a frequent topos in the Gospel of Mark, and also finds expression at Jn 14:9, 'Have I been with you so long, and yet you do not know me, Philip?' This agraphon takes up in concentrated form an important trait in the gospels' portrait of the disciples.

(18) Belief in signs

Our first example of traditions about Jesus in Islam which are not found in the canonical gospels is Sure 3.49 in the Koran:

I come to you with a sign from your Lord: I make something for you out of clay that looks like birds. Then I breathe into it, and if God wills, the clay will turn into real birds. And if God wills, I shall heal the blind and the lepers, and make the dead alive. And I will tell you what you eat and store up in your houses. If you believe, this is a sign for you.

The surprising element in this Sure is not the allusion to Jesus' miracles of feeding the crowds, but the reference to the remarkable visual miracle of breathing life into birds formed of clay. This is related in the Infancy Gospel of Thomas (2:2–4; see ch. 5b below), and this is surely the source on which the Koran draws, just as the nearby Sure 3.44 reflects the episode in the Protevangelium of James (8–9; cf. ch. 5b below) in which lots are drawn. Much of what the Koran knows about Jesus has passed through the filter of apocryphal traditions.

(19) Jesus as forerunner

The Koran contains other agrapha (cf. Sure 5.72; 43.63; 61.14), but we quote here only Sure 61.6, since Jesus is interpreted here as the forerunner of Muhammad. This lets us see how obvious theological interests could contribute to the production of new agrapha:

And then Jesus, the son of Mary, said: 'Children of Israel! I have been sent to you by God, in order to confirm what went before me, that is the Torah, and to proclaim a messenger with a highly blessed name who will come after me.'

(20) The world as a bridge

One Islamic agraphon has become famous, thanks to the unusual circumstances of its discovery in 1900 in an inscription on a mosque at Fathpur Sikri in India; allegedly, it can still be read there today. The inscription dates from 1601, but the logion is attested in Islamic writers at a much earlier date (cf. nr. 46 and nr. 75 in the collection by Michael Asin y Palacios). It runs as follows:

Jesus, on whom be peace, said: 'The world is a bridge. Go over it – do not settle on it!'

There is a shorter parallel to the contents of this logion, with its impressive warning against excessive entanglement in the things of this world, in nr. 42 of the Gospel of Thomas: 'Be passers-by!'

(21) A modest lifestyle

We conclude with one more Islamic story about Jesus. It does not indeed contain a direct logion, but as we shall see, it would not have been difficult to formulate one. The text is nr. 81 in Asin y Palacios:

The only things the Messiah carried on his person were a comb and a drinking vessel. When he saw a man combing his beard with his fingers, [the Messiah] immediately threw away the comb. When he saw another taking water with his hands from a river to drink, [the Messiah] immediately threw away the drinking vessel.

Here, a comparison with the *Lives of the Philosophers* of Diogenes Laertius shows that a 'wandering legend' has been applied to Jesus. We are told about the Cynic Diogenes of Sinope (*Vitae Philosophorum* 6.37):

Once he saw a child drinking from its cupped hands, and he threw away the cup from his knapsack and said: 'A child has been content with less than I.' He also threw away his bowl when he saw a child that had broken its own plate and now used a hollow piece of bread as a vessel to hold its lentil broth.

In the Islamic version, the bowl has merely been replaced by a comb. Diogenes Laertius' version also shows that the narrative really demands an apophthegmatic logion in direct speech.

(22) Getting up again after a fall

It is impossible to estimate even roughly the antiquity of an agraphon found in the ancient Greek rite of anointing the sick. It forms a catena with three logia found in the gospels; all four are introduced by the same formula (cf. J. Karawidopulos, 'Ein Agraphon in einem liturgischen Text der griechischen Kirche', ZNW 62 [1971] 299f.):

You [Jesus] who said: 'Whenever you fall, get up again, and you will be saved' ...

Here too, the biblical background is not difficult to discern: in Jer 8:4, we read: 'Thus says the Lord: "When men fall, do they not rise again? If one turns away, does he not return?"' The words ascribed to Jesus here have a clear theological meaning: they intend to hold open the possibility of repentance and penance for Christians who have committed grave sins after receiving baptism.

(c) Summary

This chapter has demonstrated the great variety of sources in which we find agrapha; let us recapitulate briefly.

In the New Testament, we have the Acts of the Apostles and the epistolary literature (for example, 1 Pet 4:8, 'Love covers a multitude of sins', and Eph 4:26, 'Let not the sun go down on your wrath', have become words of Jesus), as well as the manuscript tradition of the Gospels – one example might be the three short logia in the 'homeless' pericope about Jesus and the woman taken in adultery (Jn 7:53–8:11). To these we must add the apocryphal Acts of the Apostles and liturgical texts of the early church; the works of the apostolic fathers, the apologists and patristic writers are all sources of primary importance. We also find logia in the Koran and other Islamic authors, whereas rabbinic writings have little to offer.

The logia in these sources have very different forms. We find a short imperative: 'Be good money-changers!' But we also find a relatively long discourse which paints an elaborate picture of the paradisal conditions in the messianic kingdom. Some texts are in dialogue form or framed by a rudimentary narrative, while in other cases only the logion itself has been preserved. Our selection includes a pure narrative without direct speech (cf. nr. 21); it would however be easy to add a pointed aphorism to the story, and it may be that some such logion has fallen a victim to the processes of transmission.

In many cases, we have been able to identify reasons for the secondary genesis of agrapha. Narrative accounts or indirect speech in the canonical gospels have been transposed into direct words of Jesus; some already-existing logia have been further elaborated and given a new arrangement. Words from the epistolary literature have been put on Jesus' lips. Sometimes the Old Testament was the quarry supplying the material for a logion; popular proverbs and 'wandering legends' were localized in Jesus' person. Well-intentioned theological consider-ations and clear ideological intentions inspired the imagination and thus made their own contribution to the creation of logia. Nor should we overlook one important motivating factor: an utterance presented as words of Jesus had greater authority and a higher paradigmatic value.

We cannot completely bracket off the question of historical authen-ticity. Is it possible to attribute at least some of the agrapha to Jesus himself? Are they historically genuine? This is where the critical principle of reduction, mentioned at the beginning of this chapter, comes into its own: wherever one can make a plausible case for the secondary creation of a logion, we must rule out its authenticity. No doubt there exist border cases about which one could debate endlessly. At any rate, after we have excluded all dubious instances, a number of potentially authentic logia remain. I would include among these the narrative of the man who worked on the sabbath, the logia about the far and the near and about the fire and the kingdom, and (with some reservations) the money-changers and the world as a bridge. Ultimately, however, we must admit that we do not possess any criteria that would permit a certain judgement about authenticity and inauthenticity.

The meagre harvest of the 22 logia examined here is in fact exemplary – the result would not be essentially different if we were to study 220. This means that the agrapha have only limited value for research into the historical Jesus. Despite the assertions one sometimes hears, the agrapha are not going to force a revolutionary reassessment of the picture of Jesus which we find in the canonical gospels.

Let me emphasize once again that the question of authenticity is only one aspect. *All* the agrapha retain their value for the history of tradition, when we understand them as a reflection of the fascination which the figure of Jesus has always exercised: they belong to the history of the impact he made on others. Similarly, the spiritual power in some agrapha does not depend exclusively on the question of their genuineness. One can meditate on the logia about the good money-changers and the world as a bridge, and draw helpful inspiration for one's own conduct. No matter who first coined them, they remain 'spiritual classics' and have their rightful place among the utterances of the great spiritual masters and teachers.

Bibliography

O. Hofius, in NTApo I, 88–91; A. Resch, *Agrapha*; M. Asin y Palacios, 'Logia et Agrapha Domini Jesu apud moslemicos scriptores, asceticos praesertim, usitata', *PO* 13,3 (1919) 327–431; 19,4 (1926) 528–624; K. Berger and C. Nord, *Das Neue Testament und frühchristliche Schriften*, 1112–262; W. G. Morris, *Hidden Sayings of Jesus*; J. Jeremias, *Unbekannte Jesusworte*; O. Hofius, art. 'Agrapha', *TRE* II (1978) 103–10; O. Hofius, 'Unbekannte Jesusworte', in: Idem, *Neutestamentliche Studien* (WUNT 132), Tübingen 2000, 161–88; W. D. Stroker, *Extracanonical Sayings of Jesus* (SBL, ResBibSt 18), Atlanta, Ga. 1989.

2

FRAGMENTS

Accidental discoveries and systematic searches have unearthed so many papyri in Egypt since the nineteenth century that many of them still slumber unpublished in the cellars of museums and libraries. The Christian provenance of such papyri is immediately obvious, thanks to the abbreviations they employ for the *nomina sacra*. They become accessible to a wider public, even among scholars, only when they are edited and translated. Hence it is not surprising that new Christian texts should turn up from time to time, such as the 'Unknown Berlin Gospel', discovered in 1997. Where these papyri present traditions about Jesus, it is sometimes possible to link them to an already known gospel, whether canonical or apocryphal (cf. the sections on the Gospels of Peter, Thomas and Mary, below); other material remains unidentified. The brevity of the texts and their poor condition sometimes make it impossible to tell whether we have fragments of a gospel, rather than a portion of a homily or commentary.

We select only a few of the longer fragments with clearly narrative contents for a closer examination, let us briefly mention some other papyri fragments which are occasionally discussed in secondary literature.

PMerton 51 is a third-century papyrus page written on both sides. It contains logia related to Lk 7:29f. and Lk 6:45f.

POxy 210, likewise from the third century, is mostly indecipherable. The *recto* mentions an angel, while the *verso* has the metaphor of good and bad fruits and an 'I am'-logion which recalls the Johannine *ego eimi.*

In *POxy 1224,* from a fourth-century codex, the closing lines are the most interesting, since they may contain an 'agraphon' (see ch. 1 above).

The so-called *Fayyum fragment* (PVindob G 2325) was the first such textual fragment to be discovered, in 1885. It caused a great sensation, but it consists only of an abbreviated parallel to Mk 14:27–30. Peter speaks in the first person; his name is treated as a *nomen sacrum* and written in red ink. This has recently led to the suggestion that this fragment belongs to the Gospel of Peter (see ch. 6a below).

A remarkable feature in *PBerlin 11710* (*c.* sixth century), a dialogue between Jesus and Nathanael, is the term 'rabbi', employed once in the narrative and twice in addressing Jesus. (This indicates a recent date, rather than great antiquity.)

PCairo 10735 is no older than the sixth or seventh century. The *recto* text is related to Mt 2:13, the *verso* to Lk 1:36.

Bibliography

J. Jeremias and W. Schneemelcher, in NTApo I, 92–105; D. Lührmann, *Fragmente*, 139–85; A. de Santos Otero, *Los Evangelios Apócrifos*, 76–107.

(a) Papyrus Egerton 2 (PEg 2)

(1) Basic data

Papyrus Egerton 2 owes its name to the benefactor who made it possible for the British Museum in London to purchase a collection of Egyptian papyri in 1934. These included four pages written on both sides, originally part of a codex rather than a scroll. The fibres on the *recto* run horizontally and are therefore easier to write on; those on the *verso* run vertically, against the direction of the writing. All that remains legible on the page which the *editio princeps* by Bell and Skeat calls nr. 4 is one single letter. Page 3 consists only of a scrap, but an echo of Jn 10:30–32 is recognizable on the *recto*. We can reconstruct the text: '[... I and the Father] are one', followed by the Jews' attempt to stone Jesus. The first two pages, which are better preserved, present four or five episodes from the tradition about Jesus. It is possible that they are an excerpt from a larger gospel text, but this is uncertain; it is highly improbable that they come from the Gospel of Peter (see below).

Since the manuscript has no pagination, we do not know which texts are meant to be read first; and even the sequence of *recto* and *verso* is uncertain, since the codex consisted of several layers of papyrus leaves which were folded in the middle. In the process of folding, a *recto* may have been shifted to the left or the right, thus bearing an even or an uneven page number. Here, we follow the enumeration of the first editors, although this has sometimes been disputed (e.g. by Lührmann).

The bottom left/right corner of the first page, with five or six fragmentary lines, ended up in Cologne and has been edited by Gronewald as PKöln 255. The most recent editions of the text integrate this fragment in their reconstruction of frag. 1 (cf. Lührmann).

The first editors dated the discovery to *c.* 150 CE arguing exclusively on the basis of the form of writing employed. They assumed that the text was a copy of material which might be several decades earlier than that date. Here we must rely on the verdict of papyrologists, who have become more cautious and date PEg 2 to *c.* 200. This argues against the early dating to 50 or 60 proposed by Koester, which would make PEg 2 a preliminary version or a source of the four New Testament gospels.

(2) The contents

In frag. 1 *verso*, Jesus begins by adjuring the laywers: '<Punish (*or:* convict)> every one who act<s contrary to the l>aw, but not me!' The reason is given in line 5, which is not easy to understand: 'What he does, as he does it.' This may mean: when two persons do the same thing, it is not necessarily the same action – in other words, Jesus stands above the law. He then addresses 'the rulers of the people' in words with close Johannine parallels. They must investigate the Scriptures, which bear witness to Jesus (cf. Jn 5:39). It is not Jesus who accuses them (because of their unbelief, line 18), but Moses (cf. Jn 5:45). When they object that they know Moses, but know nothing about Jesus' provenance (cf. Jn 9:29), he replies by affirming that Moses wrote about him and that faith in Moses must lead to faith in Jesus (cf. Jn 5:46).

Frag. 1 *recto* likewise presents Johannine themes: the listeners attempt to stone Jesus. The leaders of the people want to seize him and hand him over to the crowd (!), thus attributing the responsibility for Jesus' death to the Jews. However, Jesus leaves the place unhindered (cf. Jn 10:39 etc. and Lk 4:30), 'because the hour of his betrayal <was> not yet c<ome>' (lines 7f.).

This is followed in lines 7–23 of frag. 1 *recto* by the healing of a leper. Its central section is shorter than the parallel narrative in Mk 1:40–44, but the exposition is elaborated in the manner of a novel when the leper declares: 'Master Jesus, wandering with lepers and eating with <them was I> in the inn; I also <became> a le<per>' (lines 12–15). Most people took good care to avoid lepers, but this man showed solidarity and ate with them, becoming infected thereby. This predestined him to be healed by Jesus: his cleansing is the reward for his love of neighbour. At the close, Jesus says to him: 'And sin no more', which recalls Jn 5:14 (cf. 8:11).

'They', i.e. Jewish dialogue partners, address Jesus in frag. 2 with a *captatio benevolentiae,* but their intention is to trick him: 'Master Jesus, we know that you come <from God>, for what you do bears a test<imony> to you (which goes) beyond that of all the prophets' (lines 3–5; cf. Jn 3:2). The question of the denarius for the tax, familiar from Mk 12:13–17, follows in a generalized form which speaks of 'kings' rather than of 'Caesar': 'Is it admissible <to p>ay to the kings the (charges) appertaining to their rule?' (lines 6f.). Jesus is angered, and answers with a polemical quotation from Is 29:13 which is also used in the controversial debate at Mk 7:6f.: 'This <people honours> me with the<ir lips> but their heart is far from me.'

Unfortunately, frag. 2 *verso* has been considerably damaged. Here we find two pieces of tradition which are unattested elsewhere; this makes it virtually impossible to reconstruct them. They are linked by the theme of 'sowing'. Gronewald proposes that the first lines be read as follows: 'When a farmer encloses seed in a hidden place, how can he receive its incalculable weight as long as it remains invisible?' Clearly, this is based on the metaphor of sowing and an immensely rich harvest, as in the parables of the seed in Mk 4:3–20, 26–32 or the logion about the grain of wheat which must die in Jn 12:24. This seems to be the 'strange question' with which Jesus puzzles his hearers (lines 4f.).

In the second scene, Jesus passes from words to deeds. He goes to the bank of the Jordan and stretches out his right hand. All that can then be deciphered in the text is that something is sown (or sprinkled with water) and produces fruit, bringing joy to everyone. It appears that Jesus performs a spectacular miracle here. Either he sows seed in the water – a proverbial expression in classical antiquity for doing something totally futile (cf. Theognis 1.105–108; Ps.-Phocylides 152) – and meets with unexpected success; or else he sows the seed in the sand by the shore and sprinkles it with water from the river, so that it begins to grow immediately. Here we may recall the 'corn mummies' in Egypt, where our text was discovered (and possibly also written). Wooden forms meant to represent the dead Osiris were filled with earth, in which cereal grains were sown and sprinkled with water from the Nile. When the stalks began to sprout, this was interpreted as a symbol of the overcoming of death by life. Another attempt at reconstruction seems less plausible: this imports a dried-up fig tree (cf. Mk 11:20) into the text, which is then 'brought back to life'.

(3) Evaluation

The narrative in two parts on frag. 2 *verso* shows that PEg 2 also has recourse to unknown traditions about Jesus similar to those in the synoptic gospels (although these can scarcely be called historical, in the strict sense of the word). This means that we cannot simply say that PEg 2 is exclusively dependent on the four canonical gospels.

On the other hand, when we consider the affinities to John, which apparently was known in Egypt at a very early date, we must assume that the author of PEg 2 drew directly on Johannine material. The parallels involve a language and theology so typically Johannine that it is difficult to attribute them to a common source which John would simply have adopted, and to which he would owe his characteristic way of thinking. This need not however mean that the author of PEg 2 had a *literary* knowledge of the fourth gospel; a better explanation of the freedom displayed by PEg 2 in its combination of texts from disparate parts of the fourth gospel may be supplied by the concept of 'secondary orality'. In other words, Johannine material may have become known through *hearing* the gospel read in the Christian community, where its contents were passed on by word of mouth.

The same is true to a lesser extent of the use made of the synoptics in PEg 2. Here, it is arguable that the author draws on shared older traditions, rather than on the literary versions in the gospels, but – with the exception of the double episode on frag. 2 *verso* (see above) – this is never a genuinely necessary hypothesis.

Bibliography

J. Jeremias and W. Schneemelcher, in NTApo I, 96–9; D. Lührmann,

Fragmente, 142–53 (with bibliography); H. I. Bell and T. C. Skeat, *Fragments of an Unknown Gospel and Other Early Christian Papyri,* London 1935, and *The New Gospel Fragments,* London 1935; M. Gronewald, *Kölner Papyri* VI (PapyCol 7,6), Opladen 1987, 136–45 (= PKöln 255); G. Mayeda, *Das Leben-Jesu-Fragment Papyrus Egerton 2 und seine Stellung in der urchristlichen Literaturgeschichte,* Bonn 1946; H. Koester, *Gospels,* 205–216; Good photographs of the text and further information can be found in the Internet: www-user.uni-bremen.de/~wie/Egerton/Egerton_home.html.

(b) Papyrus Oxyrhynchus 840 (POxy 840)

Although it is enumerated among the papyri, POxy 840 is in fact a parchment leaf from a small codex (8.5 × 7 cm.) from the third or fourth century, which may have been used as an amulet. The *recto* begins in the middle of a sentence, with the conclusion of an admonitory sermon by Jesus about the judgement. After this, he takes his disciples with him into the inner precincts of the temple, where he has a debate about questions of purity (cf. Mk 7:1–23) with a *chief priest* who belongs to the *Pharisees.* No satisfactory explanation of this problematic combination has been suggested, and the historical authenticity of the following episode is highly doubtful.

The chief priest, whose name may have been Levi, asks Jesus in a polemical tone how he and his disciples have dared to enter the holy place and look at the sacred vessels – e.g. vessels used for drink-offerings of water, wine and oil, or for the shewbread – without first washing their feet and changing their clothes. When Jesus replies briefly: 'You are (also) here in the temple court. Are you then clean?', the priest affirms his own purity: he has washed in the pool of David (perhaps the pool of Bethesda, cf. Jn 5:2), has 'gone down by the one stair and come up by the other' (there were two staircases, so that those who sought purity and those already purified did not have to meet), and has put on clean white clothing. Jesus, whom the narrative now calls 'Saviour', reacts with a new tirade, beginning with a cry of woe. He contrasts outward and inward purity (cf. Mt 23:25–28); the 'dogs and swine' in line 33 are most likely metaphors for immoral human beings. Unfortunately, the text breaks off in mid-sentence. Lines 31–45 read:

> Woe to you, blind ones who do not see! You have bathed in water that is poured out, in which dogs and swine lie night and day, and you have washed yourself and chafed your outer skin, which prostitutes also and flute-girls anoint, bathe, chafe and rouge, in order to arouse desire in men, but within they are full of scorpions and of <bad>ness <of every kind>. You say that I and <my disciples> have not im<mersed> ourselves. But we <have been im>mersed in the liv<ing...> water which comes down from <... B>ut woe to those who ...

The 'water of eternal life', which recalls Jesus' dialogue with the

Samaritan woman about the 'living water' in Jn 4, may be an indication of the *Sitz-im-Leben* of this text. Bovon is surely right to locate its origin in debates about ritual purity and correct baptismal praxis in Jewish-Christian baptist groups of the second or third century. In this controversy, the author plays down the importance of ritual and emphasizes rather the spiritual dimension.

Bibliography

J. Jeremias and W. Schneemelcher, in: NTApo I, 94f.; D. Lührmann, *Fragmente*, 164–9; J. Jeremias, *Unbekannte Jesusworte*, 50–60, 98f.; F. Bovon, '*Fragment Oxyrhynchus 840*, Fragment of a Lost Gospel, Witness of an Early Christian Controversy over Purity', *JBL* 119 (2000) 705–28.

(c) The Strasbourg Coptic papyrus

The 'Strasbourg Coptic papyrus' consists of two very poorly preserved leaves from a papyrus codex of the fifth or sixth century, written on both sides. Recently, scholars have paid this text renewed attention, since its contents are strikingly similar to those of the 'Unknown Berlin Gospel' (UBG, see below). The *recto* of the first page presents a farewell prayer of Jesus with distant echoes of Jn 17 and clearer borrowings from 1 Cor 15: 'You will place [all things] in subjection to me ... Through whom will [the last] enemy be destroyed? ... Through whom will the sting of death be [destroyed]?' When we compare this text with UBG, we should note that every sentence in this prayer ends with a responsorial 'Amen'.

The *verso* text has a stronger Matthaean orientation. The scene is Gethsemane: 'The hour is near at hand when I shall be taken away from you. The spirit [is] willing, but the flesh [is] weak. Remain now and stay awake [with me]' (cf. Mt 26:38, 41, 45). It is significant that the 'apostles' use the 'we'-form here: 'But we, the apost[les, we] wept [when we] said [to him] ...' This continues on the *verso* of the second page, which relates a visionary experience of the apostles: 'Our eyes penetrated everywhere, we saw the glory of his divinity and all the glory of [his] sovereignty.' Only UBG makes a relatively certain localization of this vision within a narrative of Jesus' life possible; on the question whether the Strasbourg fragment belongs to the Unknown Berlin Gospel, see the recent essay by Emmel.

Bibliography

W. Schneemelcher, in: NTApo I, 103–5; D. A. Bertrand, in: *Ecrits apocryphes chrétiens*, 425–8; S. Emmel, 'Unbekanntes Berliner Evangelium = The Strasbourg Coptic Gospel: Prolegomena to a New Edition of the Strasbourg Fragments,' in H. G. Bethge *et al.* (eds.), *For the Children, Perfect Instruction* (Festschrift for H. M. Schenke) (NHMS 54), Berlin 2002, 353–74.

(d) The 'Unknown Berlin Gospel' (UBG = PBerol 22220)

(1) Basic data

In 1961, the Egyptian Museum in Berlin acquired remnants of a parchment codex from a second-hand dealer. Although an unidentified archivist had immediately recorded in a note that it contained 'A New Testament apocryphon (alleged discourses of Jesus)', the text lay unnoticed among other materials in the museum, awaiting an editor and conservator, until the American specialist Paul A. Mirecki discovered it while working in libraries in Berlin in 1991. When news of the manuscript emerged in 1997, newspapers spoke of an unknown gospel that would shed a completely new light on the origins of Christianity. But the little sensation promised did not materialize, and the publication of the text in 1999 attracted virtually no attention in the media.

External indications suggest a dating of the codex between the fourth and seventh centuries; the balance of probabilities tilts slightly towards the sixth century. A number of linguistic peculiarities show that the Coptic text has been translated from Greek, but only internal indications help date the original Greek version. Initially, an early date (between 100 and 150 CE) was suggested, but more cautious counsels have prevailed: the earliest plausible date is the close of the second or early third century. It appears to draw on the Gospel of Peter, and its contents are related to the Strasbourg Coptic gospel fragment. The title 'Gospel of the Saviour' comes from the editors, who observe that the narrative mostly calls Jesus *sôtêr* ('saviour, redeemer'), though 'Lord' (as throughout the Gospel of Peter) and 'Son' are also used. Here, we prefer to retain the more neutral name 'Unknown Berlin Gospel'.

We know that the codex originally contained more than 100 pages, since two page-numbers (99/100 and 107/108) can be deciphered. Remnants of about 30 pages have survived, but only three double pages and two single pages are legible. Twenty-nine smaller fragments exist, some of them with only a few letters preserved. Apart from the numbered pages, the textual sequence is uncertain; scholarly reconstructions diverge in their arrangement of the individual pages. Since there is no definitive enumeration, the textual sequence, enumeration and translation in this section follow Plisch.

(2) The contents

The state of transmission makes it impossible to determine the extent of the whole gospel to which our fragments belong. We do not know whether it contained a narrative about the public ministry of Jesus, nor whether it went on to speak of Easter apparitions. It is, however, possible to locate the surviving section very precisely: it belongs to the passion narrative, presenting discourses on the lips of Jesus and dialogues with the apostles (the word 'disciples' is not used in this text) in the brief interval between the Last Supper and the crucifixion, including the Gethsemane episode; the situation is similar to that of the farewell discourses in Jn 14–17, located between the events leading up to the passion in Jn 12–13 (entry to Jerusalem, farewell meal) and the continuation in Jn 18–19 (arrest, trial and crucifixion), and thus differs markedly from the gnostic gospels, which prefer to situate such dialogues in the period between the resurrection and the ascension. This warns against a purely gnostic interpretation of the newly discovered text.

In §1, the 'Saviour' utters a beattitude: 'Blessed is the one who shall eat with me in the kingdom of heaven' (cf. Lk 14:15) and speaks of a 'garment of the kingdom which I have received (?) in the blood of the grape.' The reference to Jacob's blessing of Judah at Gen 49:11 would be even clearer if we read 'washed' instead of 'received'; an allusion to the eucharist is also probable. In §2, Andrew speaks, but the text containing his words has been broken off. §3 contains a clear prediction of Christ's descent to the underworld:

After I have served the inhabitants of this world, it is also necessary that I descend into the realm of the dead, for the sake of the souls who are fettered in that place.

§4 skilfully links the prediction of the apostles' flight (Mk 14:27f., quoting Zech 13:7) and the transition in Mk 14:42 with Johannine themes; indeed, it is typical of UBG, which has a Johannine orientation, to link synoptic and Johannine words of Jesus:

You will all flee and leave me alone, but I do not remain alone, for my Father is with me. I and my Father, we are one single person ... But I am the good shepherd and will give my life for you. You too must give your lives for your friends, so that you may be pleasing to my Father, for there is no greater commandment than this: that I give my life for human beings. This is why my Father loves me, because I fulfil his will, since I am God and became a human being ... (cf. Jn 16:32; 10:30; 10:11; 15:13).

The last sentence, speaking of the incarnation of God, coins a new, concise formula for the Johannine christology of pre-existence, and especially the 'becoming flesh' of the Logos (Jn 1:14). In §5, an anxious disciple asks whether Jesus will send for them and take them out of the world to himself (cf. Jn 14:2f.). In §6, Jesus addresses his apostles: 'O my sacred members, my blessed seeds!' This may be derived from Paul's image of the community as the body of Christ and the believers as Abraham's 'seed'; the first part of the address occurs several times on Jesus' lips in UBG. §7 merits special attention:

[...] on the mountain. We too became like spiritual bodies, and our eyes were opened in all directions, and the entire place lay open before us. We drew near to the heavens, [while] one heaven opened up to the next. The gatekeepers tottered. The angels were afraid and fled . . . We saw how our Redeemer passed through all the heavens [*About half a column is missing at this point* . . .] from all the heavens. Then this world became like darkness before us, the apostles. We became like [those] who are in the aeons of glory, while our [eyes] penetrated [all] the heavens and [grace?] clothed us with our apostolate. And we saw our Redeemer, as he reached the seventh heaven . . .

The text now becomes increasingly illegible, but it mentions angels, archangels and cherubim who throw down their crowns before the Father's throne (cf. Rev 4:10). The first significant point is the narrative perspective: the apostles speak in the 'we'-form (although this does not entitle us to accept the suggestion that the text is part of the 'Gospel of the Apostles' or 'Gospel of the Twelve' which some church fathers mention). The Saviour takes the apostles with him on a heavenly journey (cf. Paul's experience in 2 Cor 12:1–4) into the throne-room of God. One may be initially inclined to think that this refers to the resurrection and ascension of Christ, with the apostles as immediate witnesses, but the structure of UGB as a whole does not permit this interpretation. The only remaining point of contact with the canonical gospels is the transfiguration of Jesus on a mountain, in the presence of three of the twelve disciples: this is widened here to take on cosmic dimensions, becoming a heavenly journey shared by all twelve apostles. This is when they are appointed as apostles, indicated by the words: '. . . and [grace?] clothed us with our apostolate.'

Although this vision is linked to the Gethsemane pericope in such a manner that little remains of the occasion when those disciples whom Jesus had singled out from among the twelve disgraced themselves by falling asleep, §8 does speak of Jesus' distress as he struggles in prayer in the garden. The exclusive cause of his distress is, however, his knowledge that he 'will be killed by the people of Israel,' and it is this that leads him to pray: 'O my [Father], if it is possible, let this chalice pass me by. May I be [killed] by another people – a sinful people.' Apparently, this prayer will not be granted, although Jesus insists anew on his request:

[I] will die happily and pour out my blood for the human race, but I weep only for those whom I love: [Abraham], Isaac and Jacob, for [when they] appear before me [on] the day of judgement and I sit on my throne and judge the world, they will say to me [*unfortunately, the text breaks off at this point*].

Little can be gleaned from what remains of the text in §§9 and 10. In §11, Jesus is questioned by the apostles ('We said to him') and then by John about his return. His reply begins with words from Jn 20:17, which are addressed in the canonical gospel only to Mary Magdalene: 'But do not touch me until I have ascended to my Father, who is also your Father, and to [my God], who is also your God.' This is followed by words found as an agraphon and in GThom 82: 'I am the blazing fire. The one [who is close to me, is] close to the fire. The one who is far from me, is far from life.'

§13 presents a remarkable dialogue which recalls a scene of worship. In my view, it is more plausible to interpret the text to mean that the choir of apostles respond with 'Amen' to each utterance of the Saviour, but since the change of subject is not clear in the text itself, it is possible that Jesus himself says the 'Amen' in confirmation of his words (cf. also the dance and song in Acts of John 94–96). This passage speaks of the crucifixion which will soon take place, and it is striking how narrative or commentary from the canonical accounts of the passion are transformed into literal direct speech on the lips of Jesus. This can be seen most clearly in the author's treatment of the lance and the witness (Jn 19:34f.):

'... I am the king.' – 'Amen.' – 'I am the son of the King.' – 'Amen.' – 'I fight together with you. You too: fight!' – 'Amen.' – 'I shall be sent, and I shall send you.' – 'Amen.' ... 'Weep no more, but rejoice!' – 'Amen.' – 'I have conquered the world. Do not allow the world to conquer you!' – 'Amen.' – 'My side will be pierced with a lance. The one who has seen it must bear testimony. And his testimony is true.' – 'Amen.' – 'The one who does not receive my body and my blood is a stranger to me.' – 'Amen.' ...

The last sentence (cf. Jn 6:53f.) shows that the group for which UBG was written celebrated the eucharist; this may be the reason for the liturgical style of this entire section. The crucifixion does not immediately follow this antiphonal song; in §14, the last surviving portion of the text, Jesus addresses the cross, which appears to be thought of as a living dialogue-partner which proceeds him to Golgotha:

... Rise up to heaven, for this is your will, O cross. Do not be afraid! I am rich and I will fill you with my riches. [I] will ascend you, O cross ... Do [not] weep, O [cross], but rejoice and recognise what the Lord possesses when he glorifies you, since he is rich ... They await you: one who laughs and rejoices, another who weeps, [mourns] and laments. Go ahead of me now, O cross, just as I will go ahead of you and leave this one.'

The cross is mentioned several times in the many small fragments. Before we turn to the evaluation of the text, let us mention some elements found in the fragments (we follow the enumeration of Hedrick and Mirecki): the 'holy limbs' (9H); the (new) city of Jerusalem (14F); the throne of the Father (17H); the widow (19F); milk and honey and the source of the water of life (19H); words addressed by Jesus to Judas (20F); and the word 'pound' (*litra*), found four times in 24H, which may be connected with the burial of Jesus.

(3) Evaluation

Towards the end of Jesus' address to the cross, we find a mysterious pair: 'one who laughs and rejoices, another who weeps, [mourns] and laments.' If this designates the heavenly Christ (who is not at all affected by the crucifixion) and the one who takes his place on earth, it would be an example of the docetic christology which employed similar devices to avoid attributing suffering to the Redeemer; but since the text contains no other unambiguous signals pointing in this direction, it is better to attempt another interpretation. The reference may be to the two men crucified along with Jesus, only one of whom understands what is happening; or to the variety of reactions on the part of the onlookers – while some mock and jeer (Mk 15:29–32), others weep and lament (Lk 23:27). This would enable us to avoid a gnostic interpretation of UBG.

Nevertheless, we must insist on the great reticence with which this text deals with the suffering of the Saviour. We see this in the version of the Gethsemane pericope, which is ultimately watered down by being linked to the transfiguration and changed into a heavenly journey; and in the anticipation of the crucifixion in the antiphonal song and the Saviour's address to his cross, which turn it into a celebration of redemption.

When he says to the cross: 'just as I will go ahead of you', this probably refers to the resurrection, when the risen Jesus will walk before the cross – precisely as we read in the Gospel of Peter (see ch. 6a below). The simplest explanation of these links is to postulate that UGB made use of the earlier Gospel of Peter. The links with the Strasbourg Coptic papyrus are even closer; it is possible that both texts attest a particular gospel type in which the apostles are eye-witness narrators and in which the harshness of the crucifixion is somewhat toned down.

Bibliography

C. K. Hedrick and P. A. Mirecki, *Gospel of the Savior. A New Ancient Gospel*, Santa Rosa, Calif. 1999; U. K. Plisch, *Verborgene Worte Jesu*, 27–35; H. M. Schenke, 'Das sogenannte "Unbekannte Berliner Evangelium" (UBE)', *Zeitschrift für Antike und Christentum* 2 (1998) 199–213; J. Frey, 'Leidenskampf und Himmelreise. Das Berliner Evangelienfragment (Papyrus Berolinensis 22220) und die Gethsemani-Tradition', *BZ* new series 46 (2002) 71–96; S. Emmel, 'The Recently Published *Gospel of the Savior* ("Unbekanntes Berliner Evangelium"): Righting the Order of Pages and Events', *HThR* 95 (2002) 45–72; P. Nagel, ' "Gespräche Jesu mit seinen Jüngern vor der Auferstehung" – zur Herkunft und Datierung des "Unbekannten Berliner Evangeliums" ', *ZNW* 94 (2003) 215–47.

(e) The 'Secret Gospel of Mark'

(1) The circumstances of the discovery

In 1958, while the American scholar Morton Smith was cataloguing books and manuscripts in the monastery of Mar Saba in the desert near Jerusalem, he discovered a handwritten text on the last free page and the inside-back cover of a printed seventeenth-century edition of the letters of Ignatius. On examination, this proved to be a hitherto unknown letter by Clement of Alexandria, quoting from a 'mystic' Gospel of Mark which was read in circles of initiates in Alexandria. Smith published his discovery in 1973, using photographs which he had taken. Between 1958 and 1973, a number of experts had confirmed that Clement was the probable author of the text itself, while the manuscript clearly indicated an eighteenth-century provenance; it was apparently common practice at that period in Mar Saba to write on blank pages and gaps in books and to copy fragmentary ancient texts. In the eighth century, John Damascene had worked in this monastery, and he mentions that he knew letters of Clement. This allows the construction of a slender line of transmission which lends a remote plausibility to the hypothesis that a letter of Clement was indeed handed on in this unusual manner.

Unfortunately, Smith linked his *editio princeps* to far-reaching conclusions about the picture of Jesus (further developed in his book *Jesus the Magician,* London 1978); the impression was given – although Smith himself does not actually declare this explicitly – that the text implies a homosexual relationship between Jesus and at least one of his disciples. This is one main reason why doubts about the status of this discovery have never been completely silenced. More fundamental questions are raised too; the whole thing may be a clever forgery composed at any time between late antiquity and the twentieth century. Assessment is made more difficult by the fact that, apart from Smith, no scholar has ever seen the original. All that investigations have shown is that the volume was transported from Mar Saba to the Orthodox patriarchate in Jerusalem, where the handwritten leaves were detached from the book in order to be better conserved. At the present date, however, the patriarchal librarian is unable to produce these pages, although it appears that older photographs taken by his predecessor have now been discovered. The Secret Gospel has its own homepage, with regular updates, detailing the various incidents in this *chronique scandaleuse.*

(2) The contents

In the letter, addressed to a certain Theodore, Clement attacks the gnostic Carpocratian group, whom he accuses of holding a libertine position on questions of sexual morality. Since they appeal to a particular version of the Gospel of Mark, he begins by recalling the genesis of this text in the circle around Peter in Rome. Subsequently, Mark brought further notes of Peter's words to Alexandria, where he composed a second, more spiritual version of his gospel for perfect believers. (In his account of these events, Clement employs the language of the mystery cults, as he does elsewhere.) Carpocrates got hold of this secret gospel and distorted it. There are, in other words, three versions of the Gospel of Mark: (a) the first version which Mark wrote in Rome, the canonical text with which we are familiar; (b) a second, more spiritual version, which he produced in Alexandria; and (c) a third edition expanded by Carpocrates in keeping with his own ideas.

At the end of the second page and on the third page of the copy of Clement's letter, we are told what Clement found in the second version of Mark, which he himself accepted as authentic. A text is inserted in the narrative gap between Mk 10:34 and 10:35, beginning with the raising to life of a young man who had died. This takes place in Bethany, recalling the raising of Lazarus in Jn 11, but with one interesting difference: the young man's voice is heard from inside the tomb before Jesus himself rolls the stone away from the entrance, takes him by the hand and raises him up. The young man's reaction is described as follows: 'And the young man looked at him, loved him, and began to ask that he might stay with him' (III 4f.). They enter the house of the young man, and we are now told that he was rich (cf. Lk 18:23; also Mk 10:21, where the evangelist says that Jesus 'looking upon him loved him').

The next scene takes place some time later. It is here that we find a section peculiar to the Secret Gospel, which gave rise to various suspicions (III 6–9):

And six days later, Jesus gave him a charge. And when it was late, the young man came to him, his naked body clothed with only one garment. And he remained with him that night; for Jesus taught him the mystery of the kingdom of God.

Mk 4:11 speaks of Jesus' instruction about the 'mystery' of the kingdom of God, and the nocturnal visit of the young man to Jesus recalls Nicodemus in Jn 3. Above all, however, we are reminded of the puzzling passage in Mk 14:51, where Jesus is arrested and a young man wearing only a garment on his naked body initially attempts to follow him, but is seized and saves his life by fleeing naked and abandoning his garment.

Clement goes on to quote another verse from the 'Secret Gospel', from a passage located after the semicolon in Mk 10:46, between Jesus' coming to Jericho and his immediate departure from the city: 'And they came to Jericho; and as he was leaving Jericho ...' In the city, Jesus meets the sister of the young man, his mother, and Salome, but we are surprised to read: 'But Jesus did not receive them' (III 16). This may be because he was interested only in the young man, who was a genuine disciple. Clement designates as falsehood all the other interpolations to which the Carpocratians appealed. He gives one example: only the Carpocratian version, not his own, includes the phrase 'one naked man with another naked man', which makes the nocturnal 'mystery' appear even more offensive. If one seeks to give a serious (rather than a trivial) interpretation of the nakedness, it should be understood in a baptismal context: the one who received baptism, and sometimes also the one who baptized, took off their garments and went down naked into the water. In other words, the initiation into the mystery of the kingdom of God takes place in the celebration of baptism. This would account for the many allusions in the text to the language of the mystery cults and their initiations; this narrative is a 'rite of institution' of Christian baptism.

(3) Evaluation

'Secret Mark' has given rise not only to questionable historical reconstructions, but also to far-reaching tradition- and redactional-historical
hypotheses, e.g. the claim that our canonical Gospel of Mark abbre-
viates and tones down the 'Secret Gospel', which in turn is based on an
'Ur-Mark'. Thus we are told (cf. Meyer) that the 'young man' is the rich
man from Mk 10:17–22. Initially, he does not respond to the love Jesus
has for him, and goes away; but after he is raised from the dead (in
'Secret Mark'), he responds to Jesus' love and becomes the 'beloved
disciple'. When Jesus is arrested, he at first endeavours to follow him,
but then loses his courage and flees (Mk 14:51). However, he is definitively rehabilitated by his presence in the empty tomb (Mk 16:5), which
demonstrates his willingness to share Jesus' death.

We must affirm that the text itself does not warrant the construction
of such bold hypotheses. Even if we accept the authenticity of the letter
of Clement and grant that he knew a 'Secret Gospel', it suffices to posit
a mid-second-century date for its composition. Classical rhetoric was
familiar with the stylistic device of 'amplification', i.e. the expansion
and elaboration of existing texts, and it is possible that a redactor in
Alexandria took Mark's narrative as his basis and amplified this with
other material, including Johannine elements. Since, however, the
genuineness of the text remains an open question, it is doubtful whether
there is much point in speculating on these matters.

Bibliography

H. Merkel, in NTApo I, 106–9; D. Lührmann, *Fragmente*, 182–85; M.
Smith, *Clement of Alexandria and a Secret Gospel of Mark*,
Cambridge, Mass. 1973 (academic); Idem, *The Secret Gospel: The
Discovery and Interpretation of the Secret Gospel According to Mark*,
New York 1973 (popular); H. Merkel, 'Auf den Spuren des Urmarkus?
Ein neuer Fund und seine Beurteilung', ZThK 71 (1974) 123–44; M.
W. Meyer, 'The Youth in the *Secret Gospel of Mark*', Semeia 49 (1990)
129–53; S. G. Brown, 'On the Composition History of the Longer
("Secret") Gospel of Mark', *JBL* 122 (2003) 89–110. – www-user.uni-
bremen.de/~wie/Secret/ secmark_home.html.

3

JEWISH-CHRISTIAN GOSPELS

Since Christianity came into existence as a movement within Judaism, the first Christians were all Jews. The question for historians is how and why the Gentile church came into existence, and why Judaism and Christianity parted company.

When we speak today of 'Jewish Christianity', we employ a narrower concept, which presupposes that the process of separation already lies in the past. The term 'Jewish Christian' is applied to groups which believed in Jesus Christ while maintaining the Jewish manner of life, celebrating the sabbath, practising circumcision and observing the dietary regulations. As time went on, they fell between the stools, since both Gentile Christians and Jews suspected them of heresy. Nevertheless, the existence of Jewish-Christian communities in various places can be demonstrated with certainty until the fourth or fifth century, and it is possible that Islamic sources attest their survival at an even later date.

We must assume that these groups had a literature of their own, but unfortunately no original texts survive – not as much as one single fragment on a papyrus leaf or a parchment page. All we have are quotations in the church fathers, and this poses a number of problems, as we see in a passage from Jerome's *Adversus Pelagianos* (3.2) to which we shall return below. He introduces the pericope about Jesus' baptism as follows:

In the Gospel according to the Hebrews, which is written in the Chaldaean and Syrian language but with Hebrew letters, and is employed to this day by the Nazaraeans, the Gospel according to the Apostles – or, as many hold, according to Matthew – which is also found in the library at Caesarea ...

Here we encounter a 'Gospel of the Hebrews', written with Hebrew block characters but in Aramaic (the terms 'Chaldaean' and 'Syrian' refer to this language, also frequently called 'Hebrew'). This Gospel is used by the Nazaraeans; an alternative title is 'Gospel of the Apostles'. Jerome also mentions the possibility that this text is identical with the original Hebrew text of Matthew, the existence of which was postulated by Papias of Hierapolis in the early second century.

This description appears very precise, and is echoed in other works of Jerome. In reality, however, it has led to a considerable measure of confusion. At any rate, one of the few points on which scholars agree is that the Gospel of the Hebrews is not to be equated with an 'Ur-Matthew'.

Although Jerome speaks of the Gospel of the Hebrews in a variety of terms, depending on the context of his writing, it is clear that he knows only one Jewish-Christian gospel. Patristic writers always call this text the 'Gospel of the Hebrews'; the name 'Gospel of the Nazaraeans' is found only in mediaeval sources. Despite this, it has become almost canonical in twentieth-century scholarship to speak of three Jewish-Christian gospels: a Gospel of the Hebrews (EvHeb), a Gospel of the Nazaraeans (EvNaz) and a Gospel of the Ebionites (EvEb; this name was coined only in the nineteenth and twentieth centuries). While EvEb is attested only by Epiphanius of Salamis, Clement of Alexandria and Origen used an EvHeb in the period before Jerome. Textual attestation of EvNaz is attained by dividing passages in Jerome between EvHeb and EvNaz (and scholars have not hesitated to accuse Jerome of supplying erroneous or even consciously false information on this point).

In more recent years (cf. Schmidt), in a pendulum swing away from this scepticism, there has been a tendency to regard Jerome as more trustworthy. Materials which earlier scholars had apportioned between EvHeb and EvNaz are now attributed to EvHeb alone, so that we are left with only two Jewish-Christian gospels, EvEb and EvHeb. Against this hypothesis, however, it must be pointed out that we possess three extra-canonical narratives of the baptism of Jesus (see below) which vary to such an extent that they cannot come from one or even two gospels alone. Rather, they presuppose three independent contexts.

I have no intention of intensifying the confusion which already exists. In this chapter, I present the material according to the conventional division into three gospels, but I add a question mark in brackets to the title EvNaz, in order to indicate the precarious status of this text.

The solution is not to reduce everything to one single EvHeb. We must assume the existence of a broader stream of transmission, with oral traditions and a larger number of literary sources than merely two or three texts (or than a variety of redactions of those two or three texts). The texts are usually dated to the first half of the second century. The original language may have been Aramaic or Greek; in some instances, we may posit composition in Aramaic, then translation into Greek, then a subsequent translation from Greek back into Aramaic.

Bibliography

P. Vielhauer and G. Strecker, in: NTApo I, 134–78; D. Lührmann, *Fragmente*, 32–55; S. C. Mimouni, *Le judéo-christianisme*; A. F. J. Klijn and G. J. Reininck, *Patristic Evidence for Jewish-Christian Sects* (NT.S 36), Leiden 1973; A. F. J. Klijn, 'Das Hebräer- und das Nazoräerevangelium', *ANRW* II/25.5 (1988) 3997–4033; J. Carleton Paget, 'Jewish Christianity', *CHJud* III (1999) 731–75; P. L. Schmidt, '"Und es war geschrieben auf Hebräisch, Griechisch und Lateinisch": Hieronymus, das Hebräer-Evangelium und seine mittelalterliche Rezeption', *Filologia mediolatina* 5 (1998) 49–93.

(a) The Gospel of the Hebrews (EvHeb)

We find the earliest relatively certain attestation of EvHeb in the Alexandrian theologians Clement and Origen. It seems that EvHeb was written in Egypt, unless we wish to assume an historical kernel in the legendary account of the visit to India by their teacher, Pantaenus. According to Eusebius (*Historia Ecclesiastica* 5.10.3), Pantaenus found there Matthew's Gospel in the Hebrew language, which had been brought to India by the apostle Bartholomew. This might indicate that EvHeb was composed elsewhere and brought to Egypt at a secondary stage.

There is no doubt that Clement and Origen read EvHeb in Greek. Its composition can be dated to the first decades of the second century. Jerome too, who was in Egypt from 385 to 386, came to know EvHeb in Alexandria.

We should note that neither the Alexandrians nor later writers treat EvHeb as heretical testimony. They are indeed unwilling to accord it the same status as the canonical gospels, but they quote from it with respect, probably because this text was inextricably linked in their minds with the Hebrew 'Ur-Matthew'.

(1) 'Seeking and finding' in Clement of Alexandria

A beautiful logion which Clement of Alexandria twice quotes (attributing it in one passage to EvHeb) has now been identified as nr. 2 in the Greek and Coptic versions of the Gospel of Thomas (cf. ch. 7a below); this logion may have been present in both gospels. We begin our discussion with a synopsis of these four attestations (opposite): the first two are from Clement's *Stromateis,* the third is based on Coptic Thomas, and the fourth on the (partly reconstructed) Greek version.

Let us combine the four versions into a long form of the logion which attempts to integrate all the various elements:

> The one who seeks must not cease to seek until he finds.
> When he has found, he will be disturbed.
> When he is disturbed, he will begin to be astonished.
> When he begins to be astonished, he will reign.
> When he begins to reign, he will find rest.

This logion has the form of a *sorites,* where the last word in one line is taken up at the beginning of the next line. The effect of this rhetorical device is to create the impression of a compelling necessity, where one line leads logically to the next.

Behind the contents of this logion (though at some distance) stands Jesus' logion about seeking and finding (Mt 7:7, cf. also Mt 11:28f.). But this is not the only quarry: Clement quotes the logion in the context of a quotation from Plato, for whom 'astonishment' is the beginning of all philosophy. 'Reigning' recalls the central message of Jesus' preaching, viz.

Strom. 2.45.5	Strom. 5.96.3	GThom 2	POxy 654.5–9
As it is also written in the Gospel of the Hebrews:	*The following word is like these (words):*	*Jesus said:*	*Jesus says:*
	The seeker must not cease until he finds;	The one who seeks must not cease seeking until he finds;	The seeker must not cease seeking until he finds;
	but when he has found, he will be disturbed;	and when he finds, he will be perturbed;	and when he has found, he will be disturbed;
	but when he is disturbed,	and when he is perturbed,	and when he is disturbed,
The one who has begun to be astonished		he will be astonished,	
will reign;	he will reign;	and he will reign over the universe.	he will reign;
and the one who has begun to reign will find rest.	and when he has begun to reign, he will find rest.		and when he has begun to reign, he will find rest.

the sovereignty of God, in which all who are saved will have a share; our logion, however, does not understand this 'reigning' in an eschatological sense, but as something that is present now, or else is timeless. Besides this, one basic principle of Cynic-Stoic philosophy (embraced by Philo of Alexandria too) is that only the wise man truly reigns as king. Gnostics came more and more to identify 'rest' as the highest gift of salvation.

The logion contains an intentional paradox: only the restless activity of seeking leads to the rest for which one yearns. But what ought one to seek? If we take the Gospel of Thomas as the framework for our interpretation, the task is to uncover the deeper meaning of the words of Jesus; this can be extended to Scripture as a whole, or else to the question of the meaning of one's own existence. In Jewish wisdom literature, divine wisdom is the object of human seeking, and Sir 6:27f. shows how the various elements in our logion can find a point of reference in this sapiential tradition:

Search out and seek, and she (wisdom) will become known to you;
and when you get hold of her, do not let her go.

For at last you will find the rest she gives,
and she will be changed into joy for you.

(2) The 'mother' of Jesus in Origen

It would seem that one logion in EvHeb made a particularly great impact, since Origen quotes it twice and Jerome three times. The following passage in Origen's commentary on John mentions the source of the logion (*In Johannem* 2.12):

> But if one accepts the Gospel of the Hebrews, where the Saviour himself says: 'Recently, my mother the Holy Spirit took me by one of the hairs on my head and bore me off to the great mountain Tabor', he must ask how the Holy Spirit, who came into being through the Logos, can be the 'mother' of Christ.

Origen, who clearly disapproved of the role attributed to the Spirit in this text, nevertheless found himself obliged to discuss it. To speak of the Spirit as Jesus' 'mother' presupposes semitic thinking; in semitic languages (unlike Greek and Latin), the word for 'spirit' is feminine. Mount Tabor will probably suggest to us the transfiguration of Jesus, but a tradition localized an event from the temptation narrative there too. Where Mt 4:8 says that 'The devil took him to a very high mountain', EvHeb speaks of the Spirit (cf. Mt 4:1), and the perspective of the speaker in the logion makes sense, if EvHeb does indeed have the temptation in mind: the inner circle of three disciples were present at the transfiguration, but not at the temptation, and this is why Jesus subsequently tells his disciples what happened on that occasion.

Biblical texts relate that the prophets Ezekiel and Habakkuk are lifted by the hair and transported to another place (Ezek 8:3, Dan 14:36), but there is no exact parallel to the affirmation that Jesus is borne off by one single hair. Arnold Meyer comments: 'Clearly, the intention is to state that Jesus did not need to be pulled away; thanks to an inner impulsion, he automatically followed the flight of the Spirit, so that it sufficed for him to be led very gently, as if by one single little hair' (in: *Handbuch zu den Neutestamentlichen Apokryphen*, Tübingen 1904, 28).

(3) Jesus and the sinful woman according to Didymus the Blind

Eusebius attributes to EvHeb a narrative preserved by Papias about a woman who was brought to Jesus, accused of many sins (*Historia Ecclesiastica* 3.39.19). This most likely refers to the 'homeless' pericope (or 'apocryphal', if one prefers the term) about Jesus and the sinful woman, which ended up only by chance in John's Gospel (8:3–11), although some scholars have suggested that Papias refers to Lk 7:36–50. New papyrus discoveries have revealed another version, in a biblical commentary by Didymus the Blind, the Alexandrian scholar who was the teacher of Jerome and of Rufinus (who translated Origen into Latin). This is frag. 3b in Lührmann's enumeration:

It is related in some gospels that a woman was condemned by the Jews because of a sin and was taken to the customary place of stoning, in order that she might be stoned. We are told that when the Saviour caught sight of her and saw that they were ready to stone her, he said to those who wanted to throw stones at her: 'Let the one who has not sinned, lift a stone and throw it. If someone is certain that he has not sinned, let him take a stone and hit her.' And no one dared to do so. When they examined themselves and recognized that they too bore responsibility for certain actions, they did not dare (to stone) her.

While this version is clearly shorter than that in Jn 8:3–11, the words of Jesus display an unnecessary doublet; this makes evaluation difficult. It is probably not an abbreviated version of Jn 8:3–11, but an independent variant tradition, found by Didymus in a non-canonical gospel which was available in Alexandria.

(4) The baptism of Jesus in Jerome

Two of the three non-canonical versions of the baptism of Jesus are found in Jerome. Although his introduction speaks of 'Nazaraeans', recent scholars attribute the following version to EvHeb (Jerome, *In Isaiam* 11.2):

According to the Gospel written in the Hebrew speech, which the Nazaraeans read, the whole fount of the Holy Spirit shall descend upon him ... Further in the Gospel which we have just mentioned we find the following written:

'And it came to pass when the Lord had come up out of the water, that the whole fount of the Holy Spirit descended upon him and rested on him and said to him: "My Son, in all the prophets I was waiting for you, that you should come and I might rest in you. For you are my rest; you are my firstborn Son who reigns for ever".'

When the Spirit addresses Jesus as 'my Son', we are reminded of the concept of the Spirit as his mother, discussed above.

This text shows the intersection of the prophetic and the sapiential traditions which have their roots in the Old Testament. It is not by chance that Jerome quotes this narrative of Jesus' baptism in his commentary on Is 11:2: 'The Spirit of the Lord shall rest upon him [i.e. upon the 'shoot from the stump of Jesse'], the spirit of wisdom and understanding, the spirit of counsel and might, the spirit of knowledge and the fear of the Lord.' The prophets of the old covenant received a share in this Spirit, but it is only upon Jesus that the Spirit rests in fullness – and when this fullness is called a 'fount', we may compare the expression 'fountain of wisdom' in Bar 3:12. The sapiential literature says that wisdom 'in every generation passes into holy souls and makes them friends of God and prophets' (Wis 7:27), and she herself says: 'Among all these I sought a resting place; I sought in whose territory I might lodge' (Sir 24:7).

To some extent, contradictory tendencies are at work here. On the one hand, there is no mention of a dove descending from heaven or of a voice which sounds forth from heaven: it is the Spirit who speaks directly to Jesus (perhaps as an interior voice), and this looks like a reduction of the mythological 'props'. On the other hand, we find here the wisdom myth of early Judaism, which was to unfold its full potential in Gnosis.

(5) James, the Lord's brother, in Jerome

Jerome twice quotes exhortations from EvHeb to fraternal love and mutual consideration which are particularly appropriate to a relatively small and compact group of Jewish Christians: 'As we have read in the Hebrew Gospel, the Lord says to his disciples: "And never be joyful, except when you look at your brother in love"' (*In Ephesios* 5.4); 'In the Gospel according to the Hebrews, which the Nazaraeans are wont to read, there is counted among the most grievous offences: "He who has grieved the spirit of his brother"' (*In Ezechielem* 18.7).

These two logia form a good introduction to a narrative in which James, the Lord's brother (not the apostle James from the circle of the twelve), plays a key role alongside Jesus. The scene takes place after Easter, but also refers back to the pre-Easter situation of the Last Supper (Jerome, *De viris illustribus* 2):

The Gospel called according to the Hebrews which was recently translated by me into Greek and Latin, which Origen frequently uses, records after the resurrection of the Saviour:
'And when the Lord had given the linen cloth to the servant of the priest, he went to James and appeared to him. For James had sworn that he would not eat bread from that hour in which he had drunk the cup of the Lord until he should see him risen from among those who sleep. And shortly thereafter the Lord said: "Bring a table and bread!"' And immediately it is added: 'He took the bread, blessed it and broke it and gave it to James the just and said to him: "My brother, eat your bread, for the Son of Man has risen from among those who sleep"'.

The central concern of this text is to elaborate 1 Cor 15:7 by attributing the first appearance of the risen Lord to his brother James, thus legitimating him as head of the post-Easter community. James was the great hero of Jewish Christianity, where he was called 'the just' (as in this text). So popular was this tradition among Jewish Christians that we have six attestations of it (Klijn nr. 15).

It seems strange that the risen Jesus himself should give the high priest's servant the linen cloth in which his body had been wrapped (cf. Jn 20:6f.). We may dismiss as fanciful the suggestion that it was needed as a table-cloth for the table which James was to bring into the room, since the only function of the linen cloth is to underline the reality of the resurrection. The remarks of Hans Waitz in the second edition of NTApo are still pertinent here: 'The resurrection narrative – unlike the biblical accounts – must describe how the Lord emerged from the tomb before the eyes of the soldiers who were keeping guard. He himself gives the servant his linen cloth, so that he can bring it to the high priest as evidence of the resurrection of Jesus' (Tübingen 1924, 49).

The narrative retrospect intends to assert that James, the Lord's brother, was present at the Last Supper, where he drank from the chalice of the Lord. (The other, less convincing possibility points to the chalice of suffering, as at Mk 10:38f.) James takes a vow, analogous to Jesus' vow at Mk 14:24, not to eat again unless Jesus rises from the dead. Here too, an apologetic argument can be discerned: if James – the 'just' man – deviates from his vow, the only reason can be that the resurrection has indeed taken place and the risen Lord has encouraged his brother to resume eating.

Bibliography

P. Vielhauer and G. Strecker, in: NTApo I, 172–78; D. Lührmann, *Fragmente*, 40–55; A. F. J. Klijn, *Jewish-Christian Gospel Tradition*; S. C. Mimouni, *Le judéo-christianisme*, 207–25; P. Vielhauer, *Geschichte*, 656–61.

(b) The Gospel of the Nazaraeans (?) (EvNaz)

The Gospels call Jesus a 'Nazarene' (Mk 1:4 in the Greek) or 'Nazoraean' (Mt 2:23) because of his home town of Nazareth; the latter term allows a clearer allusion to Hebrew roots meaning 'consecrated person' or 'scion'. After Easter, it appears that the terms 'Nazoraeans' or 'Nazaraeans' (both words are found) were applied for a time to his followers in general, especially in Syria; gradually, this developed into a designation for special groups of Jewish Christians in the Jordan area and Syria. Scholars call the gospel these Christians used the 'Gospel of the Nazaraeans' (a name not found in the sources), and propose a date of 150 or somewhat earlier.

Eusebius, writing in the period between the Alexandrians and Jerome, attributes knowledge of a 'Gospel of the Hebrews' to Hegesippus (c. 160–180; *Historia Ecclesiastica* 4.22.8). In a fragment called *Theophania*, he himself quotes from a 'gospel written in Hebrew characters' a moralizing non-canonical version of the parable of the talents, in which the Lord punishes, not the one who had hidden the money, but another 'who squandered the property of his master with harlots and flute-girls'.

Most modern editions relate these two pieces of information to EvNaz, but Eusebius himself does not explicitly state this. This means that we must read the following textual examples with a double reservation. (*a*) It is possible that they belong to EvHeb, enriching our knowledge of that text; or (*b*) that they come from other works and contexts which we can no longer identify. But since our main concern here is to study the contents of these traditions about Jesus, uncertainty about their exact provenance does not affect the conclusions we will draw.

(1) The rich man in Origen (?)

A parallel tradition to Mt 19:16–24 is found only in the Latin translation of Origen's commentary on Matthew. His introduction speaks of
EvHeb, but most recent scholarship attributes this text to EvNaz,
arguing that only the Latin redactor has inserted it in Origen's text. Let
us prescind from the disputed question of the provenance and present a
synopsis of this version and the pericope in Matthew.

Mt 19:16–24	Gospel of the Nazaraeans
And behold, one came up to him, saying:	The other of the two rich men spoke to him:
'Teacher, what good deed must I do, to have eternal life?'	'Teacher, what good thing ought I to do, so that I may live?'
And he said to him, 'Why do you ask me about what is good? One there is who is good.	He said to him:
If you would enter life, keep the commandments.'	'Man, fulfil the law and the prophets.'
He said to him, 'Which?'	
And Jesus said, 'You shall not kill, You shall not commit adultery, You shall not steal, You shall not bear false witness, Honour your father and your mother, and, You shall love your neighbour as yourself.'	
The young man said to him, 'All these I have observed; what do I still lack?'	He replied to him, 'I have done this.'
Jesus said to him, 'If you would be perfect, go, sell what you possess and give to the poor, and you will have treasure in heaven; and come, follow me.'	He said to him, 'Go and sell all you possess, and share it out among the poor, then come and follow me.'
When the young man heard this he went away sorrowful; for he had great possessions.	Then the rich man began to scratch his head, and it [i.e. Jesus' words] did not please him.
	And the Lord said to him: 'How can you say: "I have fulfilled the law and prophets"? For it is

	written in the law: "Love your neighbour as yourself"; and behold, many of your brothers, Abraham's sons, are stiff with dirt and die of hunger, and your house is full of many good things, yet nothing at all comes out of your house to them!'
And Jesus said to his disciples: 'Truly, I say to you, it will be hard for a rich man to enter the kingdom of heaven.	And he turned around and said to Simon, his disciple, who sat beside him:
Again I tell you, It is easier for a camel to go through the eye of a needle than for a rich man to enter the kingdom of God.'	'Simon, son of Jona, it is easier for a camel to go through the eye of a needle than for a rich man [to enter] the kingdom of heaven.'

Strictly speaking, we should also take into consideration Mk 10:17f., since there the man asks: 'Good Teacher, what must I do to inherit eternal life?', and Jesus rejects this form of address with the words: 'Why do you call me good? No one is good but God alone.' The christological problem implicit in Jesus' rejection of the attribute 'good' is defused by Matthew and EvNaz in the same way, viz. by omitting these words and employing the expression 'doing good'.

At the beginning of the text, EvNaz speaks of 'the other of the two rich men'. A preceding passage must therefore have spoken of the first of the two (unlike Matthew's text). This may indicate some kind of gospel harmony in which the present pericope was preceded by a text like Lk 12:13–21, where Jesus is asked to settle a dispute about an inheritance, and replies with the parable of the rich farmer.

A particularly striking feature of the narrative in EvNaz is the comprehensive formula: 'Man, fulfil the law and the prophets.' Why then does not Jesus quote five commandments from the decalogue and the precept of love of neighbour (Lev 19:18), as he does in Mt 19:18f.? The reason is that EvNaz is concerned not only with the decalogue, but with the Jewish law in its entirety (an attitude typical of Jewish Christians); hence there is no need to mention the ten commandments specifically.

The designation 'the rich man' is found only in EvNaz, but corresponds to Matthew's statement that 'he had great possessions' (cf. also Lk 18:23, 'for he was exceedingly *rich*'). EvNaz writes that the rich man begins to scratch his head (instead of 'going away sorrowful'); this vivid, novelistic detail cannot plausibly claim to be more original than Matthew's formulation.

Since the rich man does not go away at this point, Jesus can address him a second time, quoting the commandment to love one's neighbour (already mentioned by Matthew in v. 19b) and deriving this specifically from 'the law' (Lev 19:18). The designation of the rich man's brothers as 'sons of Abraham' is a further glimpse of the background in a Jewish-Christian community which attaches great value to the observation of the social obligations inherent in the law (cf. Deut 15:4, 'Let there be no poor among you'). The rich man's failure to live up to these precepts reveals the hollowness of his initial claim to do all that the law and the prophets demand. The parable about the rich man and Lazarus (Lk 16:19–31) is based on similar considerations.

The address 'Simon, son of Jona' in the closing verse is parallel to 'Simon Bar-Jona' at Mt 16:17. A marginal variant reading at Mt 16:17 in the gospel codex 566 appeals to *To Iudaïkon* and reads 'Simon, son of John' (as in Jn 1:42). We shall return to this interesting textual witness below.

(2) The fragments in Jerome

When scholars propose a distinction between EvHeb and EvNaz, Jerome becomes the principal witness to the latter gospel. He says that he derives his knowledge of EvNaz from people living in Beroea (near Aleppo in Syria), and three of his references to EvNaz call for particular attention.

(a)   The question why Jesus submitted to the penitential baptism of John posed a problem as early as the New Testament tradition and *a fortiori* for the early church, as we see in the second of the three non-canonical versions of the baptismal pericope which Jerome has preserved in *Adversus Pelagianos* 3.2:

Behold, the mother of the Lord and his brethren said to him: 'John the Baptist baptises for the remission of sins, let us go and be baptised by him.' But he said to them: 'What sin have I committed, that I should go and be baptised by him? Unless what I have said is ignorance (a sin in ignorance).'

The text seems simply to deny that Jesus was baptized by John, although the lack of a narrative context for this fragment makes it impossible to be certain of this; perhaps the intention is merely to insert a safety clause like that at Mt 3:15, where Jesus accepts baptism only because 'thus it is fitting to fulfil all righteousness'.

An important factor in our christological evaluation of this text is how we understand the term 'ignorance'. We should resist the temptation to refer it exclusively to Jesus' preceding question, 'What sin have I committed?', as if that question had made an erroneous presupposition; such an interpretation does nothing to explain the passage. Rather, the text assumes that while Jesus has not committed any grave, intentional sins, he has most probably sinned unintentionally and unknowingly. The Old Testament too is familiar with this differentiation: cf. the reference to 'unwitting error' in Lev 5:18. This would be a relic of an old Jewish-Christian christology which chose not to keep up with all the doctrinal developments in the church at large.

(b)   Much speculation has been devoted to the Greek word *epiousios* in the fourth petition in the Lord's Prayer, since this is otherwise unattested. Does it mean 'daily' bread, 'tomorrow's' bread, or 'necessary' or 'supernatural', or something else again? Jerome had his own view about this, but he knows of another suggestion (*In Matthaeum* 6.11):

In the so-called Gospel according to the Hebrews, I have read, instead of 'essential to existence', the word *mahar,* i.e. 'belonging to tomorrow'. The meaning would then be: 'Our bread of tomorrow' – i.e. our future bread – 'give us today.'

Jerome understood the word in an eschatological sense: 'tomorrow's bread' is our 'future' bread, the food promised us in the time of fulfilment when we will celebrate a feast together with Jesus; but it is possible that those who first handed on this interpretation understood the word literally. Homeless itinerant apostles and missionaries were glad when they had tomorrow's bread ration available today – that meant one less problem to cope with. Recent exegesis takes seriously the possibility that this may have been the original meaning of the fourth petition in the Lord's Prayer.

(c)   In Mt 12:9–14, Jesus heals a man with a withered hand on a sabbath day in the synagogue. As the reaction of the Pharisees in v. 14 shows, this is a clear infringement of the law.

EvNaz tones down the scandalous quality of Jesus' action by offering a detailed description of the life this man led. The text reveals his physical and social distress and evokes a deep sympathy with him; this accorded with Jewish-Christian sensitivity. Jerome writes (*In Matthaeum* 12.13):

In the Gospel which the Nazarenes and the Ebionites use, which we have recently translated out of Hebrew into Greek, and which is called by most people the authentic [Gospel] of Matthew, the man who had the withered hand is described as a mason who pleaded for help in the following words: 'I was a mason and earned (my) livelihood with (my) hands; I beseech you, Jesus, to restore to me my health that I may not with ignominy have to beg for my bread'.

I have intentionally included here Jerome's introduction to this quotation, since it reminds us of how problematic the search for Jewish-Christian gospels is. Here, Jerome equates the Gospel of the Nazaraeans, which is familiar to him, with the Gospel of the Ebionities, which he claims to have translated into Greek (if this is indeed true, he must have relied on helpers who knew the language); then he writes that 'most people' consider this text to be the Hebrew Ur-Matthew.

(3) The 'Zion Gospel edition'

We have already mentioned gospel codex 566. Together with a small number of other codices, it contains marginal glosses to the Gospel of Matthew which are attributed to *To Ioudaïkon*, i.e. to a Jewish gospel. Some scholars identify this with EvHeb or EvNaz, while others see it as a separate work. It is suggested that these marginal notes go back to an old gospel manuscript once kept in the basilica on Mount Zion in Jerusalem; this lost archetype is therefore given the name 'Zion gospel edition'.

Let us see some examples of its readings. At Mt 4:5, in the temptation narrative, we are told that the devil took Jesus, not *into the holy city*, but *to Jerusalem*. At 5:22, many textual witnesses read: 'Everyone who is angry against his brother *without a reason* will be liable to judgement.' A marginal gloss in codex 1424 observes that in some witnesses and 'in the Jewish gospel' the word for 'without a reason' is missing, so that all anger (even reasonable anger) is condemned by Jesus. Here, the 'Jewish gospel' has preserved the older reading, which is favoured by modern textual editions too.

Codex 899 mentions another omission in the logion about the sign of Jonah (Mt 12:40), 'For as Jonah was three days and three nights in the belly of the whale, so will the Son of Man be three days and three nights in the heart of the earth.' According to the gloss, '*To Ioudaïkon* does not read: "three days and three nights".' This is probably because a comparison with the events of Easter shows that Jesus did not in fact lie in the tomb for three days *and three nights*. If we count Good Friday and Easter Sunday as parts of days, we do indeed reach the total of three days, but only *two* nights.

An observation in the 'Jewish gospel' at Mt 27:65 about the task of the soldiers who guarded Jesus' tomb is strongly reminiscent of the Gospel of Peter: 'And he [Pilate] deliverd to them armed men that they might sit over against the cave and guard it day and night.'

Sometimes the 'Jewish Gospel' agrees with Jerome, especially in the change made to Mt 18:21f. both in Jerome (*Adversus Pelagianos* 3.2) and in codices 566 and 899:

He [Jesus] said: 'If your brother has sinned with a word and has made reparation to you, receive him seven times in a day.' Simon his disciple said to him: 'Seven times in a day?' The Lord answered and said to him: 'Yes, I say to you, up to seventy times seven times. For even in the prophets after they were anointed with the Holy Spirit, (a) *word* of sin was found.'

The expression 'word of sin' does not mean (as some translations imply) that the prophets employed the word 'sin'. No doubt they did so, but that is not what this text wishes to say: rather, it affirms that even after their vocation (symbolized in the anointing with the Spirit) the prophets were not preserved from the possibility of sin, and hence required forgiveness again and again. It is possible that their sins were only sins of the tongue (cf. Sir 19:16, 'Who has never sinned with his tongue?'), and that forgiveness by other human beings was enough. In favour of this suggestion, we may note that the introductory sentence amplifies Mt 18:21 by speaking of sin 'with a word' and of the reparation that must be made before forgiveness is granted.

One last interesting example is a logion which codex 1424 adds at Mt 7:5 from *To Ioudaïkon*, although its contents indisputably belong to Mt 7:21–23: 'If you are in my bosom and do not do the will of my Father in heaven, I will cast you out from my bosom' (quoted also in 2 Clement 4:5). In Mt 7:21, entrance to the kingdom of heaven is made conditional on doing God's will. The same principle is illustrated by this additional logion, which appeals to the image of the eschatological feast at which the elect will sit at table beside the Lord (cf. Jn 13:23).

(4) Transmission of the tradition in the middle ages

A Jewish-Christian gospel – more precisely, the Jewish-Christian gospel which was understood to form a literary unity, relying on the authority of the Hebrew Ur-Matthew – continued to exert considerable influence in the middle ages and produced many new narrative shoots. It is virtually impossible to determine the age of these traditions; some may indeed go back to a lost Jewish-Christian gospel. It is here that we first find the title 'Gospel of the Nazaraeans', e.g. in Haimo of Halberstadt in the ninth century: 'As it is said in the *Gospel of the Nazaraeans*: "At this word of the Lord many thousands of the Jews who were standing around the cross became believers" ' (Klijn nr. 47). This certainly refers to the word of the Lord at Lk 23:34, 'Father, forgive them, for they know not what they do.' We may compare the 'many thousands' of converts here to the accounts of successful preaching in the Acts of the Apostles (e.g. 2:41). The title is found for the second time (in the plural) in a marginal note in a manuscript of a twelfth-century work by Peter of Riga: 'In the *Gospel* books which the *Nazarenes* use we read: "Rays went forth from his eyes, by which they were frightened and fled" ' (Klijn nr. 46); this may refer to the cleansing of the temple.

Appeal is often made to an EvNaz or EvHeb in order to add details and resolve exegetical difficulties. For example, we are told that the many miracles performed by Jesus in Chorazim and Bethsaida (Lk 10:13) were 53 in number (perhaps this should really be 153, like the fish in Jn 21:11). – Names are supplied for nameless personages: the woman with the flow of blood (Mt 9:20) is given the name 'Mariosa', the man with the withered hand (Mt 12:10), described (as in Jerome: cf. above) as a mason, is called 'Malchus', and the queen of the South (Mt 12:42) is called 'Meroe'.

Jesus' confiscation of two animals at his entry to Jerusalem (Mt 21:1–3) posed difficulties which were resolved as follows: 'But these animals were sent back by the Saviour to their owners, as we read in the Gospel according to the Hebrews' (Klijn nr. 56). And how was it possible for John the beloved disciple to gain admission to the court of the high priest, who knew him – while Peter had to stay outside (Jn 18:16)? A mediaeval *Historia Passionis Domini* supplies the explanation (Klijn nr. 54):

In the *Gospel of the Nazaraeans,* we are told how John had become acquainted with the high priest. He was the son of the poor fisherman Zebedee and had often brought fish to the palace of the high priests Annas and Caiaphas. John went out to the girl who kept the door and persuaded her to admit his companion Peter, who stood outside the gate weeping loudly.

New errors are also introduced. Hugh of St Cher (thirteenth century) attributes to the Gospel of the Nazaraeans the affirmation – which he himself considers incorrect – that the risen Jesus showed himself first to his mother Mary (Klijn nr. 50); here there is a confusion with Mary Magdalene. Hugh relates that, in the same source, Jesus appears first to Joseph of Arimathea, who has been imprisoned because of Jesus, before showing himself to Mary Magdalene (Klijn nr. 49); and that after the resurrection, two holy men who had been dead for about 40 years enter the temple and declare that they wish to go to Pergamum (Klijn nr. 48). There are obvious connections between these pieces of information and the Gospel of Nicodemus (see ch. 6b below), which may indeed be their source, rather than a 'Gospel of the Nazaraeans'.

We see that lengthy narratives are uncommon. One exception is found in Sedulius Scottus (ninth century), who devotes considerable space in his commentary on Matthew to an alternative version of Mt 2:1–12 (Klijn nr. 41):

For thus the Gospel which is entitled 'According to the Hebrews' reports:
'When Joseph looked out with his eyes, he saw a crowd of pilgrims who were coming in company to the cave, and he said: "I will arise and go out to meet them." And when Joseph went out, he said to Simon [his adult son: cf. Mk 6:3], "It seems to me as if those coming were soothsayers [*augures*], for lo, every moment they look up to heaven and confer with one another. But they seem also to be strangers, for their appearance differs from ours; for their dress is very rich and their complexion quite dark; they have caps [*pileos*] on their heads and their garments seem to me to be silky, and they have breeches [*saraballae,* a Persian loan-word] on their legs. And lo, they have halted and are looking at me, and lo, they have again set themselves in motion and are coming here."
'From these words it is clear that not merely three men, but a crowd of pilgrims came to the Lord, even if according to some the foremost leaders of this crowd were named with the definite names Melchus, Caspar and Phadizarda.'

The fine portrait of the foreign astrologers ('at every moment they look up to heaven') which Joseph formulates in direct speech points to Persia, not least because of the caps and breeches. The main point for the narrator is that more than three wise men travelled to Bethlehem; here, he is in agreement with Mt 2:1–12, which never mentions 'three kings'. Nevertheless, three of them are singled out as leaders and given specific names, which in part are still familiar to us – Caspar, Melchior and Balthasar. How is it that Joseph has an adult son? We shall learn the answer in the Protevangelium of James (see ch. 5a).

Bibliography

P. Vielhauer and G. Strecker, in: NTApo I 154–65; A. F. J. Klijn, *Jewish-Christian Gospel Tradition*; P. Vielhauer, *Geschichte*, 648–52; S. C. Mimouni, *Le judéo-christianisme*, 207–25; J. Frey, 'Die Scholien nach dem "jüdischen Evangelium" und das so genannte Nazoräerevangelium', ZNW 94 (2003) 122–37.

(c) The Gospel of the Ebionites (EvEb)

For information about EvEb, we must turn to Epiphanius, bishop of Salamis on Cyprus from 366 to 403, where he composed his major work, the *Panarion* ('medicine-chest against all the heresies'). In Book 30, from which we quote in this section, he discusses the Ebionites or Ebionaeans, attributing the origin of this sect to a founder called 'Ebion' (an error Epiphanius shares with other fathers). In reality, the name is based on the Hebrew word *ebionim*, 'the poor', an honorific title among pious Jews.

According to Epiphanius, these Ebionites, who probably lived in Transjordania, used a gospel which they themselves called the 'Gospel of Matthew' or 'Hebrew' Gospel (13.2). This was an early attempt at a synoptic gospel harmony, excluding John but perhaps including the Acts of the Apostles, composed most probably in the mid-second century.

Epiphanius accuses the Ebionites of employing a 'forged and mutilated' gospel (13.2) without an infancy narrative or genealogy as in Mt 1–2 (13.6; 14.3). This indicates Jewish-Christian reservations about the doctrine of the virginal conception of Jesus. EvEb begins, like Mark, with the appearance of John the Baptist. Epiphanius writes (13.4f.):

And his food, we are told, was wild honey, the taste of which was that of manna, as a cake [*egkris*] dipped in oil. Thus they were resolved to pervert the word of truth into a lie and to put a cake in the place of 'locusts' [*akrides*, in the singular *akris*].

The first point we note is the play on words: *egkris/akris*. Since this works only in Greek, it follows that EvEb as Epiphanius knew it was a Greek text. It was probably also originally written in Greek, based on the Greek texts of the synoptic gospels.

In the Old Testament, we read that the manna tasted like 'cakes baked with oil' (Num 11:8) or 'wafers made with honey' (Ex 16:31). An even more decisive reason for the replacement of the roasted locusts with honey cakes in EvEb was the strict vegetarianism of the Ebionites, who could not accept even the hint that John or Jesus ate meat, as we see in the following text (22.4f.), which takes up Lk 22:15:

But they abandon the proper sequence of the words and pervert what is said, although this is plain to all from the words which belong together. They have the disciples say: 'Where do you wish us to prepare the passover meal for you?' They have Jesus reply as follows: 'Surely I do not desire with desire to eat meat with you at this passover?' But is not their folly perfectly obvious? The sequence of the text cries out that the *mu* and the *eta* are an addition – they have added the word 'not' to Jesus' words: 'I have desired.' In reality, he said: 'I have desired with desire to eat this passover with you.' But those who add the word 'meat' have fallen into a foolish error and written: 'Surely I do not desire with desire to eat meat with you at this passover?'

The Greek letters *mu* and *eta* form the negation *mē*. Jesus' words at Lk 22:15 are expanded to specify that the *meat* of the paschal lamb is consumed at the passover meal, and the *negation* of the entire sentence offers a strong argument against eating meat and in favour of vegetarianism. This vegetarian lifestyle had its primary source in a radicalization of Jewish regulations about diet and purity, which the Ebionites continued to observe. Besides this, one could never be certain in a predominantly non-Jewish world whether meat came from an impure animal or had come into contact with sacrifices to the gods. Complete abstinence from meat was a reliable alternative to such uncertainties.

This may be one aspect of the criticism of sacrifices which EvEb attributes to Jesus (16.5): 'I came to do away with sacrifices, and if you do not cease to sacrifice, the wrath will not depart from you.' We also find in other Jewish-Christian texts a vigorous polemic, not only against pagan sacrifices, but also against the Old Testament sacrificial cult within Judaism. This polemic arose after the destruction of the temple had put an end *de facto* to Jewish sacrificial praxis.

EvEb contains the third non-canonical parallel to the narrative of the baptism of Jesus by John (13.7f.):

When the people were baptized, Jesus also came and was baptized by John. And as he came up from the water, the heavens were opened and he saw the Holy Spirit in the form of a dove that descended and entered into him. And a voice said from heaven: 'You are my beloved Son, in you I am well pleased.' And again: '*This day I have begotten you.*' And immediately a great light shone round about the place. When John saw this, we are told, he said to him: 'Who are you, Lord?' And again a voice from heaven [said] to him: 'This is my beloved Son in whom I am well pleased.' And then, we are told, John fell down before him and said: 'I beseech you, Lord, baptize me.' But he prevented him and said: 'Let it be so, for thus it is fitting that everything should be fulfilled.'

The special elements in this baptismal pericope include the union between the Spirit and Jesus, the great light which suddenly shines out, and the doubling of the heavenly voice, which speaks first to Jesus and then to the Baptist. His reluctance to perform the baptism, and Jesus' reply, are reminiscent of Mt 3:14f.

The dynamite in this version of the baptism narrative is the fact that the heavenly voice is not content to quote only the first half of the verse from Ps 2 ('You are my son'), but employs a transitional formula to add the second half: 'This day I have begotten you' (some manuscripts of Lk 3:22 do the same; we may note that many specific traits of the apocryphal gospels are also found in the New Testament textual tradition). This addition – '*Today* I have begotten you' – makes possible an adoptionist or even a docetic interpretation of the baptismal scene. The former would say that it is only at his baptism that God adopts and publicly acclaims the man Jesus of Nazareth as his Son; the docetic reading would emphasize the fusion with the Spirit and say that it is only at his baptism that a heavenly spiritual being enters the man Jesus.

It is obvious that the rigidly orthodox Epiphanius must reject this christology as defective. He identifies other defects too, when he asserts that the Ebionites explicitly deny the humanity of Jesus (14.5) and attributes to them the belief that Jesus was not 'born of God the Father, but created like one of the archangels' (16.4). Thus it is possible that the model of an 'angelic christology' had survived among the Ebionites, who understood Jesus as the great angel of God, analogous to Michael.

One final passage from Epiphanius' account of the Ebionites has been accorded greater importance by scholars than its problematic nature deserves (13.2f.):

There appeared a certain man named Jesus of about thirty years of age, who chose *us*. And when he came to Capernaum, he entered into the house of Simon whose surname was Peter, and opened his mouth and said: 'As I passed along the Lake of Tiberias, I chose John and James the sons of Zebedee, and Simon and Andrew and Thaddaeus and Simon the Zealot and Judas Iscariot, and you, Matthew, I called while you sat in the customs house, and you followed me. I wish you therefore to be twelve apostles for a testimony to Israel.'

The closing sentence speaks of twelve apostles, although only eight names have been mentioned, but this is only a minor blemish. Jesus himself recapitulates here in direct speech his calling of the apostles, as related in the synoptic gospels, so that he might prepare them for their mission. We have already seen a similar transformation of narrative into direct speech on the lips of Jesus in the 'Unknown Berlin Gospel' (see ch. 2d above). The position at the end of the discourse and the individual details supplied emphasize the calling of the 'tax collector' Matthew, which would certainly make sense in a 'Gospel according to Matthew'. The unmistakable Jewish-Christian character of this pericope is seen in the fact that the twelve are to be 'a testimony to Israel'.

One other detail, at the very beginning of the text, is striking: Jesus 'chose *us*'. The first person plural means that the narrative is related from the perspective of eyewitnesses (possibly with Matthew as their spokesman). Since these eyewitnesses are the apostles, many scholars have identified EvEb with the 'Gospel of the twelve apostles' (or 'of the twelve', or 'of the apostles') which is mentioned by Origen and Jerome. However, if that were true, we should expect to find the entire EvEb in the 'we'-form; the few surviving fragments neither demonstrate this with certainty nor allow us to exclude the hypothesis completely. One possibility is an abrupt transition from a personal ('we') to a neutral ('he') narrative perspective, but here too, the appropriate response seems to be scepticism. It is also possible that this pericope does not come from the same gospel as the other fragments. (In his introduction to the last quotation at 13.2, cited above, Epiphanius speaks both of 'the Gospel of Matthew' and of a 'Hebrew gospel'. These need not necessarily be the same text – even if Epiphanius himself thought they were.)

We have now examined the basic materials which scholars attribute to the specific Jewish-Christian tradition about Jesus. We have seen the fragmentary condition of the texts and the problems involved in their classification; these make it extremely difficult to evaluate their tradition-history with any measure of certainty. In general, we may say that they present a strange mixture of predominantly secondary traits and many archaic survivals. The threefold baptismal pericope illustrates this point well. No doubt, most of its material is shared with the synoptics, and it is broadly based on the canonical gospels – but does this suffice to explain the question in the pericope whether Jesus might have committed unwitting sins? Alfred Resch held that: 'Jewish Christianity has already come so far at this stage that it dares to take up the question of Jesus' sinlessness', though as yet only 'in a coy manner' (*Agrapha*, 234), but this view need not be correct. On the contrary, it seems more plausible that this element derives from an early stage of tradition and from a milieu where the idea of a Jesus who was aware of being a sinner was indeed felt to be problematic, but not yet as offensive and heretical as it later became in the church at large.

Little is gained by calling the Jewish Christianity which produced these texts 'heretical' and 'syncretistic-gnostic'. It would be more helpful to accept the theological impulses which the texts offer and to make use of them in today's dialogue between Jews and Christians.

Bibliography

P. Vielhauer and G. Strecker, in: NTApo I, 166–71; D. Lührmann, *Fragmente*, 32–9; A. F. J. Klijn, *Jewish-Christian Gospel Tradition*, 65–77; S. C. Mimouni, *Le judéo-christianisme*, 257–72; D. A. Bertrand, 'L'Evangile des Ebionites: Une harmonie évangélique antérieure au Diatessaron', *NTS* 26 (1980) 548–63: G. Howard, 'The Gospel of the Ebionites', *ANRW* II/25.5 (1988) 4034–53.

4

TWO GOSPELS OF THE EGYPTIANS

It has become misleading to speak of 'the' Gospel of the Egyptians in the singular, since we now possess two unrelated texts with this title. One 'Gospel of the Egyptians', some fragments of which are quoted in Greek by Clement of Alexandria, has been known for a long time, and is found in every collection of New Testament apocrypha; the second 'Gospel of the Egyptians' is a Coptic text which became accessible only in the mid-twentieth century, when it was discovered at Nag Hammadi.

It is true that the literary genre of this second text is not that of a genuine gospel, and we shall discuss Nag Hammadi in ch. 7 of this book. But the identity in name suggests that we offer a foretaste of the Nag Hammadi codices (NHC) by presenting their 'Gospel of the Egyptians' in the present chapter.

(a) The Greek text in Clement of Alexandria (EvEg [Gr])

(1) Contextual information

Origen was acquainted with a gospel 'According to the Egyptians', but refused to make use of it, since it did not belong to the four canonical gospels (*In Lucam* 1.2). According to Hippolytus, the gnostic Naassene group appealed to EvEg in support of their special doctrine about the soul (*Refutatio* 5.7.8f.), and Epiphanius mentions its title when he discusses the sect of the Sabellians in his *Panarion* (42.2.4). These three authors evaluate EvEg as a text which is no longer orthodox.

Clement of Alexandria takes a different position. In Book 3 of his *Carpets,* where he discusses questions about marriage and sexuality, he takes issue with encratites, i.e. Christians who abstained from intercourse even in marriage since they rejected sexuality and procreation. They had drawn radical inferences from Paul's incipient recommendations in 1 Cor 7, and appealed to EvEg in support of their views. Clement intends to refute this argument by demonstrating that they have misunderstood EvEg. This complicated series of refractions makes it difficult to uncover the original intention of the statements in EvEg.

Since Clement is familiar with the text, it must have been composed in the second century, probably before 150. Its title led earlier scholars to assume that it was the gospel of Gentile Christians in Egypt, as the Gospel of the Hebrews was the gospel of Jewish Christians in Egypt; but it is possible that the title 'According to the Egyptians' was acquired only outside Egypt, e.g. in Rome, and recent scholars are more cautious in their affirmations about the diffusion of EvEg. It suffices to see it as the basic text of an autochthonous Egyptian group in Alexandria. (On this and on the following questions, cf. especially Petersen.)

(2) The contents

The logia which Clement quotes from EvEg seem to come from one single context, viz. a dialogue in which Jesus instructs Salome. It is unclear whether it is the risen Lord or the earthly Jesus who speaks with her; in the former case, the text would be a 'dialogue gospel' (cf. ch. 8 below). Salome is a disciple of Jesus, one of the women who stood at a distance and saw him hanging on the cross (Mk 15:40), and went on Sunday morning to the tomb (Mk 16:1). At Mt 27:56, the parallel text to Mk 15:40, she is not called 'Salome', but 'the mother of the sons of Zebedee', James and John (cf. also Mt 20:20). It is difficult to assess whether this implicit equation of the two women is historically correct; at any rate, later tradition tended to retain such identifications and to introduce new ones. If Salome is understood by EvEg to be the mother of James and John, this affects our understanding of one particular text (see below).

Although the order of texts may have been different in EvEg itself, we follow here the sequence of quotations in Clement. The first text is a brief dialogue between Salome and Jesus (*Stromateis* 3.45.3; quotations from EvEg in italics):

When Salome asked, 'How long will death have power?', the Lord answered: 'So long as you women bear children.' [He did not say this] because life itself was evil and the creation bad, but in order to teach the natural sequence – for what comes into being always ceases to be.

Salome's initial question is found later in the form: 'How long will people die?' (3.64.1), asking about the duration of this earthly time where death holds sway. The meaning of Jesus' mysterious reply becomes clearer in the course of the subsequent argumentation, but we may begin by recalling God's words to the woman at Gen 3:16, 'I will greatly multiply your pain in childbearing; in pain you shall bring forth children.' Since childbirth is a characteristic of the fallen world, Clement's opponents infer that one should abstain from marital intercourse. He himself understands the logion in sapiential terms, as a description of the necessary sequence of the generations, and he refuses to draw negative consequences about the created order, to which gender duality belongs.

A further logion continues this topic and raises the argument to a higher pitch (*Stromateis* 3.63.1):

Those who are opposed to God's creation because of continence, which has a fair-sounding name, also quote the words addressed to Salome which I mentioned earlier. They are handed down, as I believe, in the Gospel of the Egyptians. For, they say, the Saviour himself said, *'I am come to undo the works of the female'*, by the female meaning lust, and by the works birth and decay.

This has a programmatic sound to it – 'to undo the works of the female' – but Clement edulcorates the logion by means of an allegorical and moralizing exegesis: he specifies that 'the female' denotes such passions as avarice, pride, vainglory and pederasty, from which Christians should now abstain. However, even his opponents' exegesis in terms of sexual abstinence falls short of the original intention of EvEg, which envisaged a fundamental abolition of gender duality: although this was indeed laid down at creation, it is the mark of a negative division and separation which will be reassumed into an overarching unity at the end of time. Why is it 'the female', rather than 'the male', that must be overcome? This is because of the patriarchal societal context in which the masculine was evaluated more highly than the feminine; besides this, in the second creation narrative in Gen 2, it is the male human being, Adam, who is created first, and only then the female, Eve. Hence, a return to the origins would mean a return to the male principle.

According to Clement, his opponents have omitted to quote Salome's obvious reaction, and the subsequent reply of the Lord. This means that he does not owe his knowledge of EvEg exclusively to their writings (*Stromateis* 3.66.1f.):

Why do they [i.e. the encratites] not also adduce what follows the words spoken to Salome, these people who do anything but walk by the gospel rule according to truth? For when she said, '*I have then done well in not bearing children*', as if it were improper to engage in procreation, then the Lord answered and said, '*Eat every plant, but that which has bitterness eat not.*'

Salome's words are usually translated: 'I have then done well in not bearing children'; in other words, she is childless. If however EvEg understands her as the mother of the sons of Zebedee, we would have to read these words (as is philologically possible) as the expression of an unreal wish ('I would have done well, had I not borne children'). They would then be the expression of Salome's repentance at having given birth to her two important sons.

Once again, Jesus' reply is mysterious. Clement himself may have read it in sapiential terms, as Petersen (p. 211) suggests: 'You can do whatever you wish, but be aware of the consequences!' This, however, is not likely. In the context of EvEg, the 'bitter plant' must be related to sexuality, and above all to childbirth, which can be called 'bitter' because of what it entails – the pangs of birth, the labour involved in bringing up children, and the subordination to one's husband which was expected in classical antiquity. Here too, we should recall Gen 3:16: 'I will greatly multiply your pain in childbearing; in pain you shall bring forth children, yet your desire shall be for your husband, and he shall rule over you.' The grammatical construction of the logion also recalls Gen 2:16f.: 'You may freely eat of every tree in the garden; but of the tree of the knowledge of good and evil you shall not eat ... [otherwise] you shall die.' EvEg employs the metaphor of the bitter plant for the entire complex of fall, gender duality, childbirth and death. Accordingly, it is better to abstain from all of this and to attempt to return to that state which existed before human beings were divided into male and female. This, of course, means that EvEg was a much more encratite document than Clement was willing to recognize. Encratite does not, however, necessarily mean gnostic; it was Clement's gnostic opponents who first read a dualistic rejection of the world into EvEg.

Finally, Clement mentions the name of his opponent, viz. the Alexandrian theologian Julius Cassian in his book *On continence or on castration* (*Stromateis* 3.92.2–93.1):

> Therefore Cassian now says, *When Salome asked when what she had inquired about would be known, the Lord said, 'When you have trampled on the garment of shame and when the two become one and the male with the female [is] neither male nor female.'* Now in the first place we have not this word in the four Gospels that have been handed down to us, but in the Gospel of the Egyptians. Further he seems to me to fail to recognise that by the male impulse is meant wrath and by the female lust.

Clement's first move is a 'canonical' argument: these words are found only in EvEg, not in the New Testament gospels. His second move is, once again, an allegorical exposition: 'male' denotes wrath, 'female' denotes lust. The logion in EvEg takes its starting-point in the first creation narrative, where the human being is created as man and woman (Gen 1:27). This gives it a more egalitarian tone, like Paul's programmatic affirmation in Gal 3:28, 'There is *neither male nor female*' (for the logion as a whole, cf. also the metaphor of clothing in the previous verse – 'You have put on Christ' – and the theme of unity in 3:28, 'You are all *one* in Christ Jesus'). 'The garment of shame' in EvEg is the human body. This is a further reference to the fall, which entailed the end of the state described in Gen 2:25: 'And the man and his wife were both naked, and were not ashamed.' This logion expresses, even more clearly than the earlier logion about 'the works of the female', the yearning that gender duality may be overcome.

This logion has a parallel in the second (pseudepigraphical) Letter of Clement of Rome (2 Clem 12:2):

> For the Lord himself, on being asked by someone when his kingdom should come, said: 'When the two shall be one and that which is without as that which is within, and the male with the female neither male nor female.'

These words and their subject matter have many parallels in the logia in the Gospel of Thomas (cf. especially EvThom 22 and 37); since we shall return to this text in ch. 7a below, we content ourselves here with the question of how the various versions of this one logion are related. While we cannot wholly exclude the possibility that the author of 2 Clement has taken it directly from EvEg (or *vice versa*), it is equally possible that this was a widely diffused logion which was made accessible to its witnesses at least in part by a continuing oral tradition.

Bibliography

W. Schneemelcher, in: NTApo I, 209–15; D. Lührmann, *Fragmente*, 26–31; P. Vielhauer, *Geschichte*, 662–65; S. Petersen, *'Zerstört die Werke der Weiblichkeit!'*, 77–9, 195–200.

(b) The Coptic text from Nag Hammadi (EvEg [NHC])

(1) Contextual information

Around the middle of the twentieth century, thirteen codices containing texts in the Coptic language were found near Nag Hammadi in Egypt. Most had gnostic contents; we shall return to these in ch. 7 below. Two treatises with identical contents are found as the second text in the third codex (page 40, line 12 to page 69, line 20: abbreviated as NHC III, 2: 40, 12–69, 20) and as the second text in the fourth codex (page 50, line 1 to page 81, line 2: abbreviated as NHC IV, 2: 50, 1–81, 2). The relationship between these texts is not one of direct dependence; rather, they present two independent translations of the same Greek text, with divergences due, not only to the fact that two separate translators were at work, but also to textual transmission. This means that our two Coptic texts were not translated from exactly the same Greek archetype; rather, they reproduce older Coptic manuscripts which themselves may be based on various Greek manuscripts.

This complicated translation process must be borne in mind, when we attempt to determine the age of the work; we must distinguish between the text as it now stands and its contents. Our manuscripts are from the mid-fourth century, but the various intermediary stages bring us back to a date in the early third or the second century for the composition of the original work.

Since IV,2 is very badly preserved (although it is more precise in terms of the substance of the work), we shall refer primarily to III,2. The colophon (i.e. concluding formula) of this text calls the version in III,2 'The Gospel of the Egyptians' (69,6). This may indicate that the treatise was written, and above all read, in Egypt, but it is not the real title. This is presented, in keeping with classical custom, as a *subscriptio* (a 'sub-title', so to speak, not a 'sur-title') and reads: 'The Holy Book of the Great Invisible Spirit' (69,18–20). The *incipit,* the beginning of the book at 40,12–14, corresponds to this: 'The [holy] book [of the Egyptians] about the great invisible [Spirit, the] Father whose name cannot be uttered ...' The title 'Gospel' may have been added at a later stage, perhaps in order to make it acceptable to members of the worldwide church.

This is not a 'gospel' in our sense of the word; while Jesus Christ is not wholly missing, he plays only a secondary role, and the emphatic language of the colophon is exceptional (69,14f.): 'Jesus Christ, Son of God, Saviour, Ichthus' (i.e. 'fish', a symbol of Christ). The central figure is the great Seth, Adam's son (cf. Gen 5:3). 'Seth' is, however, also the name of a local Egyptian deity who embodies the evil opposing power. Gnosis loves to undertake radical re-evaluations and see things in a new light – for example, the present tractate has Seth settle his descendants in Sodom and Gomorrah, of all places. This means that the double meaning of the name 'Seth' is intentional, and envisages an Egyptian readership. Here, we enter the sphere of the exuberant gnostic mythology which was to some extent an artificial creation.

Why then is such a work called a 'gospel'? The concept is employed here by way of analogy: the Coptic gnostic Gospel of the Egyptians is concerned about salvation history in the widest sense of the term. The origins of salvation history are pursued back to a time before the creation of the world; but the same can be observed, albeit much more briefly, in the prologue to John's Gospel. Further, the Nag Hammadi Gospel of the Egyptians depicts the path taken by a redeemer figure named Seth, and the salvation of all who adhere to him.

When we read such works, which are difficult to understand and initially seem repellent, it is important to remember that we need not share the world-view elaborated by the authors. The first step is simply to discover what this world-view was, and to endeavour to understand what the texts wish to convey.

(2) The contents

The work can be subdivided into four main sections, with two longer and two shorter parts. The first extensive section deals with the origin of the heavenly world (41,8–55,16), and the second with the path taken by Seth and his descendants (55,16–66,8). This is followed by a shorter hymnic section containing prayers (66,8–67,26) and a similarly short closing section (68,1–69,20).

– On the origin of the heavenly world

At the beginning stands the Father God, the invisible Spirit who lives in perfect light and silence, and about whom only negative affirmations can be made. From him there proceeds a strange Trinity which includes another Father lower in degree (although this is not said explicitly in the text: 41,7–12):

Three powers came forth from him; they are the Father, the Mother, (and) the Son, from the living silence, what came forth from the incorruptible Father. These came [forth from] the silence of the unknown Father.

We are then told that these three entities are 'ogdoads', i.e. eightfold entities containing other powers which they can emit from themselves, thus generating continuous emanations and articulations within the heavenly world; the text devotes many pages to these, since the underlying concern is to build a bridge across the seemingly infinite distance which separates the highest God from the world of human beings.

Among the many figures who gradually appear on the scene are the '[great] Christ whom the [great] invisible Spirit had anointed' (44,22–24) and 'Adamas' (49,8f.), the first human being, who plays an important role as the narrative unfolds. The decisive turning-point comes at 51,5–14:

The incorruptible man Adamas asked for them a son out of himself, in order that he (the son) may become father of the immovable, incorruptible race, so that, through it (the race), the silence and the voice may appear, and through it, the dead aeon may raise itself, so that it may dissolve.

The self-*dissolution* of the dead world is not seen as a punishment, but as a necessary component of *redemption*. Adamas' son is Seth (Gen 5:3), and his race are the gnostics who look forward to perfection. At present, however, it is only 'the incorruptible, spiritual church' (55,3f.) that exists in the heavenly world.

– Seth and his descendants

The main character in the second principal section of the text is the great Seth, who yearns for his 'seed', i.e. his descendants. Only now is the world created by the great angel Sakla and the great demon Nebruel. Although Sakla has some traits of the Bible's divine creator, the fact that the creation of the world was an unintended error means that he is separated far from the highest Father and is accused of arrogance (58,23–59,4):

And after the founding [of the world] Sakla said to his [angels], 'I, I am a [jealous] god, and apart from me nothing has [come into being,' since he] trusted in his nature. Then a voice came from on high, saying, 'The Man exists, and the Son of the Man.'

The heavenly voice announces the coming into existence of the earthly human being. Along with him, Metanoia, the personification of repentance, comes into existence; her very name indicates that this phase of the creation remains defective and must be overcome.

The basic structure of the history of salvation and damnation sketched in the second principal section is paradoxical: although Seth's descendants are the immovable and incorruptible race, they are exposed to hostilities and dangers. The devil and his helpers take on many disguises and employ a multitude of tricks to divert Seth's adherents from their path; Seth sends 'guardians' to help them, and finally himself comes to save them.

One of the forms in which Seth appears is Jesus Christ. The text hints at this when it speaks of the 'Logos-begotten body which the great Seth prepared for himself, secretly through the virgin' (63.10–13), and it is affirmed clearly in expressions such as 'Jesus the living one, even he whom the great Seth has put on' (64,1–3). The long list of redeemer figures who are revealed begins at 64,9–11 with the strange name

'Yesseus Mazareus Yessedekeus', which doubtless conceals the name of Jesus; it also includes 'Jesus, who possesses the life and who came and crucified that which is in the law' (65,17f.). We may note that the crucifixion is interpreted here, not as passive suffering, but as an active deed. The consequence of all of this for the 'Sethians' (if we may use this name) is: 'These will by no means taste death' (66,7f.).

– Hymnic section and conclusion

The response to this message of salvation is the praise uttered in the hymnic section, where language is taken to its limits – and beyond (69,9–22):

Really truly,
O Yesseus Mazareus Yessedekeus,
O living water,
O child of the child,
O glorious name!

Really truly,
O existing aeon,
iiii ēēēē oooo uuuu ōōōō aaaa.

Really truly,
ēi aaaa ōōōō,
O existing one who sees the aeons!

Really truly,
aee ēēē iiii uuuuuu ōōōōōōōō,
who is eternally eternal.

Really truly,
iēa aiō, in the heart,
who exists, uaei eisaei, eioei, eiosei.

These vowel sequences, which reduce language to its naked essence as sound, are related to the early Christian phenomenon of 'speaking in tongues' about which Paul writes in 1 Cor 14. In general, one need not look for any specific meaning, although with a little imagination one can read the vowels in the last line as Greek, expand them a little, and group them as follows: *(h)u(os) aei eis aei, ei o ei, ei os ei* – 'who exists as Son for ever and ever. You are what you are, you are who you are.'

The concluding section juxtaposes a first and a second conclusion to the book, finishing with the colophon and *subscriptio* mentioned above. Here we learn more about the composition of the text: 'This is the book which the great Seth wrote, and placed it in high mountains' (68,1–3). It took him 130 years to write it, and his primary intention is to proclaim that this incorruptible, holy race of his descendants already exists.

Bibliography

A. Böhlig and F. Wisse, in: NHL 208–19; U. K. Plisch, in: *Nag Hammadi Deutsch* I, 239–321; G. Lüdemann and M. Janssen, *Bibel der Häretiker*, 230–46; A. Böhlig and F. Wisse, *Nag Hammadi Codices III,2 and IV,2* (NHS 4), Leiden 1975; A. Böhlig, 'Das Ägypterevangelium als ein Dokument der mythologischen Gnosis', in: Idem, *Gnosis und Synkretismus* (WUNT 47), Tübingen 1989, 341–70; H. J. Klauck, 'Von Kassandra bis zur Gnosis. Im Umfeld der frühchristlichen Glossolalie', *ThQ* 179 (1999), 289–312, at 305–10.

It is scarcely possible to draw up a comparison between the two gospels which we have studied in this chapter, since the state of their preservation and transmission is so different: on the one hand we have an entire Coptic text of some considerable length, preserved in two separate versions, while on the other hand we have only a few Greek fragments quoted by a church father. Thus, while we see that EvEg (NHC) does not contain any discussion of gender polarity and sexual continence, we do not know whether this was in fact as prominent a theme in EvEg (Gr) as the deliberately selected quotations in Clement suggest.

At any rate, however, we cannot overlook the great divergence in the atmosphere of the two works, which is concretized above all in the position attributed to Jesus Christ. There is no question that he is the authoritative speaker and the main character in EvEg (Gr), but the figure of Seth in EvEg (NHC) completely marginalizes him; or, to put it more accurately, he is given a marginal position by being integrated into a system in which Seth had the central role *a priori*.

This shows us that gnosis knew and employed a variety of redeemer figures, or a variety of names for the manifestation of the redeemer. We also see here how wide a spectrum is covered by the collective term 'early Christian apocrypha'; the discoveries at Nag Hammadi have considerably broadened our perspective on this point.

5

INFANCY GOSPELS

Strictly speaking, an 'infancy gospel' is a contradiction in terms. The name 'gospel' was initially applied by the first Christians to the oral proclamation of Jesus' death on the cross and his resurection; Mark was the first to employ it for a narrative account of the story of Jesus from the appearance of John the Baptist to the discovery of the empty grave, and it developed into the designation of a literary genre which never placed its primary emphasis on the *birth* of Jesus. Matthew and Luke do indeed give information about his birth in the two chapters which introduce each of their gospels; but the evangelists understand these texts as a prelude or 'trial run' preceding their real subject, viz. the public ministry and the passion of Jesus.

There is an obvious link, demonstrable at many points, between the so-called apocryphal 'infancy gospels' and the infancy narratives in Mt 1–2 and Lk 1–2. Why were they composed? One important factor was the desire to fill the narrative gaps in Matthew and Luke; besides this, a comparison of these two very different accounts of Jesus' birth indicated a number of open questions, and people felt a need to know more about the main characters. Stories were told about the years in which Jesus was growing to manhood, and the story of his mother Mary's childhood was related, while a biographical excursus could be devoted to figures such as Joseph or John the Baptist.

The authors of the infancy gospels draw their material not only from Mt 1–2 and Lk 1–2, but from the entire New Testament, as well as from the Greek version of the Old Testament and from the biographical literature of late antiquity, which had developed fixed *topoi* to describe the provenance of great personalities. One may well have theological reservations about what happened when the preparatory phase in Jesus' life was detached and isolated from the kernel of the oral and written gospel, and this phase underwent an inflationary expansion (in rhetorical terms, an *amplificatio*). One should not expect historically reliable information, even in exceptional cases, from this literature. It adds nothing to our knowledge of Jesus' human origins.

Bibliography

F. Bovon, 'Die Geburt und die Kindheit Jesu', *BiKi* 42 (1987), 162–70; R. F. Hock, *The Infancy Gospels of James and Thomas* (The Scholars Bible 2), Santa Rosa, Calif. 1995; G. Schneider, *Evangelia Infantiae Apocrypha/Apokryphe Kindheitsevangelien* (FC 18), Freiburg i.Br. 1995.

(a) The Protevangelium of James (Protev)

(1) *Contextual information*

The name 'Protevangelium' (i.e. 'first gospel') was first given to this text in the sixteenth century when it was rediscovered and made accessible to the West by the French humanist Guillaume Postel. The name seems to have been suggested by the idea that this text served as an introduction to Mark, whose gospel begins rather abruptly in 1:1–8 with the appearance of John the Baptist. In the oldest manuscript, PBodmer V (early fourth century), its main title is 'The Birth of Mary', with an additional secondary title: 'Revelation of James'. This is not the son of Zebedee, one of the twelve (Mk 3:17), but James the brother of the Lord (Mk 6:3), although some scholars have preferred to identify him as 'James the younger' (Mk 15:40). At any rate, this transparent authorial fiction is found in the text itself: 'Now I, *James*, who wrote this history ...' (25:1). The Protevangelium was composed between 150 and 200 in an unknown place; Egypt has been suggested, but Syria or Asia Minor would also be possible.

The large number of surviving Greek manuscripts (*c.* 140) and numerous translations into oriental languages attest the popularity of this text in the east. The textual form is not wholly fixed; we find abbreviations, expansions and paraphrases, and even the oldest textual witness, PBodmer V, displays traces of considerable interventions, mostly intended to shorten the text. Only a few fragments of a Latin translation have survived, thanks to the condemnation of the Protevangelium as a dangerous apocryphal writing by the Gelasian Decree, a list of canonical books drawn up in the western church (see Introduction, above). Objection was taken to the fact that the Protevangelium interprets the 'brothers' of Jesus in the same way as the eastern church up to the present day: Joseph was a widower when he married Mary, and the 'brothers' were sons from his first marriage. The western church adopted the interpretation favoured by Jerome, understanding the 'brothers and sisters' of Jesus as his cousins.

This already gives us a glimpse of the contents and the source of the Protevangelium. In chs. 11–21, it attempts with an astonishing measure of success to combine the disparate narrative cycles of Lk 1–2 and Mt 1–2 into one coherent story. Additional material is employed; sometimes other traditions, e.g. the birth of Jesus in a cave, are preferred to Luke's account. The account of the conception and birth of Jesus is preceded in chs. 1–10 by a still earlier 'prior history' which concentrates on the birth of Mary. Her parents are presented, and we learn hitherto unknown details about her early years. Apart from the pious imagination, the main source here is the Septuagint, the Greek translation of the Old Testament, from which the author derives the names of his characters and a number of Jewish customs, some of which are described in a distorted form. In chs. 21–24, he relates how Herod's slaughter of the holy innocents threatened the life of John the Baptist too, and how his father Zechariah consequently died as a martyr at the hands of the king. In a brief epilogue (ch. 25), the narrator reveals his own identity in the first person singular; otherwise (apart from the section 18:2–19:1, see below), he writes in the third person.

This work has many charming touches, and apart from the scene involving Salome in chs. 19–20, it avoids gross exaggerations. The best way to characterize its general intention is to call it 'praise of Mary'. It intends to demonstrate with all desirable clarity the purity of Mary, the new 'Eve', from her own conception and birth, in her earliest childhood, her years as a 'temple virgin', and in her 'fictitious' marriage to Joseph, until the birth of Jesus. Apologetic interests have been suspected here, e.g. a reaction to the accusations of the pagan philosopher Celsus, who mocked the lowly social origins of Jesus and laughed at the very idea of a virginal conception. Celsus' book was written between 170 and 180 and is known to us from the response it provoked in Origen's *Contra Celsum*. In the Protevangelium, Mary's parents enjoy a high social position, and her virginity is repeatedly confirmed by a variety of witnesses – the angel, Joseph, the priest and the people, not forgetting the midwives.

One other tendency is, however, surely just as important. The Protevangelium offers an encomium of Mary, a laudatory address which follows the rules of rhetoric applicable to this genre, beginning with her noble origins (*genos*), her birth (*genesis*), her education (*paideia*) and her deeds (*praxeis*).

(1) The contents

– Prior history

Chapter 1 presents Joachim, the future father of Mary. He is called 'very rich' (1:1), recalling Joakim, the husband of Susanna in Dan 13:1–4, whose name he borrows; Anne, Joachim's wife, is given the same name as Hannah in 1 Sam 1–2. When sacrifice is offered on a feast day, Reubel/Reuben, who functions as Israel's spokesman, reproaches the kind and generous Joachim on account of his childlessness. Joachim withdraws in sadness to the wilderness, where he fasts for forty days. He is consoled when he remembers that God gave the patriarch Abraham a son even in his old age.

In the meantime, Anne's maid makes similar reproaches on account of her childlessness. She turns in prayer to God, who 'blessed the womb of our mother Sarah and gave her a son, Isaac' (2:4; cf. also Tobit 3:7–15). In a moving hymn in several strophes, taking up the genre of the Old Testament cries of lamentation, Anne compares the fruitfulness of nature in Joachim's great garden, where she is sitting, with her own barrenness (ch. 3). An angel of the Lord appears and addresses her with words which recall Lk 1:26–31: 'Anne, Anne, the Lord has heard your prayer. You *shall* conceive and bear, and your offspring shall be spoken of in the whole world' (4:1). Anne promises that she will consecrate the child, whether boy or girl, to serve in the temple (cf. 1 Sam 1:11). Another angel tells Joachim: 'Behold, your wife Anne *has* conceived' (variant reading: '*will* conceive'), and urges him to return from the wilderness to which he had withdrawn.

– A virginal conception?

The text-critical question about the tense of the verbs italicized in our quotations recurs at 4:4, when Anne recounts her encounter with Joachim. Are we to read: 'I *have* conceived', or: 'I *shall* conceive'? The reading in the past tense is probably older, and elevates the conception of Mary in the absence of Joachim to a miraculous conception without male involvement. In other words, the claim found in some of the New Testament traditions, that Jesus was virginally conceived, is now transposed to Mary.

If this interpretation is incorrect, we would have to understand the statement: 'And Joachim rested the first day in his house' (4:4) as a curtain drawn discreetly in front of a conception in the normal manner, and the verbs in the perfect tense as concealed (so-called 'prophetic') affirmations about future events. Even if we understand the text to speak of a virginal conception, this does not yet amount to an affirmation of the 'immaculate' conception of Mary. The latter term refers to her freedom from original sin rather than to a conception without sexual intercourse on the part of her parents. However, when we bear in mind the link Augustine makes between original sin and concupiscence, and the corresponding devaluation of sexuality, we see that it was easy to move from the one affirmation to the other.

On the following day, Joachim offers a great sacrifice in the temple, which in some obscure way confirms his freedom from sin (5:1). The sin in question may perhaps have been the fact that he was in reality the father of Mary. The frontlet of the priest (Ex 28:36–38) functions here as an oracle. Presumably, this resembled a mirror of metal which became brighter or darker as a reaction or answer to changing situations and issues.

– Birth and early childhood

In the seventh month, a daughter is born miraculously and is given the name Mary (5:2). Six months later, she takes her first seven steps. Anne then turns her bedchamber into a sanctuary and chooses 'the undefiled daughters of the Hebrews' to keep Mary company (6:1).

On the child's first birthday, Joachim invites all the people and all the office-bearers to a great feast (cf. Gen 21:8), during which the priests and chief priests invoke God's blessing on Mary (6:2). This prompts

Anne to withdraw into her bedchamber and sing her own 'Magnificat': 'I will sing praises to the Lord my God, for he has visited me and taken away from me the reproach of my enemies ...' (6:3).

When Mary is two years old, Joachim proposes that Anne's vow be fulfilled and the child handed over to the temple, but Anne's moving plea obtains a postponement of one more year: 'Let us wait until the third year, that the child may then no more long after her father and mother' (7:1; cf. 1 Sam 1:21–24).

When Mary is three years old, she is led to the temple by the Hebrew virgins, who bear burning torches (cf. Mt 25:1–12?). Here, the priest greets her with words taken from Lk 1:48, and Mary delights all who are present by dancing on the steps of the altar.

– The oracle of the rod

All we are told about the ensuing years is that Mary lives as a temple virgin 'like a dove' (the anachronism reflects the later Christian ideal of virginity), and that 'she received food from the hand of an angel' (8:1). When she is twelve, however, the priests must face the problem that she might defile the Lord's temple (the text passes over in silence the reason, viz. her first menstruation). They urge the high priest Zechariah – identified by the author of the Protevangelium with the father of John the Baptist (Lk 1:5–25; cf. his temporary dumbness at Protev 10:2) – to enter the Holy of Holies and seek divine counsel. An angel charges him to call together all the widowers in Israel. Each is to bring his rod, since God will give a sign through these rods. The priest takes them with him when he goes into the temple to pray, and then hands them out again (cf. the 'oracle of the rod of Aaron', Num 17:16–28).

Joseph too lays down his axe, the tool of his trade, and obeys this summons (9:1). 'Joseph received the last rod, and behold, a dove came out of the rod and flew on to Joseph's head' (cf. Mk 1:10), indicating that he has been chosen to take 'the virgin of the Lord' as his wife, while preserving her as a virgin for God.

Joseph initially protests, pointing out that he is an elderly man with sons of his own; he does not want to be mocked by the people. Finally, when the high priest threatens him with God's punitive judgement, he gives in and takes Mary to his house (which the author clearly locates in Jerusalem), then sets out on his travels 'to build my buildings'.

– The conception of Jesus

The primary function of ch. 10 is to affirm that Mary remained a virgin during the following years; according to 12:3, she is sixteen years old when Jesus is conceived. Since she more than adequately fulfils the qualifications required, she is given the task, along with seven virgins from the tribe of David (!), of making the precious curtain for the temple (cf. Ex 35:25). She carries out this work in her own home.

Ch. 11, which keeps closely to its model in Lk 1:26–38, announces the miraculous conception of Jesus through the 'Logos' of God (11:2). The angel speaks to Mary while she is drawing water and spinning in her house. This is followed in ch. 12 by a free version of Mary's visit to her relative Elizabeth from Lk 1:39–56.

– The crisis

The crisis occurs when Joseph returns home in the sixth month of Mary's pregnancy and at once sees her condition. He utters bitter lamentations (13:1):

Who has done this evil in my house and defiled the virgin? Has the story (of Adam) been repeated in me? For as Adam was (absent) in the hour of his prayer and the serpent came and found Eve alone and deceived her and defiled her, so also has it happened to me

(cf. Gen 3:13 and the tradition of Jewish exegesis up to 2 Cor 11:3; this passage implicitly calls Mary the new Eve). According to 12:2, Mary has in fact 'forgotten' the mysterious words spoken to her by the angel; she is completely silent about these matters, and can only declare that she is innocent. Joseph begins to reflect on the situation, wondering whether Mary's child 'may have sprung from the angels' (14:1; this picks up the story of the fall of the angels in Gen 6:1–4 and gives it a positive turn). He is reluctant to hand her over to a court, which would be obliged to sentence her to death. This allows the author of the Protevangelium to introduce material from Mt 1:18–25: an angel reveals the truth to Joseph in a dream (14:2).

– The ordeal

On the next day, Annas the scribe visits the house and discovers that Mary is pregnant. He informs the high priest, voicing the obvious suspicion – which the high priest too accepts – that Joseph has secretly had intercourse with the virgin and that the child is his. (The expression: 'he has stolen marriage with her, and *has not disclosed it to the children of Israel*' at 15:2 and 15:4 appears to mean that he would have been allowed to have a 'normal' marriage with Mary, provided that this was made public in the proper manner.)

When Mary and Joseph are confronted singly with this accusation, all they can do is to affirm their innocence. The 'water of conviction', prescribed by Num 5:11–31 for cases where a woman is suspected of adultery, resolves the situation. In a changed version of the rite, each separately drinks the water of conviction, goes off into the wilderness, and returns 'whole', i.e. without the bodily symptoms threatened in Num 5:21f. This is sufficient evidence of their innocence.

– The journey to Bethlehem

At 17:1f., Joseph and Mary, accompanied by the sons from Joseph's first marriage, set out for Bethlehem to be enrolled in the census ordered by Augustus. During the journey, Mary weeps and laughs, because she sees 'two peoples, one weeping and lamenting and one rejoicing and exulting' (i.e. unbelievers and believers; cf. Lk 2:34 and Gen 25:23). At the halfway point (reckoning either from Jerusalem or from the place of this vision), near the tomb of Rachel outside Bethlehem, Mary's birth pangs begin. Joseph finds a cave for her to shelter in, and goes to look for a midwife.

Here there is a remarkable divergence between the manuscripts. A longer text, beginning at 18:2, has Joseph speak (for the first time in the Protevangelium) in the first person singular. We are reminded of 'Sleeping Beauty' as he relates how everything stands still in hushed expectancy. All nature holds its breath as it awaits the great event that is now to take place. Both the longer version and the shorter text in PBodmer V (which knows nothing of this sudden change in the narrative perspective) agree that Joseph meets a midwife who is just coming down from the hill country (19:1). Strictly speaking, however, her services are not needed. All she does is to stand there and see how the cloud lying over the cave gives way to a great light that shines out in the cave and in turn vanishes when the child 'appears' (19:2).

– The midwife and Salome

As she leaves the cave, the midwife meets another woman named Salome, whom the author may originally have cast as a daughter of Joseph, rather than as a second midwife. 'She said to her: "Salome, Salome, I have a new sight to tell you; a virgin has brought forth" ' – and, as the continuation of the text makes clear, this mother has remained a virgin. Salome reacts like Thomas the 'doubter' in Jn 20:25, 'Unless I put (forward) my finger and test her condition, I will not believe' (19:3).

She is permitted to carry out her investigation in ch. 20, and she confirms that Mary's virginity remains intact even after she has given birth, so that we now have two competent witnesses to this fact, viz. the midwife and Salome. But Salome's curiosity has serious consequences: the hand with which she 'tested' Mary is consumed by fire, and she must recognize that it was *God* she put to the test. An angel tells her to touch the child, and she is healed when she does so. The composition of this episode no doubt owes much to dogmatic reflections on the virginity of Mary both while giving birth (*in partu*) and afterwards (*post partum*).

– The children are endangered

Chapter 21 takes up the narrative of Mt 2 and speaks of the magi and king Herod, but the murder of the holy innocents does not lead in the

Protevangelium to a flight into Egypt. Rather, Mary 'took the child and wrapped him in swaddling clothes and laid him in an ox-manger' (22:2). The manger (cf. Lk 2:7) serves here as a hiding place; the mention of the 'ox' is the first step on a path that will lead to the depiction of ox and ass on either side of the Christmas crib. The omission of the flight into Egypt is motivated by apologetic interests: critics such as Celsus had declared that Jesus was able to work miracles in his public ministry only because he had learned the magic arts in Egypt in his youth.

Herod's action endangers the lives of others too: the king is also searching for John the Baptist (whose birth has been passed over in silence), because he is afraid that John, as the son of a high priest, may be the royal Messiah whose coming was announced (23:2). Elizabeth flees with her son into the hill country, where a fissure opens in a mountain to receive them (22:3).

– The martyrdom of Zechariah

Herod now sends his henchmen twice to the temple, but the high priest Zechariah refuses both times to reveal where his son is hiding. The second time, he replies as follows (23:3):

I am a martyr of God. Take my blood! But my spirit the Lord will receive, for you shed innocent blood in the forecourt of the temple of the Lord

(cf. 2 Chron 24:20–22 and Mt 23:35, where another 'Zechariah' too meets a bloody end 'between the sanctuary and the altar'). Zechariah is killed immediately. The other priests wait in vain at the appointed hour for him to emerge and join in prayer with them. One ventures into the temple, sees the blood beside the altar (which the author wrongly locates within the sanctuary), and hears a voice say: 'Zechariah has been slain, and his blood shall not be wiped away until his avenger comes' (24:2; the 'avenger' may be Christ, or God as judge, or the Roman general Titus who is to destroy the temple). The other priests observe that the blood has now turned into stone, but they do not find the corpse of Zechariah (probably because the murderers have removed it; but cf. the unknown grave of Moses at Deut 34:6 and the vain search for Elijah at 2 Kg 2:16f.). 'All the tribes of the people' mourn him for three days. Then the lot falls on Simeon (from Lk 2:25f.), and he succeeds Zechariah as high priest.

– Conclusion

In the closing chapter, the narrator speaks in the first person singular, before ending his book with a doxology and a blessing: 'Now I, James, who wrote this history, when a tumult arose in Jerusalem on the death of Herod, withdrew into the wilderness ...' (25:1), where he found enough time and peace to compose the Protevangelium. The literary fiction probably identifies him with one of the sons of Joseph mentioned at 17:1f., so that he would be an eyewitness of some of the events related; and the reference to the death of Herod the Great suggests that he is writing at a date when Jesus himself was still only a small child.

(3) Summary

We can scarcely ask for any greater degree of authenticity than this; but one who tries too hard to establish his own authorial authority ends up by establishing nothing at all. What remains is the narrative world of his text, which is generated by biblical models and his own rich imagination.

The Protevangelium also prompts wider-reaching theological questions, however. *First,* is the form of mariology which we meet here still compatible with the testimony of Scripture? This a question which must be answered in the negative, even if dogmatic theology has not yet wholly abandoned its reluctance to accept such a conclusion. *Secondly,* what of the christology of the Protevangelium? When the child Jesus 'appears' at 19:2 and we are given such an emphatic demonstration that his mother remains *virgo intacta,* this is surely reminiscent of docetism – in other words, this Christ was able to pass through his mother without leaving any physical traces behind him, because he has merely the outward appearance of a body. However, the elaboration of these motifs is not clear enough to confirm this suspicion, not least because the Protevangelium is silent about the adult Jesus and his suffering.

It is scarcely possible to underestimate the influence of the Protevangelium on subsequent church history, especially in the fields of mariology, iconography and liturgy (e.g. the feasts of the 'Presentation of Our Lady in the temple', of 'Saints Joachim and Anne', or even, though rather indirectly, the 'Immaculate conception'). Despite the scepticism mentioned above, it became influential in the West too, since other widely-read infancy gospels such as Ps.-Matthew (see below) had drawn much of their contents from the Protevangelium.

Bibliography

O. Cullmann, in: NTApo I, 421–39; R. F. Hock, *Infancy Gospels,* 2–81; G. Schneider, *Kindheitsevangelien,* 95–145; H. R. Smid, *Protevangelium Jacobi. A Commentary* (ANT 1), Assen 1965; E. de Strycker, *La forme la plus ancienne du Protévangile de Jacques. Recherches sur le Papyrus Bodmer 5 avec une édition critique du texte grec et une traduction annotée* (SHG 33), Brussels 1961.

(b) The Infancy Gospel of Thomas (IGTh)

(1) Contextual information

The manuscripts of the infancy narrative of Thomas give the work a variety of titles; the central designation includes the term *paidika*, i.e. 'things (events, deeds) from the childhood (of the Lord)'. The title's attribution to Thomas, one of the twelve, which is repeated in ch. 1, is a later addition; indeed, the preamble as a whole (ch. 1) is a secondary interpolation. Other manuscripts attribute the work to figures such as James. The oldest version was probably anonymous, and the work began with our ch. 2.

The first problem is the fluidity of the text, which exists in three separate recensions, A, B and C. A (printed by Tischendorf) is a longer Greek version containing chs. 1–19, which we mostly follow here. B is a shorter Greek version with many divergent readings. C is a Greek manuscript whose beginning agrees with the Latin translation; it fills the gap between 6:2 and 6:3 in A in the same way as the Slavonic version. We also have a number of other translations, e.g. into Syriac, Ethiopian and Georgian, some of which are older than the fifteenth-century Greek manuscripts on which the reconstruction of A is based.

The variety in length is connected with another factor. IGTh offers 'snapshots' from the life of Jesus between the ages of five and twelve (clearly, no one was particularly interested in what happened to him between the ages of twelve and thirty), showing him performing miracles and outdoing a total of three teachers in disputations. Since most of the individual narratives are self-contained units, they can wander from one manuscript to another, and can be added or dropped in the process of transmission. Information about Jesus' age, the repeated emphasis on the efficacy of his words, and the repetition of a number of motifs are employed in the attempt to create an overarching structure that holds the individual narratives together.

The Old Testament, which is so important for the Protevangelium, plays no role in IGTh. The only direct loan from the New Testament is the pericope about the twelve-year-old Jesus in the temple (Lk 2:41–52, in IGTh 19) – with good reason, since this is the obvious nucleus from which the whole work has grown. New material fills the gap in Lk 1–2 between the birth of Jesus and his public appearance at the age of twelve, and here the New Testament supplies some individual expressions and personal names, patterns of speech and narrative motifs. For example, some stories imitate the healings and raisings of the dead in the canonical gospels, and we are sometimes reminded of miracles in the Acts of the Apostles. We also find in IGTh characteristic elements of the miracle narratives, e.g. a description of human distress, a word which brings about the miracle, the observation that the miracle has indeed taken place, a demonstration and a concluding chorus.

The vivid style of the narrative is sometimes interrupted by speculative and apparently profound words uttered by Jesus. The most important of these is his exegesis of the letter A in ch. 6. Irenaeus of Lyons says that this episode is found in a work used by the gnostics (*Adversus haereses* 1.20.1; cf. Epistula Apostolorum 4:1–5), and this has led some scholars to propose that IGTh as a whole originally had a much more gnostic tone, which was largely eliminated by an orthodox reworking of the text; all that was left was the narrative itself (which the gnostics viewed as only the surface).

Dates from the second to the fifth century have been suggested for the composition of IGTh; however, the parallel to Irenaeus certainly justifies dating the basic material of the text to the late second century.

(2) The contents

– Jesus at the age of five

In the preamble, the author presents himself as 'Thomas the Israelite' and declares his intention of making known to 'the brethren from among the Gentiles' the mighty deeds which Jesus performed in his childhood. He begins with episodes from the life of the five-year-old Jesus, who plays by a brook on the sabbath day, gathers the water into pools, and fashions twelve sparrows from the moist clay. When his father Joseph rebukes him for profaning the sabbath day, Jesus claps his hands, and the sparrows come to life and fly away (2:1–5; this may be meant as a presage of the sending of the twelve apostles).

In ch. 3, the son of Annas the scribe disperses the water which Jesus had gathered, so that the pools dry up. As a fitting punishment, his entire body withers up (cf. Mk 11:20f.), and his distraught parents must take away his corpse for burial. Another child has the misfortune to bump into Jesus as he is running through the village: he drops dead on the spot (4:1), and when his parents complain to Joseph, Jesus strikes them with blindness (5:1). This illustrates the efficacy of his words – 'From where does this child spring, since his every word is an accomplished deed?' (4:1; repeated at 17:2). Joseph is angry, and twists Jesus by the ear. The child protests in words which are difficult to interpret; but at any rate he refrains from punishing Joseph (5:2f.).

– The first teacher

After this first series of miracles, a teacher named Zacchaeus shows an interest in the child and wishes to teach him the alphabet. When Jesus asks whether he himself knows the mystery of the Alpha, Zacchaeus is unable to answer. Jesus then gives the following allegorical (cf. 7:1!) explanation before a great crowd of hearers (6:4):

Hear, teacher, the arrangement of the first letter, and pay heed to this, how it has lines and a middle mark which goes through the pair of lines which you see, (how these lines) converge, rise, turn in the dance, three signs of the same kind, subject to and supporting one another, of equal proportions; here you have the lines of the Alpha.

Much of this is incomprehensible, but it seems to indicate that the three straight lines which make up the letter Alpha are to be interpreted in a trinitarian sense. (Another Greek textual recension and the Slavonic version have a longer text at this point, probably influenced by gnosticism, in which Jesus also says: 'I swear to you, teacher, that I already existed before you were born', and: 'When the world was created, I already existed together with the one who sent me to you.')

Zacchaeus despairs of fulfilling his task, and asks Joseph to take the child back. He also gives voice to a suspicion: 'This child is not earth-born ... Perhaps he was begotten even before the creation of the world' (7:2); he 'is something great, a god or an angel or what I should say I do not know' (7:4; repeated at 17:2). With a laugh, Jesus confirms (in Johannine diction) that he has 'come from above' in order to 'call to the things above' those destined to receive them, and he revokes the punishments he has earlier inflicted, so that all are healed (8:1f.).

– Miracles of rescue

Jesus continues this positive action in miracles which help others. When one of his playmates falls from a flat rooftop and is killed, the parents blame Jesus, since his earlier punitive miracles have made them aware of his powers. Jesus cries with a loud voice and summons the dead child back to life, in order that he himself may confirm the true course of events. The parents praise *God* for this miracle, and fall down before *Jesus* (9:1–3; cf. the story of Eutychus at Acts 20:9–12).

A young man cuts his foot with his axe while chopping wood, and nearly bleeds to death – but Jesus takes hold of the foot and heals the wound. The crowd react with the choral conclusion: 'Truly the Spirit of God dwells in this child' (10:2).

When Jesus is six years old, his mother sends him to fetch water. In the press of the crowd, the pitcher is broken, but Jesus brings the water safely home in the folds of his outer garment (11:1f.).

At the age of eight, he goes out with his father to the field in the time of sowing and sows one single grain of wheat (other textual witnesses read: 'a measure' of wheat). This produces such a rich harvest ('a hundred measures') that the poor in the village can be given wheat, while the rest suffices for Jesus' own family (12:1f.).

Joseph the carpenter, who usually makes ploughs and yokes, is commissioned to make a bed for a rich man. One of the two beams is shorter than the corresponding beam, but Jesus takes it and stretches it until they are equal in length (13:1f.).

– The second and third teachers

In ch. 14, Joseph takes Jesus to a new teacher, who says: 'First I will teach him Greek, and then Hebrew' (an indication of the author's linguistic context). But when Jesus repeats the challenge he had issued to his first teacher – 'Tell me the meaning of the Alpha' – the teacher is 'annoyed' and strikes Jesus on the head. Jesus is hurt and curses him, and the teacher at once swoons and falls to the ground (14:1f.).

Another schoolmaster, this time 'a good friend of Joseph', makes a last attempt. Inspired by the Holy Spirit, Jesus explains the law in fluent language to a great crowd of hearers in the schoolhouse (cf. Lk 4:16–22), and the teacher acknowledges Jesus' superiority. This time, the story has a happy ending, and even the teacher from the previous scene awakens from his faint (15:1–4).

– Miracles

It is clear that the two 'school stories' in chs. 14 and 15 are intentionally framed by the three miracles in chs. 11–13 and three new miracles in chs. 16–18.

In 16:1f., Jesus accompanies his brother James when he is sent to collect wood. A poisonous snake, which had lain hidden among the sticks, bites James' hand, and he is on the point of death when Jesus breathes on the bite. James is at once restored to health (cf. Acts 28:2–6).

After this, a sick child in the neighbourhood dies. Jesus is drawn to the scene by the loud cries of lamentation. He touches the child's breast and commands him to live. At once, the child opens his eyes and laughs (17:1).

One year later, when a man is killed in an accident while building a house, Jesus takes his hand and 'leads' him back to life (18:1). Once again, we should note the choral conclusion on the part of the crowd: 'This child is from heaven, for he has saved many souls from death, and is able to save them all his life long' (18:2).

– Conclusion

IGTh ends in ch. 19 with the narrative which was the inspiration for the composition of all these stories. The text reproduces, with only a few expansions, the account in Lk 2:41–52 of how the twelve-year-old Jesus demonstrates his quality as a teacher in the temple. The most striking difference from Luke is perhaps that, where the evangelist has *Elizabeth* praise Mary (cf. Lk 1:42), now it is the *scribes* who pronounce a blessing (19:4):

Blessed are you among women, because the Lord has blessed the fruit of your womb. For such glory and such excellence and wisdom we have never seen or heard.

This is clearly the conclusion of the work, confirmed by a brief doxology: 'To him be glory for ever and ever. Amen.' In view of this, it is highly improbable that the three chapters which follow in the Slavonic version belonged to the oldest version of the book. In ch. 20, Jesus passes a temple of pagan idols and destroys it by his word alone;

in ch. 21, he assists a doctor and heals a man who is half blind; in ch. 22, he changes Jewish children into pigs (the anti-Jewish tendency makes this narrative even more objectionable than it would otherwise be).

Let us mention one more miracle, found in this form only in the material which the Greek recension C inserts at the beginning of the text, and in the Latin translation. Here, the two- and three-year-old Jesus is in Egypt. While playing with other children, Jesus takes a dried fish, throws it into a pool and commands it to breathe and to exude the salt it contains. The fish immediately obeys, but this so terrifies the widow who rents a room to the holy family that she hastens to throw them out of her house.

(3) Conclusion

We cannot call the tendency of the individual narratives and of IGTh as a whole 'edifying' – on the contrary, the child Jesus in these stories has been described as ill-tempered, unkind and arrogant, in short 'a highly dangerous being who terrifies his neighbours, and whose parents do not understand him' (in Vielhauer's words), and Schneider has called the theological content of IGTh 'extraordinarily banal'. We need not dispute this, nor attempt to gloss over the problems. At the same time, however, we must bear in mind the cultural expectations and literary conventions which helped to generate such a picture of Jesus' character. Biographies of important persons in classical antiquity tended to see the future deeds of their hero presaged in his childhood and youth. This is why the child Jesus is shown as a great wonder-worker and superior teacher: God is recognized already in the child. It is not by accident that we can observe many parallels in pagan mythology and in fairy-tales to the portrait of the 'arrogant divine child' (Cullmann's phrase) in IGTh. Similar traits have been adduced from Indian legends about Krishna and Buddha, but an example closer to home is the Greek god Hermes, later the patron of thieves: as a small child, he steals a herd of cattle from Apollo, and we are told: 'As sparks fly and swirl from the eyes, so *words and deeds* were at once united in the thinking of the glorious Hermes' (Homeric Hymn 4.45f.; cf. IGTh 4:1 and 17:2).

Jesus experiences pain when the teacher strikes him on the head (14:2); accordingly, the version of IGTh which we know does not imply a docetic christology. However, a christology of pre-existence, which is not yet found in Mt 1–2 and Lk 1–2, is introduced into the infancy narratives of IGTh, and the deep allegorical exposition of the letter Alpha may indicate that a gnostic reading of IGTh was at least a possibility. The objectionable traits could then be interpreted in a symbolic manner: the revealer who comes from on high must necessarily be experienced as alien to the human world below.

Bibliography

O. Cullmann, in: NTApo I, 439–51; G. Schneider, *Kindheitsevangelien*, 147–71; R. F. Hock, *Infancy Gospels*, 84–146; A. de Santos Otero, *Das kirchenslavische Evangelium des Thomas* (PTS 6), Berlin 1967; W. Baars and J. Heldermann, 'Neue Materialien zum Text und zur Interpretation des Kindheitsevangeliums des Pseudo-Thomas', *OrChr* 77 (1993) 191–226; 78 (1994), 1–32; P. Vielhauer, *Geschichte*, 672–7.

(c) The Gospel of Pseudo-Matthew (PsMt)

(1) Contextual information

The Gospel of Ps.-Matthew, composed in Latin, takes us not only into another geographical area, viz. the West, but into another period. This means that it can be included among the 'ancient Christian apocrypha' only to a limited extent. The most recent thorough study of this work argues for a probable date of composition between 600 and 625 (Gijsel, p. 67).

The original title was probably something like *Liber de ortu beatae Mariae et de infantia Salvatoris*, 'Book about the birth of the blessed Mary and the childhood of the Saviour'. The title 'Pseudo-Matthew' has been in use for only the past 150 years, after Tischendorf included it in his influential edition on the basis of a fictitious exchange of letters between two bishops and the church father Jerome which precedes the work in some manuscripts, where it is described as the Hebrew or Aramaic Ur-Matthew, which Jerome himself had translated into Latin.

This was not the only aspect of Tischendorf's edition which was to prove highly influential. He includes a free Latin translation of the Infancy Gospel of Thomas, with occasional expansions, as chs. 25–42, the *altera pars* ('second part'); this, however, is not found in the older manuscripts.

Gijsel edits and translates only the remaining chapters (1–24), which in turn consist of two sections: chs. 1–17, a Latin version of the Greek Protevangelium, with some redactional changes and expansions, and chs. 18–24 about the experiences of the holy family in Egypt. The unknown author assuredly bases his account of the flight into Egypt on earlier texts, but since these are now lost, it is impossible to estimate even approximately the age of their contents.

(2) The contents

– Comparison with the Protevangelium

Let us begin by summarizing some of the additions and changes which PsMt makes to the material drawn from the Protevangelium. The ambiguities concerning Mary's conception are eliminated in PsMt, where an angel explicitly tells Joachim that his wife has 'conceived a daughter of your seed' (3:2: *ex semine tuo concepisse filiam*). The regular rhythm of work and prayer which characterizes Mary's time in the temple (ch. 6) recalls the monastic life and indicates a knowledge of the Rule of Benedict; and the same *Sitz-im-Leben* is suggested by the explicit vow of virginity which she takes in ch. 7, appealing to the example of two virginal persons in the Old Testament, Abel and Elijah.

In 13:3, after carrying out her investigation, the sceptical midwife affirms with lapidary concision the abiding physical virginity of Mary: *virgo concepit, virgo peperit, virgo permanet,* 'She conceived as a virgin, she gave birth as a virgin, she remains a virgin' (following Codex P; cf. the doctrinal affirmation of the Lateran Synod in 649, DS 503).

Finally, PsMt elaborates the 'ox-manger' of Protev 22:2 in a way that was to have momentous consequences for every artistic representation of the birth of Jesus in later centuries: it places the ox and ass directly alongside the crib and appeals to two quotations from the prophets (14:1):

On the third day after the birth of the Lord, Mary left the cave and went into a stable. She laid the boy in a crib, and ox and ass venerated him. This fulfilled the words of the prophet Isaiah: "The ox knows its master, and the ass knows the crib of its Lord" [Is 1:3]. The animals received him into their midst and venerated him without ceasing. This fulfilled the words of the prophet Habakkuk: "In the midst, between two animals, you shall be known" [Hab 3:2 according to the Septuagint].

– The flight into Egypt

The account of the flight into Egypt has the following high points. In ch. 18, Jesus tames many dragons which emerge from a cave and frighten the children who are travelling with the holy family (cf. Ps 148:7 according to the Vulgate). In ch. 19, he is served by lions and panthers, who show the travellers their path and refrain from molesting the oxen, asses, beasts of burden, sheep and rams which Jesus' prosperous family have taken with them. This fulfils the prophetic promise of an eschatological peace among the animals (cf. Is 11:6–7). A palm bends down so that Mary may take its fruit, and it causes springs of water to bubble forth at its roots (ch. 20). When the journey becomes too arduous, Jesus shortens the way, so that a thirty days' journey now takes only one day (ch. 22). When he enters a city of Egypt, all the idols (*idola*) crash to the ground and are broken in pieces (ch. 23, with a quotation from Is 19:1). This does not move the ruler of the city to anger; rather, he and the entire population come to faith (ch. 24).

– Additions to IGTh

Here, we mention only one new episode in chs. 35–36 of the later Latin version of IGTh. Near Jericho, Jesus enters a den of lions (cf. Dan

14:31–42). The old lions venerate him by waving their tails, while the cubs play before him. Jesus takes the entire pride of lions with him and crosses the Jordan, while the waters of the river part to right and to left before them (cf. 2 Kg 2:8).

(3) Later texts

One final point concerns the influence exercised by PsMt throughout the middle ages, thanks not least to its inclusion, in an edited form, in the *Golden Legend* of James of Voragine. Its contents belonged thereafter to the treasury of mediaeval piety which was seldom called into question.

The same general evaluation is applicable to PsMt, the Protevangelium (a text which survived in the West largely thanks to PsMt) and IGTh. Let us look briefly at later texts which present infancy narratives of one kind or another.

The Marian sections of PsMt were detached, probably in the ninth century, to form a new work called *Libellus de nativitate Sanctae Mariae* (cf. Beyers).

The *Arabic Infancy Gospel* (Schneider, pp. 47–55, 173–95) is based on a Syriac text. This sixth-century compilation elaborates the Protevangelium and the Infancy Gospel of Thomas, and shows a number of points of contact with Pseudo-Matthew. Its middle section has a number of colourful stories which are unparalleled elsewhere. For example, the magi (cf. Mt 2) are given a nappy of Jesus in return for their gifts, and take this home with them. It possesses miraculous powers and survives unharmed when it is cast into the sacred fire in their Persian homeland (7–8). When he is in Egypt, Jesus meets the two robbers with whom he will later be crucified (23); the water in which he washes cleanses a girl from leprosy (17), and his perspiration produces balsam (24). When he returns to his home, he encounters Judas Iscariot as a child, and Judas' subsequent betrayal is foreshadowed (35). An incident in a dyer's workshop, where Jesus throws all the cloths into a cauldron full of indigo, then draws each cloth out in the colour desired (37), is paralleled in EvPhil 54.

Two manuscripts in England (Arundel 404 and Codex Hereford), probably dating from between the seventh and the ninth centuries, preserve a *Latin Infancy Gospel* (Schneider, pp. 55–9, 197–211). The strong docetic traits in the narrative of Jesus' birth are remarkable. Out of deep silence there emerges a light which becomes stronger and stronger, filling the cave in which Mary lies with brightness and a sweet fragrance, until the rays are transformed into the resemblance of a child (72–74).

Jesus and Mary are not the only figures from the infancy narratives in Mt 1–2 and Lk 1–2 to be honoured with narrative cycles of their own, some of which continue the story beyond the childhood of Jesus. A relatively early date, in the last third of the fourth century, has been proposed for the core material in the *History of Joseph the Carpenter* (Schneider, pp. 69–73, 271–83), which is found only in Coptic (cf. S. Morenz, *Die Geschichte von Joseph dem Zimmermann* [TU 56], Berlin 1951, pp. 110–12 and frequently), although considerably later dates have also been suggested. It is Jesus himself who relates this story to his disciples on the Mount of Olives.

A last example is the *Life of John the Baptist* (Schneider, pp. 73–76, 285–305). This survives in Syriac, but its first editor held it to be a translation from Greek and dated it to between 385 and 395. The address to hearers and the rhetorical device of *apostrophe* (turning to characters in the story and speaking to them directly) show that this is a homily on the feast of dedication of a church of St John. This text also mentions Ain Karem or Karim, which even today is presented to pilgrims as the home of John the Baptist.

Bibliography

O. Cullmann, in: NTApo I, 456–65; C. von Tischendorf, *Evangelia Apocrypha*, 51–112; G. Schneider, *Kindheitsevangelien*, 213–55; J. Gijsel and R. Beyers, *Libri de nativitate Mariae: Pseudo-Matthaei Evangelium/Libellus de nativitate Sanctae Mariae* (CChr.SA 9–10), Brepols 1997.

6

GOSPELS ABOUT JESUS' DEATH AND RESURRECTION

Not only the beginning of the canonical gospel material, concerning the birth and childhood of Jesus, but also the conclusion, the narratives of his death and resurrection, offered opportunities for expansion, as we can see when we compare the Gospel of Mark, which ends with the discovery of the empty tomb, with the three later gospels, all of which contain accounts of the apparition of the risen Jesus to the disciples. Expansions take place within the passion narrative too: for example, the trial before Pilate in Jn 18:28–19:16 is roughly twice as long as the account in Mk 15:1–15. The secondary conclusion to Mark (16:9–20) is an example of the apocryphal expansion of the gospel tradition. This was composed in the second century on the basis of the Easter narratives of the other three canonical gospels in order to supply events felt to be lacking in Mark, e.g. Easter appearances, a discourse in which Jesus sends out the disciples, and an ascension. There is no sharply demarcated boundary between such texts and the so-called 'dialogue gospels' which have nothing at all to say about the passion of Jesus and are content to present conversations between the risen Lord and his disciples; these are discussed in ch. 8 below.

The second Letter of Peter – the last text in the New Testament where we might have expected it – shows us something that is important for our understanding of the first text which we shall study in the present chapter, viz. the Gospel of Peter. The unknown author borrows the name of the apostle Simon Peter. After explicitly claiming to be an eyewitness (1:16), he gives a free account of the chosen disciples' experience of Jesus' transfiguration (1:17f.) which heightens the impression, already present in the synoptics (cf. Mk 9:2–8), that this story was originally a post-Easter narrative.

(a) The Gospel of Peter (EvPet)

(1) Contextual information

The most important patristic information about a 'Gospel of Peter' is found in Eusebius' *Historia Ecclesiastica* (6.12.1–6): Serapion, bishop of Antioch at the end of the second century, had permitted the neighbouring community of Rhossus to read a gospel which went by the name of Peter, although he himself did not know this text. Later, however, he was annoyed to discover that docetic groups – those who held that Jesus had possessed only the outward appearance of a body – favoured this gospel and appealed to its authority. After reading the gospel, he retracted his previous permission, since (in his own words) 'Although most of it agrees with the true teaching of our Redeemer, some of it deviates from this teaching. For your information, we append a list.' Unfortunately, Eusebius does not quote Serapion's list of these few passages which put forward problematic views.

The text known today as EvPet comes from a parchment codex, PCair 10759 from the fifth or sixth century (much secondary literature dates it to the eighth century, but this is incorrect), found in 1886/1887 in the tomb of a monk at Akhmim in Upper Egypt; the parchment also includes the Apocalypse of Peter. The text begins and ends in mid-sentence. This means that it presents only one section of the original work; however, the ornamentation at the beginning and close of this section show that nothing more was available to the copyist of the codex. Its identity as a 'Gospel of Peter' is deduced from the fact that Peter twice speaks in the first person singular (at 7:26 and 14:60), a stylistic device intended to confirm the affirmations of the text by an appeal to the chief of the apostolic eyewitnesses – and clearly going one step higher than the authority of the Gospel of Mark, which according to tradition was written 'only' by Peter's disciple. The identification of the work from which this gospel fragment comes with the EvPet mentioned by Eusebius and other patristic sources is a plausible hypothesis which most scholars accept.

The papyrus fragments POxy 2949 and perhaps POxy 4009 likewise come from EvPet (cf. Lührmann, who also refers to PVindob G 2325 and an ostrakon from Egypt which depicts Peter as evangelist and mentions his gospel). In terms of content, these add little, but the first fragment, POxy 2949, is significant because it makes it certain that EvPet was written before 200. The probable date of composition lies between 100 and 150. Since the textual form of POxy 2949 clearly diverges from that of the parallels in the Akhmim text (EvPet 2:3–5), we must assume that PCair 10759 preserves, not the oldest textual form, but a version altered by repeated copying. We must therefore be cautious when we attempt to draw inferences from EvPet.

Peter speaks in the first person singular in the few and poorly preserved lines in the second-century POxy 4009; this makes it at least possible that this text too comes from EvPet. It is a fragment from a discourse in which Jesus sends out the apostles. We follow Lührmann's translation (p. 78):

'... the harvest.
5   But be without deceit like the do-
ves and cunning as
the serpents. You will be like
lambs among the wolves'.
I said to him: 'But what if we
10   are torn to pieces?'
But he answered and said to me: 'When
the wolves have torn the

lamb, there is nothing more they can
do to it. There-
15   fore I tell you: Do not fear
those who kill you
and after killing
cannot do anything more ...'

If this discourse of Jesus is situated before Easter, and if the manuscript belongs to EvPet, this would mean that the narrative of the passion and resurrection – all that is contained in PCair 10759 – would have been preceded by an account of the deeds of Jesus during his earthly life. If, however, these words come from a dialogue between the risen Jesus and his disciples, such a conclusion would not be justified.

Some scholars, such as Crossan, propose an extremely early dating between 50 and 70 for EvPet (or for older sections in it). This is closely linked to the question of the relation between EvPet and the canonical gospels, and we shall return to this after presenting the contents of the work.

The first scholars to study EvPet divided it either into 14 chapters (Robinson) or 60 shorter paragraphs (Harnack). Today, scholars tend to give both enumerations: these overlap in such a way that, for example, 5:20 is followed by 6:21.

(2) The contents

– 'Brother Pilate'

The narration begins abruptly with the statement: 'None of the Jews washed their hands, neither Herod nor any one of his [i.e. Jesus'] judges' (1:1). Pilate then arises and gives Herod the command to lead Jesus away (1:2; note that the name 'Jesus' is never used in the text, which prefers to call him 'the Lord'). From the outset we can see a tendency to transfer responsibility for Jesus' death from Pilate to the Jews and Herod; later, a distinction is drawn between the people of the Jews and their leaders.

In the next scene (2:3–5), Joseph of Arimathea, a 'friend of Pilate and of the Lord', asks for Jesus' body even before he is crucified. Pilate sends word to Herod, who addresses him as 'Brother Pilate' and informs him that they (i.e. the Jews under the king's leadership) have already ensured that Jesus will be buried, since the sabbath will soon begin and one may not allow the sun to go down over one who has been executed (cf. Deut 21:22f.). Apparently, it is once again the Jews who torture and mock Jesus, *inter alia* by seating him on a seat of judgement (3:7). We may compare Jn 19:13, which is probably to be translated: 'He [Pilate] took his place on the seat of judgement', although some scholars have proposed: 'He [Pilate] seated him [Jesus] on the seat of judgement'.

– The crucifixion

When they – the Jews – crucify Jesus between two malefactors (cf. Lk 23:40–43), he reacts as follows: 'But he held his peace, as if he felt no pain' (4:10). This need not be understood in a docetic sense, as if the Redeemer were incapable of suffering; it may be intended to emphasize his heroic attitude. But it does at least show how EvPet could have won acceptance among docetics.

One of the two malefactors rebukes the Jews (4:13), who 'became angry with him and commanded that his legs should not be broken, so that he might die in torments' (4:14; cf. Jn 19:32f.). The grammatical construction suggests that it is the malefactor's legs that are not to be broken as a punishment for the reproaches he utters, but we cannot rule out the possibility, favoured by some scholars, that these words refer to Jesus himself. When the lower legs of a crucified man were broken, he was unable to support his body on his feet and death came more quickly. One whose legs were unbroken died in greater torments (9:34).

– Last words

At midday, it becomes so dark in the whole land (5:15) that people go about with lamps, supposing that night has already fallen (5:18). Those who have been detailed to crucify Jesus panic, because they fear that they will not be able to take him down from the cross before sunset (5:15). This is why they give him a drink of 'gall with vinegar' (5:16), understood here as a poison that will swiftly kill him.

It is far from easy to interpret the last words of Jesus: 'My power, O power, you have forsaken me!', especially since the author immediately states: 'And having said this he was taken up' (5:19). 'Power' (*dunamis*) may be a paraphrase or a variant translation of the divine name in the traditional Ps 22:2, especially when we bear in mind that there is no unambiguous evidence in favour of a purely docetic reading – viz. that the heavenly spiritual being would be separated from the human being Jesus at this point. But what of 'he was taken up'? This seems to imply a resurrection and ascension directly from the cross, something contradicted by the detailed description of the resurrection later on in EvPet. Could the author not make up his mind on this point, or did he not see this as a contradiction (cf. the equally difficult text at Lk 23:43)? Or has the text been altered by an editor? If we want to harmonize these statements on the synchronous level, we must interpret 'he was taken up' as a paraphrase for 'he died', with a choice of words which already hint at what is still to come.

– Jesus is taken down from the cross and buried

When Jesus' body is taken down and laid on the ground, the earth shakes (cf. Mt 27:51) and the sun begins to shine again (6:21f.). The Jews who had been responsible for his death beat their breasts (cf. Lk 23:48) and fear that the final judgement has drawn near (7:25). Peter relates: 'But I mourned with my fellows, and being wounded in heart we hid ourselves, for we were sought after by them as evildoers and as persons who wanted to set fire to the temple' (7:26). Here, Jesus' critical attitude to the temple is transposed to his disciples, perhaps with a hidden allusion to the accusation that it was the Christians who had set fire to Rome.

In view of the signs that take place at Jesus' death, the people begin to murmur and to beat their breasts in repentance (8:28). Their spokesmen begin to be afraid, and demand from Pilate (8:30–33):

'Give us soldiers that we may watch his sepulchre for three days, lest his disciples come and steal him away and the people suppose that he is risen from the dead, and do us harm.' And Pilate gave them Petronius the centurion with soldiers to watch the sepulchre. And with them there came elders and scribes to the sepulchre. And all who were there, together with the centurion and the soldiers, rolled thither a great stone and laid it against the entrance to the sepulchre and put on it seven seals, pitched a tent and kept watch

(cf. the special Matthaean material at Mt 27:62–66 and 28:11–15).

On the sabbath morning, a crowd of people from Jerusalem inspect the sealed tomb.

– The resurrection

Two soldiers keep watch on the sabbath night. These men hear a loud voice and see how the heavens open and two men descend. The stone rolls of its own accord from before the grave, and the two 'young men' (as the heavenly beings are now called; cf. Mk 16:5) enter (9:34–37). The watchmen waken the centurion and the elders of the Jews,

And while they were relating what they had seen, they saw again three men come out from the sepulchre, and two of them sustaining the other, and a cross following them, and the heads of the two reaching to heaven, but that of him whom they led by the hand overpassing the heavens. And they heard a voice out of the heavens crying, 'Have you preached to those who had fallen asleep?', and from the cross there was heard the answer: 'Yes.' (10:39–42)

Here we note, not only the clear reference to Christ's prior 'descent into hell', but also something not yet found in the canonical gospels, viz. direct witnesses to the event of the resurrection itself. The two angels do not really support and lead the risen Jesus, who is far taller than they are; it seems rather that they accompany him as a 'guard of honour'. The cross – which had not in fact been buried with Jesus – has now become an active symbol for the crucified Lord, and can even reply on his behalf.

Yet another man descends from heaven at 11:44 and enters the tomb, where the women will encounter him when they visit the grave of Jesus. All the watchmen hasten to Pilate and confess: 'In truth he was the Son of God' (11:45). Pilate professes his innocence: 'I am clean from the blood of the Son of God ...' (11:46; cf. Mt 27:24). They agree that no word of this must become known (11:47–49).

– The women and the other disciples

At 12:50, Mary Magdalene, the 'woman disciple of the Lord', takes women friends (either her own, or those of Jesus) and goes to the tomb. The differences from the Markan tradition are not so pronounced in this section, apart from the fact that the women apparently do not intend to anoint the body, but only to bring funeral gifts 'in memory of him' and to 'weep and lament' at great length (12:54); here we see clear traces of the cult of the dead and of graves in antiquity as a whole. In the tomb, the women see a young man in a shining garment who proclaims the message of the resurrection to them in direct speech. This, however, only leads them to flee in fear (13:35–37; cf. Mk 16:5–8).

At 14:58, the feast of unleavened bread (which in fact lasted for a week) ends, and it seems that it is only at this point that the *twelve* disciples leave the city and return home like the other pilgrims who had come to the feast. The number 'twelve' is surprising here: is Judas still in their company? It is unclear whether this passage means that the author excludes apparitions of the risen Jesus in Jerusalem, or that he keeps a space open for them but does not mention them explicitly.

The last verse reads: 'But I, Simon Peter, and my brother Andrew took our nets and went to the sea. And there was with us Levi, the son of Alphaeus, whom the Lord ...' (14:60). This may well have been followed by the account of an apparition some time after the events in the Jerusalem, either by the Sea of Gennesareth (cf. Jn 21) or in the house of Levi (as in the Syriac *Didascalia*).

(3) Evaluation

Recent attempts (see Crossan) to identify and distil from EvPet the oldest stratum of the passion tradition, on which the New Testament gospels too would have based their accounts, do not stand up to a closer examination of the text. We should also be sceptical of an early dating for a text which contains a number of traits customarily found only at a late stage of tradition-history: the fact that Jesus is consistently called 'the Lord', the lack of knowledge of Jewish customs, the transfer of responsibility for his death from Pilate to Herod and the Jews (a motif which is also dubious on theological grounds), the intensification of apologetic motifs to such a degree that alleged eyewitnesses of the resurrection are produced, and finally the emphasis on the miraculous elements in the narrative of the resurrection, with the descent into hell, huge angelic beings and a cross that speaks.

It is obvious that some of this lies on the trajectory of developments which begin in Matthew, Luke and John; it is not by chance that we find parallels in other apocryphal works such as the 'Unknown Berlin Gospel'. This does not lend plausibility to the thesis that EvPet is completely independent of the New Testament gospels and autonomously reproduces older traditions. At most, one might concede the presence of archaic traits in individual instances – though it is difficult to specify one single passage to which this judgement would apply.

This need not mean that the canonical gospels were available to the author of EvPet in written form and that he composed his own work as a simple mosaic or cento drawn from the New Testament. The specific character of EvPet is better explained on the hypothesis that its author remembered the other gospels with a greater or lesser degree of precision and used them as models for a work in which the individual elements, no matter where they came from, could take on a new pattern.

The presence of docetism in EvPet has been much discussed. Here we must be cautious, since the few passages adduced in support of this interpretation are not truly clear. Nevertheless, such passages may have drawn docetics to appreciate EvPet highly – and bishop Serapion of Antioch did not in fact claim more than this (see above).

Bibliography

C. Maurer and W. Schneemelcher, in: NTApo I, 216–27; D. Lührmann, *Fragmente*, 72–93; K. Beyschlag, *Verborgene Überlieferung*, 27–64; R. Brown, *The Death of the Messiah: From Gethsemane to the Grave* (AncB Reference Library), New York *et al.* 1994, 1317–49 (with references back); J. D. Crossan, *The Cross That Spoke: The Origins of the Passion Narrative,* San Francisco, Calif. 1988; A. Fuchs, *Das Petrusevangelium* (SNTU.B 12), Linz 1978 (concordance); M. G. Mara, *Evangile de Pierre* (SC 201), Paris 1973; L. Vaganay, *L'Evangile de Pierre* (EtB), Paris 1930; T. Nicklas, 'Ein "neutesta-mentliches Apokryphon"? Zum umstrittenen Kanonbezug des sog. "Petrusevangeliums" ', *VigChr* 56 (2002) 260–72.

(b) The Gospel of Nicodemus (Acts of Pilate) (EvNic/ActPil)

(1) Contextual information

The Gospel according to Nicodemus is the perfect example of a gospel devoted exclusively to the passion and resurrection. After a lengthy prologue in several paragraphs, it begins with the trial before Pilate, which is followed by the crucifixion and the resurrection of Jesus. Chapters 12–16 relate what then happened to Joseph of Arimathea, while chs. 17–27 describe the descent of Christ into the world of the dead. A number of signals *en route* indicate the end of the work: for example, ch. 16 closes with a doxology and ch. 27 has a concluding redactional note, but the various textual versions diverge here. This leads us to the closely interconnected problems posed by EvNic: its title, its composition, the history of its transmission, its language and origin, and not least the age of its individual parts.

An analysis of the prologue and of its various forms gives us some initial data. We begin by reproducing at full length two versions of the prologue, first that in the older *Latin* recension A (in the edition by Gounelle and Izydorczyk), then the better-known version in the more recent *Greek* recension A (in NTApo, following Tischendorf). This shows how widely the various versions diverge; and there are many further recensions in Latin and Greek alone.

Latin A: In the name of the most holy Trinity. The beginning of the deeds and actions of our Lord and Saviour Jesus Christ, which were discovered under the emperor Theodosius the Great at Jerusalem in the praetorium of Pontius Pilate, in the public archives.

All this took place in the eighteenth year of the emperor Tiberius, the ruler over the Romans, and of Herod (Antipas), son of Herod (the Great), the ruler over Galilee, in the nineteenth year of his rule, on the eighth day before the kalends of April, i.e. on 25 March, in the consulate of Rufinus and Rubellio, in the fourth year of the two hundred and second Olympiad, under the rule of the Jewish high priests Joseph and Caiaphas.

All those matters which Nicodemus recorded after the suffering of the Lord and his death on the cross – all that was done by the high priests and the rest of the Jews – were written down by the same Nicodemus in the Hebrew language.

Greek A: I, Ananias, an officer of the guard, being learned in the law, came to know our Lord Jesus Christ from the sacred Scriptures, which I approached with faith, and was accounted worthy of holy baptism. And having searched for the reports made at that period in the time of our Lord Jesus Christ <and for that> which the Jews committed to writing under Pontius Pilate, I found these acts in the Hebrew language and according to God's good pleasure I translated them into Greek for the information of all those who call upon the name of our Lord Jesus Christ, in the eighteenth year of the reign of our emperor Flavius Theodosius and in the sixth year of the 'Nobility' of Flavius Valentinianus, in the ninth indiction.

Therefore all you who read this and copy it out, remember me and pray for me that God may be gracious to me and forgive my sins which I have sinned against him.

Peace be to those who read and hear it, and also to their servants. Amen.

In the fifteenth year of the reign of the Roman emperor Tiberius, when Herod was king of Galilee, in the nineteenth year of his rule, on the eighth day before the kalends of April, i.e. 25 March, in the consulate of Rufus and Rubellio, in the fourth year of the two hundred and second Olympiad, when Joseph Caiaphas was high priest of the Jews.

What Nicodemus after the passion of the Lord upon the cross recorded and delivered concerning the conduct of the chief priests and the rest of the Jews, the same Nicodemus (drew up his records) in the Hebrew language.'

Let us begin with the last paragraph, where both versions are in broad agreement. The text claims to be based on a Hebrew account of the passion of Jesus, composed by Nicodemus, who is known to us from John's Gospel, where he visits Jesus by night (Jn 3:1f.), speaks on his behalf in the Sanhedrin (7:50–52), and finally joins Joseph of Arimathea in ensuring that Jesus is buried with dignity (19:39f.). His involvement in Jesus' burial and his membership of the leading class among the Jews lend credibility to his testimony to the events related in the gospel which bears his name.

There is basic agreement between Latin A and Greek A on the dating of Jesus' death, which apparently takes its starting-point in the synchronized dates at Lk 3:1f., but with some inherent discrepancies. We arrive, nevertheless, at 29/30 CE – the fifteenth year of Tiberius' reign was 29, while the two hundred and second Olympiad fell in 32/33.

We are also given information about the 'discovery' of EvNic and its translation into Greek. Latin A mentions Theodosius the Great, who reigned from 379 to 395, while Greek A speaks of Theodosius II; the ninth indiction brings us roughly to the year 425. Greek A diverges from Latin A by having a first-person narrator who is presented in detail. More important, however, is the mention of Pontius Pilate in the introductory section to both versions, although only Greek A speaks directly of acts from the trial held under his rule (if such a protocol had existed, it would certainly not have been written in Hebrew).

This brings us to the second title traditionally given to this text, especially to its first part (and here especially for the nucleus of chs. 1–11, to which chs. 12–16 may have been the earliest addition): *Acta Pilati*, 'Acts of Pilate'. Sometimes the title covers both main sections: *Gesta Pilati et Descensus Christi ad Inferos*, 'Deeds of Pilate and Descent of Christ into the Underworld'; 'Gospel of Nicodemus' has been used since the middle ages as a general designation.

When was EvNic composed? The manuscript evidence for the two main sections varies in age. The manuscript of Greek A containing only chs. 1–16 (i.e. without the descensus) is no older than the twelfth century, but some Latin manuscripts are much older, providing certain attestation of chs. 1–16 from the fifth century, and of chs. 17–27 from the ninth century.

We can, however, assume an earlier date for both sections, especially since we have other sources of information about the Acts of Pilate. As early as 150–155, Justin observes in his First *Apology* (35.9; 48.3): 'You can see for yourselves that these events took place in this manner, if you consult the Acts drawn up under Pontius Pilate.' Fifty years later, Tertullian makes the same claim: 'Pilate – who himself was already a Christian, as far as his innermost conviction was concerned [!] – made a report of all that happened to Christ for Tiberius, who was emperor at that time' (*Apology* 21.24). This is most likely not evidence that Christian documents in the name of Pilate already existed; rather, these texts will have inspired the composition of the Acts of Pilate.

Eusebius mentions another reason for their composition in his *Historia Ecclesiastica* (1.9.3f.; 9.5.1; 9.7.1): when pagan Acts of Pilate, hostile to Christianity, were published *c.* 311–312, under the reign of emperor Maximinus Daia, Christians had to react to these texts. By *c.* 378, Epiphanius of Salamis clearly knows Christian Acts of Pilate, which existed in a variety of divergent versions (*Panarion* 50.1.5–8). This allows us to date the composition of the Acts of Pilate to the first decades of the fourth century; the author will have drawn on older material. For chs. 17–27 (the descent into hell), we must be content with a more general dating to the fifth or sixth century, and the prior history of the material must remain an open question.

This overview shows that the text of EvNic remained in constant evolution. This makes it almost impossible to identify or reconstruct one definitive version. The following analysis of its contents agrees with most modern translations in following Greek A for chs. 1–16 and Greek B for chs. 17–27. (We follow the text and enumeration in Tischendorf/NTApo, though conscious that this version, reconstructed on the basis of Greek A and Greek B, is an artificial product.)

(2) The contents

– Trial and death on the cross (chs. 1–11)

The narrative begins with the trial before Pilate. The Jews bring a variety of accusations against Jesus: he calls himself Son of God and king, and breaks the law by healing all kinds of sick persons on the sabbath. His accusers declare that Jesus' miracles are sorcery, the fruit of an alliance with Beelzebub. Pilate, on the other hand, shows Jesus respect and kindness from the outset. When it is alleged that Jesus is in league with 'the prince of the evil spirits', Pilate observes: 'This is not to cast out demons by an unclean spirit, but by the god Asclepius' (1:1). The messenger who is sent to fetch Jesus spreads out a cloth on the ground for him to walk on (1:2). When asked why he has done this, the messenger replies that he had been present at Jesus' solemn entry into Jerusalem (1:3f.). When Jesus enters the praetorium, the busts of the emperor on the military standards bow down before him (1:5), and they repeat this act of reverence when they are borne by twelve strong Jewish men, instead of the Roman soldiers (1:6).

Pilate's wife, called Procula in a part of the tradition, tells him of the dream in which she has received a warning (Mt 27:19). She is portrayed as sympathizing with the Jews (2:1).

The first main point of controversy is the origins of Jesus. Most of his accusers maintain that his parents were unmarried (2:3); his birth led to the murder of small children, and his parents fled with him to Egypt 'because they counted for nothing among the people' (cf. Mt 2:13–18). At this, however, twelve God-fearing men, whose names are listed, swear that they were present at the wedding of Joseph and Mary, so that Jesus was not 'born of fornication' (2:4f.).

While ch. 3 almost completely follows Jn 18, ch. 4 introduces into the trial before Pilate the accusation that Jesus wanted to destroy the temple, although this belongs in the trial before the Sanhedrin (cf. Mt 26:61). Pilate declares his own innocence, and the crowd cries: 'His blood be on us and on our children!' (Mt 27:24f.). However, Pilate also notes at 4:5 that many of the Jewish onlookers are weeping, clearly because they do not agree with the action their leaders are taking against Jesus.

In ch. 5, Nicodemus makes his first appearance and pleads in favour of Jesus: if his signs are authorized by God, 'they will stand' like the signs which Moses did, but unlike the signs of Pharaoh's sorcerers (cf. Ex 7–11). In ch. 6, a number of persons who had been healed join Nicodemus in defending Jesus: a lame man who had been bedridden for thirty-eight years (cf. Mk 2:1–12; Jn 5:5), a man born blind (Mk 10:46–52; Jn 9:1f.), a man who had been bent double (cf. Lk 13:10–13), and a leper (Mk 1:40–45). The Jewish accusers react by charging Jesus with breaking the sabbath.

The summary of healing miracles is continued in ch. 7 by a woman called Bernice (Veronica in Latin), who had suffered from a flow of blood for twelve years (Mk 5:25–34). In ch. 8, some persons in the crowd relate how Lazarus was raised (Jn 11:17–44).

In ch. 9, Pilate first consults Nicodemus and the twelve men who have taken the side of Jesus, then he speaks to the crowd and attempts to use the passover amnesty to rescue Jesus (cf. Mt 27:15–26; Jn 18:39). This does not succeed, since the crowd wants Barabbas. Pilate replies with harsh reproaches, charging the people with ingratitude towards their benefactor and God who had freed them from Egypt and led them through the wilderness (9:2); but finally he gives in, when the accusers insist that Jesus has dared to call himself a king. They confirm this by telling Pilate about the magi who came from the east and about the murder of the children in Bethlehem (Mt 2:1–18; the somewhat strange logic of their argument runs as follows: Herod the Great had rightly recognized that this newborn child would one day claim to be king). When Pilate hears that Jesus is the one whom Herod had sought (9:4), he washes his hands in innocence, while the people again call down the blood of Jesus on themselves (Mt 27:24). Pilate then utters the sentence of death in a scene remote from historical reality (9:5):

Then Pilate commanded the curtain to be drawn before the judgement-seat on which he sat, and said to Jesus: 'Your nation has convicted you of claiming to be a king. Therefore I have decreed that you should first be scourged according to the law of the pious emperors, and then hanged on the cross in the garden where you were seized. And let Dysmas and Gestas, the two malefactors, be crucified with you.'

This is the first text to give the two malefactors who are crucified to the right and the left of Jesus the personal names which will now be theirs in the tradition of Christian piety.

The narrative of the crucifixion in chs. 9–11 basically follows Luke, with smaller contributions from the other gospels. Accordingly, we find the scene with the two malefactors from Lk 23:39–43 at EvNic 10:2, and the last words of Jesus at 11:1, which are first quoted in a distorted Aramaic version, are drawn from Lk 23:46: 'Father, into your hands I commit my spirit' (cf. Ps 31:6). Pilate and his wife react with sorrow to the news of Jesus' death, and fast all that day (11:2). The final point in the account of the crucifixion – which also signals its continuation – is the burial of Jesus' body by Joseph of Arimathea (11:3).

– The story of Joseph of Arimathea (chs. 12–16)

Jesus' followers are required to give an account of their conduct in the synagogue; Nicodemus and Joseph of Arimathea are mentioned here by name, and the anger of the other Jews is directed particularly against Joseph: 'You will not even be counted worthy of burial, but we shall give your flesh to the birds of heaven' (12:1). Joseph cleverly compares this threat with the arrogant words of Goliath (1 Sam 17:8–10), and he is punished by being locked into a building without windows, with watchmen guarding the sealed door. It is not by chance that this prison – without windows, but with seals and watchmen – recalls the tomb in which Jesus' body was laid. The narrative makes a number of other statements about Joseph which, strictly speaking, apply only to Jesus. The parallels are intended to depict him as a genuine follower of the Master.

On the first day of the week, when Joseph is to be brought out for sentencing and execution, they find the seals on the door still intact, but the room itself empty (13:1; cf. Acts 5:17–24). Some of the soldiers who had guarded Jesus' tomb appear almost simultaneously on the scene and announce what happened at midnight (13:1; and for the following scene, cf. Mt 28:2–4,11–15). A great earthquake took place, and an angel descended from heaven and spoke to the women, while the guards lay on the ground like dead men. When doubts are expressed about this account, they reply (not without humour): 'Then give us Joseph, and we will give you Jesus!' They go on to defend their conviction that Jesus lives and has gone to Galilee (13:2). The Jews give them a large bribe, so that from now on they will say: 'While we were sleeping, his disciples came by night and stole him' (13:3).

A priest, a teacher and a levite now come from Galilee and report that they have seen Jesus sitting on 'the mountain which is called Mamilch' and heard him instructing his disciples (14:1; the text quotes the secondary conclusion to Mark 16:16–18); after this, he ascended into heaven from the mountain. The Jewish elders, priests and levites – a pendant to the Galilean group – offer them money to buy their silence (14:2). Hannas and Caiaphas seek to quieten the general unease by suggesting once again that the disciples of Jesus have stolen his body.

Nicodemus now reminds them of the ascension to heaven of the prophet Elijah, which likewise caused great unease (2 Kg 2:11–18). As the disciples of the prophet looked for Elijah, so now the Jewish authorities should look for Jesus on every mountain (15:1). His advice is followed, but they do not find Jesus. Instead, they find Joseph in his home town of Arimathea. They send him a penitent letter and invite him to Jerusalem (15:2). Seven friends of Joseph bring him this letter, and after reading it he praises God in language drawn from the Bible (15:3). Next morning, he saddles his ass and sets out with his seven friends. They make a solemn entrance into Jerusalem, accompanied by the entire people. Joseph and the crowd repeatedly wish one another peace (15:4; here too, the echo of Jesus' entrance into Jerusalem is obvious).

On the following day, in the house of Nicodemus, Joseph tells the council what happened to him while he was in prison (15:6; cf. Acts 16:25–34). At midnight, the prison shakes and is raised up by the four corners. The risen Lord appears to him; Joseph at first thinks he is a ghost, then he takes him for Elijah. Jesus anoints his head with oil, and confirms the reality of his resurrection by showing Joseph the empty tomb in which he had buried the Master, with the linen cloths and the cloth that had been on his face. 'And he took me by the hand and placed me in the middle of my house, with the doors shut', commanding him not to leave his house in Arimathea for forty days. When they hear this account, the rulers of the synagogue and the priests and the levites fall down like dead men (16:1; cf. Mt 28:4!).

On the following day, a sabbath, a Jewish teacher named Levi speaks of Simeon (from Lk 2:28–35), under whom he himself had studied the law (16:2f.). Simeon is mentioned here because he confirmed that the parents of Jesus were good and pious people when they presented Jesus in the temple. The sanhedrin now sends for the three Galilean witnesses from ch. 14 and asks them to come to Jerusalem again (16:3f.). Each is interrogated separately, and they relate the ascension of Jesus into heaven (16:5f.); the three witnesses are in complete agreement with one another (cf. Deut 19:15). A Jewish teacher named Abuthem adduces the example of Enoch (Gen 5:24), while another named Jairus recalls the uncertainty about the location of Moses' tomb (Deut 34:5f.).

The Jewish authorities counter with an account of the events of Jesus' passion, adding further details from the canonical gospels to the narrative already given in chs. 10–11. They also recall the curse on 'everyone who hangs on a tree' (Deut 21:23). Finally, they speak of the evidential character of the duration of the memory of Jesus: 'If Jesus is remembered after fifty years, he will reign for ever and create for himself a new people' (16:7). The text ends with a lengthy praise of God by the people, and a doxology on the part of the narrator himself (16:8).

– The descent into hell (chs. 17–27)

An appendix to EvNic relates the 'harrowing of hell', Jesus' *descensus ad inferos*. (This is somewhat more detailed in the older version in Latin A than in Greek B, which we follow here.) The figure of Simeon (from

Lk 2:28–35) has already been introduced at EvNic 16:1f., and he provides a bridge to the present narrative. We learn from Joseph of Arimathea that Simeon's two sons have died recently – but now their graves are empty, since they were raised along with many other dead persons (Mt 27:52f.!). Joseph himself can testify that they are 'alive and dwelling in Arimathea' (17:1). Latin A gives them the names 'Carinus' and 'Leucius', which must be connected in some way with Leukios Charinos, an author or editor of apocryphal Acts of the apostles. These two are now asked to draw up two separate written accounts of what they experienced in the world of the dead (17:2).

Their unanimous account begins in ch. 18. At midnight, a ray of light falls into the realm of the dead, and Abraham, the patriarchs and the prophets rejoice. Isaiah sees the fulfilment of what he had promised (Is 9:1): 'The people that sit in darkness saw a great light' (18:1; in Latin A, Simeon joins his two sons and begins to speak). John the Baptist once again prepares the way of the Lord, calling those who dwell in the underworld to repentance (18:2).

Adam and his son Seth take centre stage in ch. 19. Seth relates how he went to fetch a healing oil from the tree of mercy in paradise when Adam lay on his deathbed: the angel who kept guard over paradise told him that only 5,500 years later would the incarnate Son of God go to the dead under the earth and anoint them with that oil.

Chapter 20 relates a discussion between Satan and Hades (the personification of the realm of the dead) in which Satan cites the words of Jesus, 'My soul is sorrowful even unto death' (Mt 26:38), and draws the inference that Jesus is not the Son of God, but only a human being whom the Jews crucified 'at our [!] instigation'. This means that the realm of the dead will be able to keep him for ever (20:1). Hades interprets Jesus' alleged fear of death as a mocking game that Jesus was playing with Satan (20:2) – he has not forgotten the painful experience of having Jesus snatch Lazarus away from his grasp. This leads Hades to conclude that their game is lost (20:3).

While they are still speaking, a voice thunders the command: 'Lift up your gates, O rulers, and be lifted up, O everlasting doors, and the King of glory shall come in' (21:1; cf. Ps 24:7). The patriarchs and prophets (joined in Latin A by David) sneer at the helpless attempts of Hades to put up a resistance (21:2). The iron doors and bars, which were intended to make the entrance secure, are rent asunder, and the King of glory enters in human form (21:3). Hades attempts in vain to hold him back by posing a series of rhetorical questions about his identity (22:1). Jesus has his angels bind Satan with iron chains, and commands Hades to keep him in secure detention until his definitive parousia (22:2).

In ch. 23, Hades reproaches Satan vigorously for his false assessment of the person of Jesus and threatens him with punishment. In ch. 24, the 'King of glory' liberates the 'forefather Adam', the patriarchs, prophets, martyrs and saints (i.e., not simply all the dead, at least according to Greek B; Latin A seems to take a more universalist position) and enters paradise with him in ch. 25 (to the accompaniment of songs of praise by David, Habakkuk and Micah, according to Latin A). Here two old men come to meet them: Enoch and Elijah, who had been taken up while still alive, in order to 'withstand Antichrist and to be killed by him' at the end of time (from the standpoint of the narrative, this still lies far off in the future; in other words, EvNic has an eschatological perspective). Finally, 'a humble man' appears, 'carrying a cross on his shoulder' (ch. 26): it is the malefactor to whom Jesus had promised, 'This day you will be with me in paradise' (Lk 23:43). He did not have to go first to the underworld; he showed the angel who guarded paradise his cross, the badge of his identity.

Thus ends the double account, one copy of which is handed over in a sealed scroll to the high priests, the other to Joseph and Nicodemus. The two brothers mention in ch. 27 that Michael commanded them after their resurrection to be baptized in the Jordan and to come to Jerusalem for the celebration of 'the passover of the resurrection'. They bid farewell with the salutation from 2 Cor 13:13, and suddenly vanish.

(3) Evaluation

In terms of its influence on subsequent church history, EvNic is almost as significant as the Protevangelium of James. More than 500 manuscripts with EvNic survive in Greek, Latin and the ancient languages of the east (Coptic, Syriac, Aramaic, Armenian and Georgian), to say nothing of the numerous translations into most of the old vernacular languages of Europe (including Old Swedish and Gaelic). Certainly, part of its popularity is due to the belief that the 'Acts' of Pilate in the first section were an official pagan document which would remove any doubts about the events surrounding Jesus' death and resurrection. Furthermore, the 'harrowing of hell' offered a vivid presentation of what redemption actually means: salvation is brought even to the dead (or at least to an important part of the dead) and is imparted to the great figures of the old covenant. We are also told why it was necessary for the Son of God to become human and die on a cross: this was the device which duped Satan and cheated him all the more effectively of his prey. Although gnostic ideas might have been borrowed at this point, EvNic does not do so.

Once again, we note critically how EvNic one-sidedly blames the Jewish authorities for Jesus' death and largely absolves Pilate of responsibility (see also [4] below).

A comparison of EvNic and EvPet shows that not all apocrypha have the same status. EvPet compels us to ask whether the text transmits independent traditions about Jesus (indeed, this question sometimes seems to exclude all other interests), but such a question is superfluous in the case of EvNic, which presupposes the existence of the canonical gospels. It seeks to expand them and explain them, while clearing up some exegetical difficulties (e.g. the 'saints' who are raised at Mt

27:52f.). Minor characters in the canonical gospels such as Nicodemus, Joseph of Arimathea and Simeon are given central roles; here, Simeon suddenly appears as the father of two sons. This satisfies the reader's curiosity about what happened to these characters. EvNic gives new names to nameless characters: 'Procula', 'Veronica', 'Dysmas and Gestas', and (in a part of the tradition) 'Longinus' for the soldier who pierces Jesus' side with a lance (probably from the Greek *longkhē*, 'lance'). The 'recycling' of Simeon from Lk 2 is an example of the tendency, found in other apocryphal gospels too, to make an economic use of the New Testament characters and create a narrative world with which the reader will feel easily familiar.

From the Reformation period onwards, the detailed description of Christ's descent into hell has been the object of particular criticism. EvNic as a whole fell into disfavour, and was placed several times on the Index of Forbidden Books in the aftermath of the council of Trent (from 1558 onwards). It never recovered its former position, at any rate in the West.

Bibliography

C. von Tischendorf, *Evangelia Apocrypha,* 210–432; F. Scheidwiler, in: NTApo I, 501–26; W. Michaelis, *Die apokryphen Schriften,* 132–214; K. Ceming and J. Werlitz, *Die verbotenen Evangelien,* 162–201; J. K. Elliott, *Apocryphal New Testament,* 159–204; R. Gounelle and Z. Izydorczyk, *L'Evangile de Nicodème ou Les Actes faits sous Ponce Pilate* (Apocryphes 9), Brepols 1997.

(4) The story continues

We have mentioned that the text of EvNic was in a state of constant evolution. In one version of Latin A, it does not end with ch. 27: this is followed by a new encounter between Pilate and the representatives of the Jewish people (ch. 28). Pilate comes to the temple and asks to see the books which are kept there. At his insistence, Hannas and Caiaphas admit that it was a mistake to crucify Jesus – they too are deeply impressed by all that has happened since his death. And now they can point to many passages in Israel's Bible which confirm this. We often find a ch. 29 in which Pilate sends a *Letter to Claudius* with a brief account of the public ministry, death and resurrection of Jesus. The original Greek version of this letter is also found as chs. 40–42 in the 'Acts of Peter and Paul'.

This brings us to the vast cycle of Pilate-literature. The crass anachronism entailed by a letter of Pilate to Claudius is corrected by a *Letter of Pilate to Tiberius* with a reply by the emperor; these are probably very late compositions. We also have the *Correspondence between Pilate and Herod,* consisting of three letters.

The so-called *Anaphora Pilati* is an account of the events sent by

Pilate to Tiberius; this is closely related to the letters. More interesting is the *Paradosis Pilati,* concerning the close of his life: Pilate is summoned to Rome and bears testimony to Jesus Christ before the emperor and the senate, attaching the blame for Jesus' death exclusively to the Jewish party. The emperor issues written orders that the Jews be punished as they deserve (6):

To Licianus, chief governor of the East, greeting! At the present time the Jews who live in Jerusalem and the neighbouring towns have committed a lawless crime in forcing Pilate to crucify Jesus who was acknowledged as God. Because of this crime of theirs the world was darkened and dragged down to ruin. Therefore by this decree proceed there with all speed with a strong body of troops and take them prisoner. Obey, and advance against them, and dispersing them among all the nations enslave them, and expel them from Judaea, making the nation so insignificant that it is no longer to be seen anywhere, since they are men full of evil.

The emperor commands that Pilate be beheaded, and the sentence is carried out after Pilate has prayed to the Lord. An angel of the Lord receives his head. This is the first step along the path that led to Pilate's veneration as a saint in the Coptic church.

However, not all the accounts of his death are so positive; his person was seen with more critical eyes in the West. In the mediaeval texts *Vindicta Salvatoris* and *Mors Pilati,* Tiberius is healed by Veronica's veil with its miraculous image of Jesus. Pilate commits suicide in the *Mors Pilati.* His corpse is initially thrown into the Tiber, but since it attracts evil spirits who make a tremendous din, it is then thrown into the Rhône, and finally into a lake in the Alps near the mountain in Switzerland which bears Pilate's name. Another text which probably comes from the middle ages is the *Narration of Joseph of Arimathea,* which recounts some of these events from the perspective of the first-person narrator.

Some passages preserved in Coptic fragments of homilies have attracted the attention of modern scholars, who have given them the name *Gospel of Gamaliel* (since this Jewish teacher of the law speaks in the first person in the texts). These deal with Jesus' ministry, death and resurrection; one prominent theme is the accusation that Jesus' body was stolen by his disciples.

Bibliography

F. Scheidwiler and W. Schneemelcher, in: NTApo I, 526–36; J. K. Elliott, *Apocryphal New Testament,* 159–63, 205–25; M. A. van den Oudenrijn, *Gamaliel: Äthiopische Texte zur Pilatusliteratur* (SpicFri 4), Freiburg (Switzerland) 1959; A. Demandt, *Hände in Unschuld. Pontius Pilatus in der Geschichte,* Cologne et al. 1999, 213–20.

(c) The Gospel of Bartholomew

(1) Contextual information

Jerome and the Decretum Gelasianum know of a Gospel according to Bartholomew, and Ps.-Dionysius appeals to secret knowledge imparted to the apostle Bartholomew. A writing with this name has not been handed down to us from the early church, but we have two other texts which circulated under Bartholomew's name: (1) the 'Questions of Bartholomew' and (2) the Coptic 'Book of the resurrection of Jesus Christ, by Bartholomew the apostle'.

There is no literary dependence between these two texts; at the beginning, they draw on a common earlier tradition. It is not possible to say with certainty whether they have anything to do with the 'Gospel of Bartholomew' mentioned by Jerome and the Decretum Gelasianum. In terms of their form, they could be considered 'dialogue gospels' (i.e. texts recounting Jesus' conversations with his disciples after his resurrection: see ch. 8 below), but the visionary elements in their framework have also led to their classification as apocalypses (Elliott).

The Coptic 'Book of the resurrection of Jesus Christ' took on its present basic form in the fifth or sixth century. It is difficult to date the 'Questions of Bartholomew'; dates from the second to the sixth century have been proposed. At any rate, the version of the harrowing of hell in this text is probably older than that in EvNic, indicating that it was composed in the second century; on the other hand, this text borrows from Protev 8:1 at 2:15, and from IGTh 2 at 2:11, and this suggests a third-century date. The mariology in the 'Questions' reflects a phase of dogmatic development anterior to the Council of Ephesus (431), but it is improbable that it should be dated earlier than parallel statements in Epiphanius of Salamis (fourth century).

It may seem surprising that Bartholomew should be the favourite disciple and bearer of revelation in these two texts, given that the synoptic gospels mention nothing more than his name. His prominent role is the result of his identification with the 'Nathanael' of the Fourth Gospel, whom Jesus calls 'an Israelite without guile' (Jn 1:47), telling him that he will see 'greater things than these' (1:50). The apocryphal traditions about Bartholomew describe the fulfilment of this promise.

(2) The 'Questions of Bartholomew'

We have two Greek, two Latin and five Old Slavonic manuscripts of this work. Since the divergences are considerable, it is difficult to summarize the contents; strictly speaking, it is in fact necessary to indicate which manuscript we are following for each individual episode.

– Crucifixion and descent into hell

This uncertainty about the text begins with the very first verse, since the manuscripts locate the ensuing conversation between Jesus and the apostles both in the time before the passion and in the period after the resurrection. This means that it must be understood either as an anticipatory vision of future events or as a look back to the past. Bartholomew sees various incidents which occur when Jesus is crucified: angels descend from heaven and adore the crucified Lord (1:6), angels bring the more than life-sized figure of Adam to Golgotha (1:21), and an especially large angel cuts the veil of the temple in two with a fiery sword (1:24–27). The central role played by these angels is suggested by Jn 1:51, where Jesus tells Nathanael/Bartholomew: 'You will see heaven opened, and the angels of God ascending and descending upon the Son of Man.'

Bartholomew's first question concerns what was happening in the underworld while Jesus hung on the cross – all that the apostle heard was a voice and a din coming up to the surface world. In EvNic, others relate the story, but here it is Jesus himself who tells how he descended from the cross into the underworld before his resurrection and describes the terror and fainting that fell upon Hades and Beliar, the ruler of the underworld. Then Jesus leaves quickly for paradise, where he must welcome a special sacrifice, viz. the souls of the righteous who have died on that day. Only he can admit them to paradise (1:28–35).

– Jesus' conception by Mary

In ch. 2, Mary the mother of the Lord joins the apostles. Since Peter and John shrink from the task of asking her a question of great importance, Bartholomew once again leaps into the breach (2:4):

Bartholomew came to her with a cheerful countenance and said: 'You who are highly favoured, tabernacle of the Most High, unblemished, we, all the apostles ask you, but they have sent me to you. Tell us how you conceived the incomprehensible, or how you carried him who cannot be carried or how you bore so much greatness.'

After initially declining to answer, Mary utters a prayer in pseudo-Hebrew (2:13) – 'Elphouë zarethra charboum nemioth ...', which the narrator immediately 'translates' into Greek: 'O God exceedingly great and all-wise, king of the ages ...' – and then gives the information which Bartholomew has requested (2:15–21):

When I lived in the temple of God and received my food from the hand of an angel [cf. Protev 8:1], one day there appeared to me one in the form of an angel; but his face was indescribable and in his hand he had neither bread nor cup, as had the angel who came to me before. And immediately the veil of the temple was rent and there was a violent earthquake, and I fell to the earth, for I could not bear the sight of him. But he took me with his hand and raised me up. And I looked toward heaven; and there came a cloud of dew on my face and sprinkled me from head to foot, and he wiped me with his robe. Then he said to me: 'Hail, you who are highly favoured, the chosen vessel.' And then he struck the right side of his garment and there came forth an exceedingly large loaf, and he placed it upon the altar of the temple, and first ate of it himself and then gave to me also. And again he struck his garment, on the left side, and I looked and saw a cup full of wine. And he placed it upon the altar of the temple, and drank from it first himself and gave it also to me. And I looked and saw that the bread did not diminish and the cup was full as before. Then he said: 'Three years more, and I will send my word and you shall conceive my son, and through him the whole world shall be saved. But you will bring salvation to the world. Peace be with you, favoured one, and my peace shall be with you for ever.' And when he had said this, he vanished from my eyes and the temple was as before.

The underlying idea is both simple and impressive: the cloud with dew which descends on Mary recalls the cloud over the tent of revelation in Ex 40:34f., and illustrates the words of the angel at Lk 1:35: 'The power of the Most High will *overshadow* you.' The association of the dew with the manna in Num 11:9 and other texts brings us to the eucharistic elements of bread and wine, which permit all the believers to receive the body and blood of the Lord in the sacrament – something that happened to Mary in a unique way. Thus the shared experience of the eucharist provides a symbolic action which announces the imminent conception of the Son of God by means of the word.

– The adversary

In ch. 3, the disciples ask to be allowed to look into the 'abyss', i.e. the underworld. The angels then roll up the world like a piece of paper, but the apostles cannot bear the sight, and the abyss is covered over again.

Chapter 5 is a brief discussion of detailed questions about various categories of sin; it is obviously a subsequent addition. The concluding high-point of the 'Questions' is the very lengthy ch. 4. When Peter and Mary cannot agree about who should pose the next audacious question, Bartholomew once again puts himself forward and asks Jesus to show them the adversary, who now appears in person and (as expected) evokes terror (4:12–14):

The earth was shaken and Beliar came up, held by 660 angels and bound with fiery chains. He was 1,600 yards long and 40 yards broad. His face was like a lightning of fire, and his eyes like sparks, and from his nostrils came a stinking smoke. His mouth was like a cleft of rock and a single one of his wings was 80 yards long. As soon as the apostles saw him, they fell to the ground on their faces and became like dead men.

These lines are inspired in part by the description of Leviathan at Job 41:10–13. The Lord gives Bartholomew power over Beliar, and the apostle compels Beliar to explain how the first of God's angels to be created became what he now is: this was because the devil was unwilling to accept God's image, viz. the human being. Beliar also gives information about the creation and hierarchy of the angelic world and reveals many names of angels (e.g. 4:47, 'Mermeoth, Onomatath, Duth,

Melioth, Charouth, Graphathas, Hoethra, Nephonos and Chalkatura'). Beliar hints that the fall took place when Eve let herself be seduced and had intercourse with him.

Towards the end, Jesus speaks again and declares that these mysteries may be communicated only to believers who are worthy of trust. After the insertion of 5:1–9, the work concludes with a doxology spoken by Bartholomew with the other apostles at 5:10.

(3) The 'Book of the resurrection of Jesus Christ'

We have three incomplete manuscripts of this text, as well as a number of fragments which supply additional material. Our enumeration follows Kaestli.

– Fragments

One fragment belongs at the very beginning. A cockerel is brought to the table during a meal which Jesus holds with his disciples, and the Jews comment: 'The blood of your Master will be shed just like the blood of this cockerel' (1:2). In order to make the comparison between the fate of the bird and his own fate complete – and also because the cockerel will be needed later on, so that it can crow when Peter denies Jesus – the Lord raises it to life again and tells it to fly away.

The wife of Judas Iscariot acted as foster-mother to the seven-month-old son of Joseph of Arimathea. After Judas' betrayal, the child protests and beseeches his father to take him away from Judas' house (2:2). This is a further example of the typical apocryphal elaboration of narrative material from the New Testament, where family relationships are established between the well known biblical characters.

In ch. 3, an old man from Bethlehem named Ananias asks the Jews to be crucified instead of Jesus. The chief priests attempt in vain to stone him, and they thrown him in vain into a blazing oven for three days and three nights. Finally, they kill him with a lance, and the risen Lord takes his soul up into heaven.

– Scenes in and at the grave

The next scenes take place in Jesus' tomb, which death and his seven sons inspect, and in the underworld. Since Judas is already in Hades after committing suicide, Jesus takes the opportunity to preach to him at length about his punishment (6:4–6). After Jesus' resurrection, three souls remain in the world of the dead: those of Herod (presumably Herod the Great), of Cain and of Judas (7:4).

On the morning of the first day of the week, nine holy women come to the grave of Jesus, viz. (1) Mary Magdalene, (2) Mary the mother of James, (3) Salome from Mk 15:40, identified with the Salome who appears as a midwife in Protev 20:1, (4) Mary from Lk 10:38–42 and

(5) her sister Martha, (6) Susanna from Lk 8:3 (another manuscript adds the alternative of Johanna, from the same verse), (7) the woman with the flow of blood from Mk 5:25, now called Berenice, (8) the mother of the young man from Nain, called Lea, and (9) the nameless sinful woman from Lk 7:26–50. When we consider this panorama of women from the canonical gospels, we should note that Mary Magdalene, Mary from Lk 10 and the anonymous sinful woman from Lk 7 have not yet been confused or identified with one another. It appears, however, that Mary Magdalene is interchangeable with Mary the mother of Jesus, since the continuation of the text assumes that the latter is present (8:1).

The women encounter Philogenes, the owner of the garden, who himself works as a gardener (cf. Jn 20:15), and a conversation develops between him and Mary the mother of the Lord. He relates the events of the past night: myriads of angels were present, and a huge fiery chariot stood ready. God the Father descended from heaven and awakened his Son from the dead. Only after Philogenes has finished his account does the risen Lord himself appear. He charges his mother Mary to bring a message to the disciples.

– Bartholomew

At 10:3, Bartholomew (who has not played any role up to this point) now speaks as an eyewitness of these events. It almost seems as if he is concealed behind the gardener Philogenes, all the more so since he later calls himself a 'gardener and seller of vegetables' (17:3). It is not difficult to understand how Bartholomew became a 'gardener'. Jesus had said to Nathanael/Bartholomew, 'I saw you under the fig tree' (Jn 1:48) – and one interpretation of these words held that the disciple had been pursuing his professional work under the fig tree.

Bartholomew is given the privilege of looking into the seventh, highest heaven, where he witnesses the heavenly liturgy which is celebrated to mark the return to heaven of the risen Lord. Hymns are sung continually in chs. 12–16, and Bartholomew subsequently writes these down for his brethren, the apostles. The angels sing seven hymns; one hymn is sung by Adam, since he and Eve are now once more permitted to live close to God; and one hymn is sung by the righteous. This hymnic passage ends when the righteous and the angels resume their accustomed places.

Chapter 18 is a flashback: Bartholomew reminds his fellow apostles of an earlier scene, when Jesus spoke to the twelve in a foreign language on the Mount of Olives. On that occasion too, the heavens opened and Jesus brought it about that the Father called each of the apostles by name and blessed him. Chapters 19–20 bring us back to the narrative present: the apostles celebrate the eucharist with Mary, and the fragrance of this sacrifice rises up to the throne of God (20:1). The Father is moved and sends them the risen Lord, who appears to them in

Galilee and shows them the marks of his wounds. He also gives them the authority to preach and to heal.

– Thomas

One apostle was missing, however, viz. Thomas, who had gone to his home town, since he had heard that his son Siophanes (the original may have been 'Theophanes') had died. He arrives in the town seven days after Siophanes' death, but Thomas raises him to life in the name of Jesus Christ. Siophanes then relates what his soul experienced while his dead body lay on the earth. The archangel Michael took his soul and washed it in Acheron, and it saw the twelve glorious thrones of the twelve apostles in heaven. Siophanes wanted to take his place on the throne reserved for his father, but Michael prevented him from doing so.

The raising of Siophanes causes a tremendous commotion in the town, which intensifies all the more when he tells his story to the townspeople. Thomas baptizes 12,000 persons, lays the foundation stone for a church and ordains his son Siophanes as the first bishop. Then he ascends a cloud, which takes him to the other apostles on the Mount of Olives. When he hears the good news that Jesus Christ is risen from the dead and has appeared to the disciples, Thomas reacts with his proverbial lack of faith. The other apostles try to convince him, and Bartholomew on his own tries once again to exhort him and make him change his mind. Then the risen Jesus himself appears. Thomas is allowed to touch the wound in his side and make the sign of the cross upon himself with the blood that flows from this wound.

After Jesus has departed into heaven, the apostles celebrate the eucharist together before departing to the four corners of the world to preach the gospel. The narrative indicates that from now on, the eucharist is the way in which Jesus, as risen Lord, will be present for them with his flesh and his blood, and will accompany them on every path they take.

In the wide spectrum of early Christian apocrypha, the 'Book of the resurrection of Jesus Christ' presents a transitional form from the 'gospel' to another genre. The striking interest which this text shows in what happened to individual apostles – here not so much Bartholomew, as Thomas and his son – strongly recalls the apocryphal Acts of the Apostles, a prominent example of which are the Acts of Thomas.

Bibliography

F. Scheidwiler and W. Schneemelcher, in: NTApo I, 537–57; J. K. Elliott, *Apocryphal New Testament,* 652–72; J. D. Kaestli, in: *Ecrits apocryphes chrétiens,* 255–356; J. D. Kaestli and P. Cherix, *L'Evangile de Barthélemy* (Apocryphes 1), Brepols 1993.

7

GOSPELS FROM NAG HAMMADI

In December 1945, an Egyptian farm worker in search of fertile humus near Nag Hammadi in Upper Egypt discovered a clay jar containing thirteen leather-bound codices with texts in the Coptic language (as the name itself indicates, Coptic is a late form of Egyptian). A number of difficulties slowed down the full scholarly evaluation of this discovery, which is comparable only to the discovery of the Qumran writings, and it took fifty years to bring the initial phase more or less to a conclusion, with the publication of critical editions of the texts, translations and provisional commentaries.

The thirteen codices (quoted as NHC [Nag Hammadi Codices] I–XIII) contain about 50 texts, mostly of a Christian gnostic character. The codices were produced *c.* 350, as we see from dated receipts and contracts which were torn into strips and used to strengthen the bindings; this, however, says nothing about the age of the individual writings, especially since their original language was not Coptic. All these texts are translations from Greek (only a few scholars have suggested that a text such as the Gospel of Thomas may have been written in Syriac). We do not know who translated, copied, collected, bound, used and finally buried the texts. It has been plausibly suggested that this was the work of monks in nearby ancient monasteries, but this cannot be proved.

The Nag Hammadi texts have opened up completely new sources for our knowledge of gnosis. Hitherto, the primary sources were polemical texts in which the church fathers vigorously attacked what they saw as a gnostic infiltration of the Christian faith. In most (though not all) of the newly discovered texts, gnostic authors themselves present their convictions; some of the patristic statements are confirmed and others corrected, and many matters take on a wholly new precision, since we can see more clearly that gnosis is fundamentally based on a dualistic world-view and an understanding of existence which can be described in terms such as alienation and the solitude of the individual. The individual no longer feels at home in this world, but aims to return to his origin outside the world, which he considers to be his true homeland, now lost. He is saved by the knowledge about his true condition – this is precisely what is affirmed by the Greek word *gnōsis*, 'knowledge'. The spiritual fascination which is still exercised by some of these texts, with their greater or lesser degree of gnostic influence, suggests that today's readers find in them an echo of the way they too feel about the world and about the project of their own lives.

The discoveries at Nag Hammadi have also expanded our library of ancient Christian apocrypha. The following genres are represented: gospels (see below), apocalypses (e.g. 'The Apocalypse of Paul', NHC

V,2 [i.e. second text in the fifth codex]), letters (e.g., 'The letter to Rheginus about the resurrection', NHC I,4), and acts of the apostles ('The Acts of Peter and the Twelve Apostles', NHC VI,1). We also find prayers (e.g. 'The Prayer of the Apostle Paul', I,1) and hymns for use in worship ('The Three Steles of Seth', NHC VII,5), non-gnostic collections of aphorisms ('The Sentences of Sextus', NHC XII,1), community regulations ('The Interpretation of Knowledge', NHC XI,1), revelatory discourses ('Trimorphic Protennoia', NHC XIII,1), theological treatises ('Zostrianos', NHC VIII,1), and even a poorly translated section from Plato's *Republic* (NHC VI,5 = *Republic* 588B–589B). As with ancient Christian apocrypha in general, it would be a mistake to measure the Nag Hammadi texts exclusively against the New Testament canon and to see them as the conscious attempt to construct an alternative canon. This is why Lüdemann's sensational designation of them as 'the heretics' Bible' misses the point altogether.

One general problem posed by the identification of literary genres becomes particularly acute in the case of the Nag Hammadi texts: the name an author gives his text is not identical with others' description of it. In other words, writings in the Nag Hammadi corpus called 'gospels' are not necessarily what we understand as a 'gospel', since we find no narrative elements, and these texts do not treat the public ministry and passion of Jesus Christ. We have already seen that the 'Gospel of the Egyptians' (NHC III,2 and IV,2; cf. ch. 4b above) is given this title only in the colophon, i.e. the concluding note in the manuscript, which may have been added by a translator or copyist. The same is true of the 'Gospels' of Thomas and Philip.

The 'Gospel of Truth' (NHC I,3) is a somewhat different case, since the incipit begins: 'The gospel of truth is a joy for those who have received from the Father of truth the gift of knowing him ...' (16,31–35 [i.e. page 16, lines 31–35]). It might perhaps be suggested that the noun 'gospel' in this passage has retained the original meaning, viz. the oral proclamation of salvation, while it is used only analogously in the other Nag Hammadi 'gospels' as the name for a proclamation of salvation which would enjoy the same rank as the New Testament gospels. In that case, however, one might equally well apply the term 'gospel' to writings such as 'The Exegesis on the Soul' (NHC II,6) or 'The Apocryphon of John' (attested in several versions, NHC II,1, etc.; see ch. 8d below); and the other 'dialogue gospels' (see ch. 8 below) would certainly deserve this title, even if their text does not explicitly use this word.

We must make pragmatic compromises here. The Gospel of the Egyptians has already been discussed in ch. 4b. In the present chapter, we discuss the remaining texts which use this title. Such a criterion may seem merely extrinsic, but it has the merit of concentrating our discussion on three important writings which have attracted considerable scholarly attention: the Gospel of Thomas, the Gospel of Philip and the 'Gospel of Truth'.

Bibliography

J. M. Robinson (ed.), *The Coptic Gnostic Library. A Complete Edition of the Nag Hammadi Codices* I–V, Leiden 2000; G. Lüdemann and M. Janssen, *Bibel der Häretiker*; K. Dietzfelbinger, *Apokryphe Evangelien*; W. Rebell, *Neutestamentliche Apokryphen*, 21–62; B. Layton, *The Gnostic Scriptures*, Garden City, N.Y. 1987; W. Hörmann, *Gnosis. Das Buch der verborgenen Evangelien*, Augsburg 7th edn. 1994, 106–333; M. Franzmann, *Jesus in the Nag Hammadi Writings*, Edinburgh 1996; J. D. Turner and A. McGuire (eds.), *The Nag Hammadi Library After Fifty Years* (NHMS 44), Leiden 1997.

(a) The Gospel of Thomas (EvThom)

(1) Contextual information

The Gospel of Thomas (NHC II,2) has attracted far more attention than any other of the Nag Hammadi writings, for a number of reasons.

First, a number of patristic writers mention and quote a 'Gospel of Thomas' which is distinct from the Infancy Gospel of Thomas discussed in ch. 5b above. In the course of his arguments against the Naassenes, Hippolytus quotes the sentence (*Refutatio* 5.7.20): 'The one who seeks me will find me in children from the seventh year onwards, since it is there, hidden in the fourteenth aeon, that I reveal myself', and we find a loose parallel to these words in EvThom 4. Origen seems to know our EvThom, while Clement of Alexandria attributes the logion about seeking and finding in EvThom 2 to the Gospel of the Hebrews (cf. ch. 3a, nr. 1). In the *Pistis Sophia,* another Coptic Gnostic writing from the third century, the risen Jesus charges Thomas to write down his words of revelation (1:42f.). Mani and the Manichaeans used a 'Gospel of Thomas', and it has been shown that this was our EvThom.

Secondly, EvThom consists only of logia of Jesus, occasionally with sparse indications of a situation and equally sparse elements of dialogue. These logia can be assigned to various categories known from the tradition of the words of Jesus: sapiential logia (e.g., 45, 47); prophetic logia (51, 111); 'I'-logia (61, 77); metaphors and parables (96–98); beatitudes (18f.); cries of lamentation (103); proverbs (31, 102); words of law (53, 104); and community ordinances (12, 25). EvThom is thus strikingly reminiscent of Q, the lost logia collection which scholars postulate as the second source (alongside Mark) for Matthew and Luke; most of Q consists of words of Jesus (though Q has narrative components too, more so than EVThom).

Thirdly, when the text of EvThom became available, scholars discovered that this gospel was in fact already known – though no one had realised this! So-called *Logia Iēsou* in Greek, fragmentary words of Jesus, had been published in 1897 and 1904 in the first two volumes of papyri discovered at Oxyrhynchos in Egypt. These were enumerated as POxy 1, POxy 654 and POxy 655. It was difficult to determine the provenance of these logia; some scholars suggested that they came from EvHeb. Parallels to all these logia (to the extent that the state of transmission still permits their identification) were now recognised in EvThom: POxy 654 corresponds to EvThom 1–7, POxy 1 to EvThom 26–33 and POxy 655 to EvThom 36–39.

These three papyrus fragments are independent of each other and come from three different manuscripts. Palaeographic observations date the oldest fragment, POxy 1, to *c.* 200. This means that the archetype on which the papyri are based comes from the second century. This is important, because the Coptic version – like the other Nag Hammadi texts – was copied only in the fourth century, from a text which itself was a translation from Greek into Coptic.

The long path of transmission which lies behind our Coptic EvThom has left its traces on the text; close examination shows a number of divergences on points of detail between the Greek logia from the Oxyrhynchos papyri and their Coptic pendants. Normally, it can be seen that the Greek version is older, while the Coptic traits are the product of a secondary revision. This reminds us of the need to be cautious in our study of the Coptic EvThom. For example, it has been demonstrated that it is sometimes so close to the Coptic biblical translations that it must in fact be dependent on these. This, however, tells us nothing certain about the composition of EvThom, since it may have happened only when it was translated into Coptic and then copied by a succession of scribes.

Although it was discovered in Egypt, it is most probable that EvThom was written in Syria, where the apostle Thomas was particularly venerated. Other writings linked to his name, such as the Acts of Thomas, point to Syria, and this certainly does not argue against composition of EvThom in the Greek language. Thanks to POxy 1, we must date it before 200, and even a cautious assessment of the arguments allows us to date an early version to between *c.* 120 and 140.

The dates proposed by scholars vary widely; the 50s of the first decade after Christ have also been suggested. This is linked to another problem which continues to provoke considerable controversy, viz. the relationship between EvThom and the synoptic gospels. A very early date fits better the hypothesis that EvThom is completely independent of the synoptics, while a later dating makes it easier to argue for dependence. This question concerns only some of the logia, since roughly 50 per cent have no direct parallels in the New Testament. We must make a further distinction in the remaining half between logia of a synoptic type (e.g. hitherto unknown parables) and independent revelatory logia which have a more strongly gnostic character. The best method is to evaluate each logion on its own, without presupposing a theory about the sources of EvThom; one can then see what general picture emerges. We shall return to this below.

The word 'gnostic' brings us to a second controversial point: how far is EvThom a gnostic work? Here too, everything depends on the interpretation of the individual logia. EvThom does not elaborate a coherent gnostic myth, and this makes it methodologically unwise to force all the logia into such a Procrustean bed. On the other hand, as we shall demonstrate below in the discussion of logia 28 and 50, it is simply undeniable that many logia are more easily understood if we recognize their gnostic affinities.

The lack of a narrative thread makes it difficult, indeed virtually impossible to summarize the contents of EvThom. Sometimes the logia seem juxtaposed without any inherent connection, but in other cases we can see how they are linked by prominent words (logia 25 and 26 share the concept 'brother'; logia 28 and 29 have the concept of 'flesh'; logia 36 and 37 share the theme of 'clothing'; the 'dead' are mentioned in logia 50 and 51; we find the same conclusion, like a refrain, in logia 18 and 19, 'he will not experience death'). Similarly, we find small thematic groups consisting of several logia (e.g. the three parables in logia 63, 64 and 65 all deal with the false endeavour to get hold of earthly goods; logia 68 and 69 are a collection of three beatitudes; logia 102 and 103 contrast a blessing and an invocation of woe; a fundamental idea in logia 83, 84 and 85 is that the human person is God's image). Doublets occur, especially towards the close of the work – compare 80 with 56; 81 with 2; logion 82, also known as an agraphon (see ch. 1b, nr. 8 above), 'He who is near me is near the fire, and he who is far from me is far from the kingdom', with logion 10, 'I have cast fire upon the world, and see, I am guarding it until it blazes'; the seeking and finding in logion 92 with logion 2; logion 108 with logion 13 (see below). Such doublets may indicate the attempt to construct an *inclusio* as framework for EvThom. They may also be evidence of the hand of a collector of logia who does not always follow a consistent plan.

In the next section, we shall attempt to present and discuss at least some of the major elements in EvThom, in order to give an impression of what it offers the reader. The initial logia, which develop a kind of programme, are particularly important here. We follow the customary enumeration, with 114 logia, although this was established only by the twentieth-century editors of the text. Where necessary, we indicate Bethge's subdivision of the logia into verses.

(2) *The contents*

– The incipit

Although the title 'Gospel according to Thomas' is found only in the *subscriptio*, the lengthy preamble enumerated as logion 1 includes the name of the bearer of these traditions, and also sketches a basic programme:

These are the secret sayings which the living Jesus spoke and which Didymos Judas Thomas wrote down. And he said, 'Whoever finds the interpretation of these sayings will not experience death.'

'The living Jesus' is a favourite name for the risen Lord in gnostic texts, and this would suggest a kinship between EvThom and the dialogue gospels (see ch. 8 below). However, a number of the ensuing logia are formulated from the perspective of the earthly Jesus (e.g. 12, 60f.), and it is clear that 'living' here means one who is outside or above time. The whole person of Jesus is 'living', since he is present anew in all times and places thanks to his word – when this is interpreted aright.

POxy 654 calls the bearer of tradition only 'Judas, who is also (called) Thomas'. The double name 'Judas Thomas' (whom we tend to designate by the simple name of Thomas) is found above all in the Syriac church, probably as an inference from 'Judas, not Iscariot' at Jn 14:22, where some Syriac textual witnesses read 'Judas Thomas'. While several of the disciples bear the name 'Judas', as we have seen, the epithet 'Thomas' means 'twin' in Aramaic – and this is the meaning of the Greek loan-word 'Didymos' in the Coptic text. In other words, both the names given to this Judas call him 'twin', and behind this there may lie the far-reaching conclusion drawn by the 'Book of Thomas' (see ch. 8b below) and the Syriac Acts of Thomas, viz. that Judas Thomas is the twin brother of Jesus (cf. Mk 6:3), his earthly double and representative.

From logion 2 onwards, the words of Jesus are introduced by the stereotypical formula in the present tense: 'Jesus says'. In the second half of the superscription in POxy 654, however, we find the past tense: 'he said'. This suggests that the speaker is not Jesus, but Thomas, who formulates a task – 'Whoever finds the interpretation of these sayings' – and specifies the reward promised to those who accomplish it: 'he will not experience death' (cf. Jn 8:51). The life promised here is no longer subject to death, transcending the conditions of earthly physical life. It is a spiritual reality which cannot be destroyed, since it outlasts time itself.

Why is Thomas introduced as an intermediary between Jesus and those addressed by the logia? It is because of the special character of these words, which are *hidden* (literally, 'apocryphal' in the Greek) and hence require interpretation by an expert; here, the Coptic text too employs the Greek loan-word *hermēneia*. A hermeneutical task is entailed (cf. also logion 5); it is not enough to remain on the surface level, where one may perhaps be puzzled by the apparent meaning-lessness of some of the affirmations in EvThom, for that would miss the real point. Hence, it is not by chance that EvThom so often issues the call to wake up and be attentive: 'Whoever has ears to hear, let him hear' (in 8, 21, 24, 63, 65, 96; cf. Mk 4:9, etc.).

– The kingdom

After the challenge in the preamble to 'find the interpretation of these words', logion 2 very appropriately speaks of the continuous process of seeking and finding (the text is quoted above in ch. 3a, nr. 1), which must be pursued without wearying until the promised goal is attained.

The Coptic text describes this goal as follows: 'and he will be king over the All', while POxy 654 continues: 'and he will find rest'. This 'rest', which is not mentioned in the Coptic version of logion 2, is found subsequently in logion 90: 'Come unto me, for my yoke is easy and my lordship is mild, and you will find repose for yourselves' (cf. Mt 11:28–30). The beatitude in logion 58 likewise speaks of the ceaseless work of interpreting and understanding: 'Blessed is the man who has suffered and found life.'

The conclusion of logion 2 – 'and he will be king' – is taken up in logion 3, which introduces a new leitmotif, viz. the 'kingdom':

Jesus said, 'If those who lead you [POxy 654 has: lead you astray] say to you, "See, the kingdom is in the sky," then the birds of the sky will precede you. (2) If they say to you, "It is in the sea," then the fish will precede you. (3) Rather, the kingdom is inside of you, and it is outside of you. (4) When you come to know yourselves, then you will become known [POxy 654 has the singular: the one who knows himself will *find this*], (5) and you will realize that it is you who are the sons of the living Father. (6) But if you will not know yourselves, you dwell in poverty and it is you who are that poverty.'

The synoptic apocalypse too speaks at Mk 13:21f. and parallels of those who seek to lead the disciples astray by telling them, 'See, here is the Christ – or see, there he is!' When the Coptic EvThom speaks of 'those who lead you', it may perhaps be thinking of office-bearers in the church and theologians who teach that God's royal sovereignty is a reality belonging exclusively to the sphere beyond this world. EvThom caricatures such a view when it speaks of the birds of the sky and the sea with its fish (cf. Deut 30:12f.). Verse 3 then offers a positive formulation, which is comparable to Lk 17:20f. ('The kingdom of God is not coming with signs to be observed; nor will they say, "Lo, here it is!" or "There!" for behold, the kingdom of God is in the midst of you'). EvThom 3:3 understands the presence of the kingdom both individually ('inside of you') and in a manner transcending the individual ('outside of you'). If the believer looks into his own heart, he will find the kingdom present there; but this does not exhaust the reality of the kingdom, which also has an external dimension thanks to the fact that a number of individuals (see below) share in this knowledge. Verse 5 emphasizes that the fruit of the process of seeking and finding the hidden meaning of the words of Jesus is essentially knowledge or recognition. According to v. 6, the one who lacks this insight is 'poverty itself'.

Obviously, Jesus' message of the irruption of God's sovereignty is stripped of its future contents here; the promised kingdom is reconstituted as a spiritual, timeless reality. The kingdom can be realized more or less perfectly. Other logia speaking of the kingdom (e.g. 20, 22, 27, 46, 49, 54, etc.) lead to the second-last logion in the gospel (113):

His disciples said to him: 'When will the kingdom come?' <Jesus said,> 'It will not come by waiting for it. It will not be a matter of saying, "Here it is" or "There it is." Rather, the kingdom of the Father is spread out upon the earth, and men do not see it.'

– Solitary, individual, one

The next logion immediately offers yet another leitmotif:

Jesus said, 'The man old in days will not hesitate to ask a small child seven days old about the place of life, and he will live. For many who are first will become last, and they will become a single one.'

The encounter between old man and suckling, last and first, closes a circle. This means that it is possible to go back to the beginning (cf. logion 18:3, 'Blessed is he who will take his place in the beginning; he will know the end …') or even perhaps to that beginning which is antecedent to every earthly existence (logion 19:1, 'Blessed is he who came into being before he came into being'), before the introduction of the terrible division of which logion 11:4 speaks: 'On the day when you were one you became two. But when you become two, what will you do?' Other logia confirm that the ideal state is that of the *monakhos* (from which the word 'monk' is derived), 'solitary' or 'individual': 'And they will stand solitary (*monakhos*)' (16:4), 'Blessed are the solitary and elect, for you will find the kingdom' (49:1): 'Many are standing at the door, but it is the solitary who will enter the bridal chamber' (75).

This may also be the original meaning of logion 30, which poses considerable problems in its Coptic version: 'Where there are three gods, they are gods. Where there are two or one, I am with him.' The Greek version in POxy 1 allows the reconstruction: 'Wherever there are three, they are without God. And where there is one on his own, tell him: "I am with them".' This would reverse Mt 18:20 – Jesus is not to be encountered 'where two or three are gathered in his name'; on the contrary, that is a 'godless' assembly. Jesus is present to those who are solitary.

This tells us something about the self-consciousness and experiential world of those for whom EvThom was written. They are few in number, isolated and marginal persons, but they consider this is a privilege, in keeping with Jesus' words: 'I shall choose you, one out of a thousand, and two out of ten thousand, and they shall stand as a single one' (23). It is, however, probable that these 'solitary individuals' formed small groups which led their own lives within larger groupings of communities. Where there are only a few, each one is particularly valuable. Hence the exhortation: 'Love your brother like your soul, guard him as the pupil of your eye!' (25).

– Fasting

The disciples speak for the first time in logion 6, when they ask Jesus about the three classical works of piety, viz. fasting, prayer and almsgiving. Jesus avoids giving a direct answer here – 'Do not tell lies, and do not do what you hate' – but he returns to this issue later in EvThom (cf. 14) and interprets fasting as a fundamental attitude of abstinence vis-à-vis the world, since the one who seeks must avoid getting entangled in worldly business (cf. 27 and 21:6). Logion 42 (already mentioned in our discussion of the agraphon about the world as a 'bridge', ch. 1b, nr. 20) offers a lapidary summary: 'Become passers-by.'

– Lion and human being

Logion 7 seems particularly obscure. Those who read EvThom for the first time can only shake their heads in puzzlement at these words:

Jesus said, 'Blessed is the lion which becomes man when consumed by man; and cursed is the man whom the lion consumes, and the lion becomes man.'

We must ask whether the conclusion of this logion ought not to read: 'and the man becomes a lion', since this would establish at least a verbal equivalence – when the lion is eaten by a human being, it becomes a human being, and the human being becomes a lion when eaten by a lion. In other words, the Coptic text has mistranslated the original. This would make sense in general terms: one who eats assimilates what he consumes and turns it into a component of his own self. Indeed, even the flesh of a lion, once eaten, builds up the muscles of a man. Perhaps a popular view was that such flesh would give him particular vigour and strength.

We must, however, go beyond this preliminary interpretation. The key to understanding logion 7 is the recognition that it is based on rudiments of Platonic anthropology. In the passage from the *Republic* which is included in a poor translation among the Nag Hammadi texts (588B–589B = NHC VI,5: 48,16–51,23), Plato offers a picture of the soul, which combines in itself three forms: (1) a many-headed monster, symbolizing the multiplicity of passions; (2) a lion, embodying hot-headed wrath; and (3) a human being, embodying the reason which is meant to exercise control. Accordingly, the eating of the lion by a human being symbolizes the victory of prudent reason over naked passion.

– A parable without interpretation

Logion 9 is a short version of the well known parable of the sower (Mk 4:3–8 and parallels), with no trace of the allegorical interpretation which was later added to the parable (Mk 4:14–20 and parallels). This has often led to the inference that EvThom 9 offers an older, pre-synoptic version of the parable, but this need not be the case. It is equally possible that EvThom consciously omitted both the interpret-ation and the interpretative elements in the narration of the parable,

because these anticipate the correct exegesis of these hidden words –
something the hearers of EvThom must accomplish for themselves in a
process of seeking which is open, i.e. where the direction is not laid
down in advance.

– Thomas and other disciples

In logion 12, Jesus tells the disciples to 'go to James the righteous', who
is to be the authoritative figure in the time after Easter; this indicates
that the material on which EvThom drew had been handed on in
Jewish-Christian circles. Logion 13 leaves no doubt that the real leader
is Thomas:

(1)   *Jesus* said to his disciples, 'Compare me to someone and tell me whom I
       am like.'
(2)   *Simon Peter* said to him, 'You are like a righteous angel.'
(3)   *Matthew* said to him, 'You are like a wise philosopher.'
(4)   *Thomas* said to him, 'Master, my mouth is wholly incapable of saying
       whom you are like.'
(5)   *Jesus* said, 'I am not your [sing.] master. Because you [sing.] have drunk,
       you [sing.] have become intoxicated from the bubbling spring which I have
       measured out.'
(6)   And he took him and withdrew and told him three things.
(7)   When Thomas returned to his companions, they asked him, 'What did
       Jesus say to you?'
(8)   *Thomas* said to them, 'If I tell you one of the things which he told me, you
       will pick up stones and throw them at me; a fire will come out of the stones
       and burn you up.'

The general structure of this pericope is reminiscent of the question about
Jesus' messianic identity in Caesarea Philippi (Mk 8:27–30), where Jesus
asks his disciples who the *people* think he is and *Peter* reports various
answers ('Elijah', 'one of the prophets') before himself giving the correct
assessment: 'You are the Messiah.' A comparison between these two
texts reveals a number of shifts in emphasis. In EvThom 13, the *people*
play no role. The views of a number of other *disciples* are reported, and
it is not *Peter*, but *Thomas* who gives the correct answer – in this case, an
evasive refusal to reply. In many passages in Mark (e.g. 10:10–12), after
teaching the *crowd*, Jesus takes his *disciples* aside and gives them a
private interpretation; in EvThom 13, *Thomas* is taken aside from the
group of the other *disciples* for this secret revelation. This may indicate
that the entire process of teaching is now seen as an exclusively intra-
ecclesial activity where the throng of outsiders have become irrelevant;
the disciples represent the Christians who belong to the church, while
Thomas represents a small, elite group who boast of deeper insights. For
want of a better name, we may call such a group 'gnostics'.

    The answers given by Simon Peter and Matthew are not completely
wrong; they revert to an old christology which conceived of Jesus as a

heavenly messenger or angel, and characterize Jesus as a successful philosophical teacher. However, such views do not go far enough. It is Thomas who makes the correct declaration: viz. that human speech is incapable *a priori* of formulating adequate affirmations about Jesus. This allows Jesus to reject Thomas' address of him as 'teacher' – not because this fails to do justice to his true dignity, but because Thomas no longer needs Jesus as a teacher. The metaphors in v. 5 of 'drinking' (cf. Jn 7:37f.) and the 'bubbling spring' (cf. Jn 4:14) 'measured out' by Jesus himself show that Thomas already shares in the hidden wisdom. Logion 108, towards the end of EvThom, clarifies the meaning of 13:5 by affirming that this 'drinking' produces a configuration to Christ in which one receives revelation:

Jesus said: 'He who will drink from my mouth will become like me. I myself shall become he, and the things that are hidden will be revealed to him.'

This is the reason why (according to 13:6) only Thomas is worthy of the special revelation, which consists of 'three words' so extraordinary that the other disciples may not be told of their contents. This reflects the experience of the adherents of this esoteric form of the Christian faith and life, who were unable to communicate their most important insights to the communities. Such insights were too provocative, and pious ears might even find them blasphemous. If, however, such 'normal' Christians reacted by stoning the deviants for blaspheming against God, the punishment would return upon their own heads. Silence is the best strategy for all involved.

– A quotation from Paul

At 1 Cor 2:9, Paul proclaims: '*As it is written*, "What no eye has seen, nor ear heard, nor the heart of man conceived, what God has prepared for those who love him".' Scholars have searched in vain for the source of this scriptural quotation, which is not found in our Old Testament. EvThom 17, however, relates that *Jesus* said:

I shall give you what no eye has seen and what no ear has heard and what no hand has touched and what has not occurred to the human mind.

Is Paul therefore quoting an agraphon (see ch. 1 above), a concealed logion of Jesus? It is more probable that the opposite process, discussed in ch. 1, has taken place, whereby passages from the epistolary literature in the New Testament – especially difficult texts such as this – have later been transformed into words of Jesus.

– Making the two one

The metaphor of the 'child' is used by Jesus at Mk 10:15 when he speaks of admission to the kingdom of God. The same image is taken up in the narrative framework and logion of EvThom 22:1f. The scene continues in 22:3 with a question by the disciples. The complexity of Jesus' reply is probably the result of two or three insertions. The principal theme of entering the kingdom is picked up again in 22:7:

(1)   Jesus saw infants being suckled.

(2)   He said to his disciples, 'These infants being suckled are like those who *enter the kingdom.*'

(3)   They said to him, 'Shall we then, as children, *enter the kingdom?*'

(4)   Jesus said to them, 'When you make the two one, and when you make the inside like the outside and the outside like the inside, and the above like the below,

(5)   and when you make the male and the female one and the same, so that the male not be male nor the female female;

(6)   and when you fashion eyes in place of an eye, and a hand in place of a hand, and a foot in place of a foot, and a likeness in place of a likeness;

(7)   then will you *enter [the kingdom].*'

We are already familiar with the motif of 'the two becoming one' in v. 4. Jesus' reply illustrates the deadly separation by means of the antitheses 'inside/outside' and 'above/below', which must be overcome.

The parenthesis in v. 5 gives an important new specification of this idea, drawing on a principle attested as a non-canonical logion of Jesus in the Greek Gospel of the Egyptians and 2 Clement 12:2 (see ch. 4a above). The separation entailed by the polarity of two genders – in other words, the fact that the human being is either a man or a woman – is already documented in the creation narrative at Gen 1:27. Redemption means transcending the male and female to attain a new unity. In view of logion 114 (see below), we must note that the thinking and the formulation in logion 22 are egalitarian. There is nothing to indicate a divergent evaluation of the male and the female.

The replacement of eye, hand, foot and likeness in v. 6 may be connected with the shocking aphorisms in Mk 9:43,45,47 ('If your hand causes you to sin, cut it off', etc.). The meaning is that the kingdom requires a complete renewal of the human person, who must break radically with his old existence.

– A 'gnostic' description of the situation

Logion 28 plays a central role in the controversy about the extent to which EvThom may properly be called 'gnostic':

Jesus said, 'I took my place in the midst of the world, and I appeared to them in flesh. (2) I found all of them intoxicated; I found none of them thirsty. (3) And my soul became afflicted for the sons of men, because they are blind in their hearts and do not have sight; for empty they came into the world, and empty too they seek to leave the world. (4) But for the moment they are intoxicated. When they shake off their wine, they will repent.'

Even a scholar who wishes to get away from a gnostic interpretation of

EvThom as a whole must admit: 'Of all the logia in the Gospel of Thomas, this is the one which most clearly expresses the traditional gnostic redeemer myth' (Valantasis, p. 103). In the classic gnostic texts, we repeatedly encounter a redeemer-figure who enters the world unrecognized and finds humanity drunk, intoxicated, blind and sleeping. The redeemer's primary function is to bring the summons that will awaken at least some human beings and bring them to self-knowledge.

The established repertoire of gnostic themes also includes the ascent of the soul through various heavenly realms to the highest heaven, either in a vision or as the return to the soul's origin after death. This path is risky, because the lower heavens are occupied by hostile powers to whom the soul must prove its identity by means of passwords and signs. This is precisely the constellation we find in logion 50:

Jesus said, 'If they say to you, "Where did you come from?", say to them, "We came from the light, the place where the light came into being on its own accord and established [itself] and became manifest through their image." (2) If they say to you, "Is it you?", say, "We are its children, and we are the elect of the living Father." (3) If they ask you, "What is the sign of the Father in you?", say to them, "It is movement and repose." '

One characteristic of gnosis is a dualistic cosmology in which matter and bodiliness are seen in purely negative terms. EvThom does not view the world as something wholly negative, but Jesus' words display a profoundly unhappy relationship to the world: 'Whoever has come to understand the world has found (only) a corpse, and whoever has found a corpse is superior to the world' (56; cf. 80). If we read logion 37 against the background of the metaphor of the human body as a kind of 'clothing', well known in early Christianity (cf. 2 Cor 5:1–4), the message of these words is that bodiliness must ultimately be overcome. Only so can the 'absence of shame' from Gen 2:25 be re-established:

His disciples said: 'When will you become revealed to us and when shall we see you?' (2) Jesus said, 'When you disrobe without being ashamed and take up your garments and place them under your feet like little children and tread on them, (3) then [will you see] the Son of the Living One, and you will not be afraid'

(cf. also EvThom 29). This does not mean 'that all the logia in the Gospel of Thomas are gnostic', but we may at any rate conclude 'that some logia present aspects of gnostic theology and mythology' (Valantasis, p. 103) and that it is easier to understand them against this background.

– Synoptic and Johannine materials

The brief logion 31 shows clearly why the relationship between EvThom and the synoptic Gospels is a matter of controversy:

Jesus said, 'No prophet is accepted in his own village; no physician heals those who know him.'

Jesus speaks at Mk 6:4, when he visits Nazareth, of the prophet who counts for nothing in his own home town; the narrative goes on to say that he was able nevertheless to perform a few healings there (6:5). Luke develops Jesus' visit to his home town into the great scene with his first sermon in the synagogue in Nazareth (Lk 4:16–30). This includes the logion about the prophet (4:24), but this is preceded by the anticipated objection of the people of Nazareth: 'Doubtless you will quote to me this proverb, "Physician, heal yourself!"' (4:23). One explanatory model proposes that the oldest form of this tradition is preserved in EvThom 31; while Mark has transformed the proverb about the 'physician' into an action, Luke quotes the logion in an altered form and puts the 'physician' before the 'prophet'. Our assumption is that Luke himself has created the substance of his Nazareth pericope on the basis of Mk 6:1–6, and that he introduced the well known proverb about the 'physician' here without assimilating its substance to that of the logion about the 'prophet'. This line of reasoning brings us to an alternative explanation, which I find more plausible, viz. that EvThom is a further stage on the trajectory from Mark to Luke: it isolates the two logia from the narrative context which Luke had created for them, assimilates them to one another, and reverses their order.

At Mk 12:1–9, Jesus relates the parable of the wicked husbandmen who kill the son of the owner of the vineyard. This is followed at Mk 12:10f. by an interpretative quotation from Ps 118:22f. which may have been added by Mark himself, although it is possible that the link between the parable and the quotation had already been made in the pre-Markan tradition: 'Have you not read this Scripture: "The very stone which the builders rejected has become the head of the corner; this was the Lord's doing, and it is marvellous in our eyes"?' Jesus is rejected both in the parable and in its narrative framework, where his opponents react with fury; but he is rehabilitated in the interpretative quotation. The parable of the wicked husbandmen is found in a somewhat shorter form in EvThom 65. Logion 66 follows without any linkage:

Jesus said, 'Show me the stone which the builders have rejected. That one is the cornerstone.'

When we bear in mind that no other passage in EvThom ever quotes literally from the Old Testament, it is not easy to see any reason for this quotation from the Psalm (which is not in fact signalled as a quotation). I find it incredible that it should have 'landed' here simply by chance, and that an inherent link between the parable and the quotation should have been established only at a secondary stage, in Mark's version. It seems to me much simpler to suppose that EvThom was familiar with the artificial link between the parable and the psalm-verse, but wished to reject this connection. One reason for this would be the belief that a parable needs no interpretation: the summons, 'Let him who has ears hear!', which EvThom inserts at the end of the parable, is enough.

Logion 77 hints at an almost pantheistic omnipresence of Jesus (though we should note that verses 2 and 3 are linked in POxy 1 with logion 30, not with logion 77):

Jesus said, 'It is I who am the light which is above them all. It is I who am the All. From me did the All come forth, and unto me did the All extend.' (2) 'Split a piece of wood, and I am there. (3) Lift up the stone, and you will find me there.'

It is not only the metaphor of 'light' that seems to bring us into the world of John's Gospel here (cf. Jn 8:12, 'I am the light of the world'), but also Jesus' role in the creation of the universe – we recall the words of the Johannine prologue, 'All things were made through him, and without him was not anything made that was made' (Jn 1:3; cf. 1:9f.). It is surely necessary to revise the received view that there are no immediate points of contact between EvThom and the Gospel of John.

– Two unknown parables

In addition to the parables of Jesus to which the synoptic evangelists offer parallels, EvThom contains some hitherto unknown material in logia 97 and 98, which form a trilogy of parables with logion 96 (about the 'leaven'):

(97) Jesus said, 'The kingdom of the [Father] is like a certain woman who was carrying a jar full of meal. While she was walking [on] a road, still some distance from home, the handle of the jar broke and the meal emptied out behind her on the road. She did not realize it; she had noticed no accident. When she reached her house, she set the jar down and found it empty.'

(98) Jesus said, 'The kingdom of the Father is like a certain man who wanted to kill a powerful man. In his own house he drew his sword and stuck it into the wall in order to find out whether his hand could carry through. Then he slew the powerful man.'

We may perhaps wonder why the meal trickles out of the jar when it is only the handle that has been broken; but we should remember that even familiar parables of Jesus often go far beyond our normal experience of reality. The 'jar' is a symbol of the human person who suddenly finds himself 'empty', burnt out, with no interior life: the 'contents' of his existence have vanished. The parable of the 'attacker' insists on the importance of decisiveness and self-examination in view of a great task. The metaphor recalls the defeat of the strong man at Mk 3:27 (cf. EvThom 35) and the king who resolves to go to battle at Lk 14:31f., but it remains offensive enough – like other parables of Jesus (cf. Lk 16:1–8). In other words, these unknown parables may seem so strange and alien only because of the fact that they were unknown! While it is not so certain, as some scholars suggest, that they go back to Jesus himself, or at least are very old in terms of tradition-history, the possibility cannot be dismissed out of hand.

– Glimpses of the general situation

Although the text seldom sheds a direct light on the situation of those who handed on these traditions and those who read EvThom, we have posed this question several times, and we may make some further deductions. For example, the metaphor employed in logion 34 – 'If a blind man leads a blind man, they will both fall into a pit' (cf. Lk 6:39) – may be a criticism of the claim to leadership made by an ecclesiastical hierarchy. Logion 39 (with a substantial parallel in logion 102) may be making the same point, if the Pharisees and scribes who hide the keys of knowledge and refuse entrance to seekers are office-bearers in the church. The words about the unforgivable sin against the Holy Spirit in logion 44 may be directed against critics who doubt the claim to authority made by EvThom and its message.

As I said above, the Nag Hammadi writings came to light near ancient Coptic monasteries. It is not difficult to imagine monks finding particular relevance in a logion such as EvThom 36: 'Do not be concerned from morning until evening and from evening until morning about what you will wear' (POxy 655 has a longer version). It is certainly meaningful to read all the ascetical and world-denying logia in EvThom from this perspective.

– 'Making Mary male'

This last remark could also apply to the final logion, EvThom 114: women are out of place in monasteries of men. Here we find a funda- mental trait which runs through the work as a whole, but the music here is not without dissonance:

Simon Peter said to them [i.e. the other disciples], 'Let Mary leave us, for women are not worthy of Life.' Jesus said, 'I myself shall lead her in order to make her male, so that she too may become a living spirit resembling you males. For every woman who will make herself male will enter the kingdom of heaven.'

These words refer to Mary Magdalene, whom we shall meet again below in the Gospels of Philip and of Mary. When Peter wishes to banish her from the disciples' company, he makes himself the spokesman for the official church's reluctance to accept women's active share in responsi- bility for the communities. While we note the positive point that Jesus takes Mary's side and puts her on the same level as the male disciples, there is a price to be paid. As in the Gospel of the Egyptians (see ch. 4a above), the second creation – narrative in Gen 2 leads to the idea that the male principle is the fundamental and superior reality. The 'pneumato- logical' emancipation of women can be formulated only by speaking of the overcoming of the female principle, so that women are assimilated to men. Against this, we may point to the more egalitarian language of logion 22, but these various ideas are not completely reconciled within the text itself – nor indeed in the classical world as a whole.

But what might it have meant in concrete terms to propose that women should 'become male'? If EvThom is read in the context of the radical itinerant movement in earliest Christianity, the idea is probably that women who wished to take part in this restless, homeless lifestyle should put on men's clothing. This would protect them from molestation, and they would have become 'men', as far as their outward appearance was concerned, for the sake of the kingdom of heaven (cf. S. Petersen, *'Zerstört die Werke der Weiblichkeit!'*, pp. 169–78).

Bibliography

H. G. Bethge, 'Appendix I. Das Thomas-Evangelium', in: K. Aland (ed.), *Synopsis Quattuor Evangeliorum*, Stuttgart 15th edn. 1996 (2nd corrected reprint 1997) 517–46; B. Blatz, in: NTApo I, 110–33; U. K. Plisch, *Verborgene Worte Jesu*, 93–133; D. Lührmann, *Fragmente*, 106–31 (for the Greek fragments POxy 1 and POxy 654–55); M. Fieger, *Das Thomasevangelium. Einleitung, Kommentar, Systematik* (NTA NF 21), Münster 1991; R. Valantasis, *The Gospel of Thomas* (New Testament Readings), London and New York 1997; J. Liebenberg, *The Language of the Kingdom and Jesus. Parable, Aphorism, and Metaphor in the Sayings Material Common to the Synoptic Tradition and the Gospel of Thomas* (BZNW 102), Berlin and New York 2001; Internet material: http://home.epix.net/~miser17/Thomas.html.

(3) Evaluation

The two major issues of academic controversy are: *first,* the relationship of EvThom to the canonical Gospels and *secondly,* the extent to which it can be called 'gnostic'. Our study of the logia in the previous section suggests a number of conclusions, which we shall summarize here.

First, a nuanced position on the relationship between EvThom and the canonical gospels is advisable, since individual logia point in different directions.

It is possible that some logia which resemble synoptic material, but have no parallels in the New Testament, preserve very early material which enriches our knowledge of an early stage of the tradition about Jesus.

Where EvThom has synoptic parallels, it is possible in some cases that the author had independent access to the same oral traditions which were available to the synoptic evangelists.

In some logia, however, EvThom clearly follows a wording which exegesis of the synoptic gospels normally considers the redactional creation of an evangelist (usually of Luke). In such cases, the version in EvThom must be considered secondary in terms of tradition-history.

Knowledge of the synoptic form of particular traditions does not mean that the author(s) of EvThom had access to a written text of the synoptic gospels. Here, it is very important to bear in mind the concept of secondary orality (see S. Byrskog's monograph *Story as History* in our general bibliography): even before they became 'canonical' in the true sense of this term, the use of the canonical gospels in the communities had made them *objects* of tradition. Their contents were handed on primarily by word of mouth, exposing them to new alterations, some of which harmonized divergent versions.

It is possible that material from the Gospel of John became accessible to EvThom in the same way. The typically Johannine traits of these materials exclude the possibility that we might appeal here to shared pre-Johannine traditions.

Secondly, we must admit that exaggerations have occurred, where interpreters more or less forced every logion into the constraints of a ready-made mythological pattern. There is no doubt that EvThom picks up early Jewish sapiential traditions; the affinity between logion 2, about 'seeking and finding', and Sirach 6:27f. (see ch. 3a, nr. 1) is an eloquent example. This, however, does not take us very far, since there is an increasing consensus in recent research into gnosis that the Jewish wisdom myth (linked to a Jewish apocalyptic which was understood no longer in temporal, but in spatial terms) played a role in the birth of gnosis. We may cautiously affirm that many of the central concepts employed in EvThom locate it on the path to a fully developed gnosis. I am unconvinced by the recent suggestion that the Jewish mysticism of 'ascensions' into the heavenly realms provides a better explanation, since we know even less about this particular form of mysticism than we do about gnosis – quite apart from the notorious imprecision of the concept of 'mysticism' in general.

These considerations warn against dating the composition of EvThom to the first century. The early second century is still early enough! More is expected of EvThom than the text can in fact provide, when it is claimed that its testimony to the tradition about Jesus is equal or even superior to that of the synoptics. If we free it from this intolerable burden, we ourselves are free to discover the wealth of insights which its logia offer us.

Bibliography

A. D. de Conick, *Seek to see Him. Ascent and Vision Mysticism in the Gospel of Thomas* (SVigChr 33), Leiden 1996; J. Schröter, *Erinnerung an Jesu Worte. Studien zur Rezeption der Logienüberlieferung in Markus, Q und Thomas* (WMANT 76), Neukirchen-Vluyn 1997; R. Uro (ed.), *Thomas at the Crossroads: Essays on the Gospel of Thomas* (Studies of the New Testament and Its World), Edinburgh 1998; T. Zöckler, *Jesu Lehren im Thomasevangelium* (NHS 47), Leiden 1999 (see the critical review by J. Frey, *ThLZ* 125 [2000] 1130–2).

(b) The Gospel of Philip (EvPhil)

(1) Contextual information

In the second Nag Hammadi codex, EvThom is followed immediately –
i.e. without any title – by a writing which the *subscriptio* calls 'Gospel
according to Philip' (NHC II,3: 51,29–86,19). The juxtaposition of
these two texts in NHC II is not purely accidental, since there are points
of contact between the substance of EvPhil and EvThom (cf. EvThom
19:1 and EvPhil 57; EvThom 22:4 and EvPhil 69a) and other traditions
about Thomas. In the *Pistis Sophia,* which we have mentioned in our
discussion of EvThom above, Philip is chosen before Thomas and
Matthew, and commissioned in much greater detail, to write down the
words of the Lord (1:42–44). Epiphanius quotes directly from a 'Gospel
of Philip' in his *Panarion* 26.13.2f.:

They [i.e. the gnostics] quote from another Gospel too, which was composed in the
name of the holy disciple Philip, the following words:
  'The Lord revealed to me [i.e. Philip] what the soul must say in its ascent to
heaven, and how it must answer each of the powers above:
  "I have recognized myself and gathered myself together from all sides and have
not sown children to the Archon but have uprooted his roots and have gathered the
scattered members and I know who you are; for I belong to those from above." '
  And so it is set free. But if it should prove that the soul has borne a son, it is kept
beneath until it is in a position to recover its children and bring them back to itself.

The theme of the ascent of the soul is in harmony with the world of
ideas of our Gospel of Philip, where we find an echo of the words which
the Lord tells the soul to utter, but the quotation as a whole is not
present in the Nag Hammadi text. We cannot say with certainty
whether Epiphanius knew another Gospel of Philip altogether, or
another version of the Nag Hammadi Gospel; it may simply be that he
is quoting imprecisely.
  The contents of EvPhil are clearly different from those of EvThom,
and it it is even further from our usual idea of a 'gospel'. Only a few
logia of Jesus are presented in direct speech (§§18, 54, 57, 69a, 72a),
and there are virtually no addresses to the disciples (cf. §18) or
dialogues in the form of questions and answers (only a hint in §§55b,
97). Instead, we have short sayings (most of which are puzzling) and
small theological treatises which take an increasingly independent form
towards the end of the work. This is why Hans-Martin Schenke, whose
enumeration we mostly follow here, has proposed that we should
abandon the designation 'sayings' or 'logia' for the individual units, and
speak instead of 'paragraphs'.
  Schenke calls the literary character of EvPhil a collection of excerpts
– an anthology or florilegium assembled by the author from one or
more works in the course of preparing a sermon or an instruction.
(Schenke has in mind otherwise unknown gnostic 'Acts of Philip'
containing missionary speeches.) In other words, what has survived is a

commonplace book. Martha Lee Turner has elaborated this suggestion with the hypothesis that EvPhil draws on three separate works, and her comparison with other 'file-card boxes' of authors in classical antiquity such as the *Attic Nights* of Aulus Gellius or the *Excerpta ex Theodoto* of Clement of Alexandria identifies the broader literary-historical context of EvPhil. Even if we accept Schenke's definition of the genre of EvPhil, however, we are not obliged to agree that its individual paragraphs may be interpreted only in isolation, i.e. without reference to the work as a whole. It is possible to discern link-words and thematic groups, and some ideas run with varying intensity throughout the entire work – the best example is the discussion of the sacraments, which almost gives EvPhil, taken as a whole, the appearance of a sacramental catechesis.

The title of the work is due not least to the fact that *Philip* is the only apostle to be mentioned directly (§91). It is likely that the apostle Philip, one of the twelve (Jn 14:8f., etc.; Acts 1:13) and the evangelist Philip, one of the seven (Acts 6:5; 8:5–13, etc.) are understood as one single person. EvPhil, which survives only in one Coptic manuscript, was originally composed in Greek. It is, however, possible that the work was written in Syria, since a number of passages display a striking interest in etymologies which make sense only in Syriac (cf. esp. §53, with an image recalling the 'spreading out' of Jesus' arms on the cross: 'The eucharist is Jesus. For he is called in Syriac *Pharisatha*, which is "the one who is spread out", for Jesus came crucifying the world.').

Some theological statements in EvPhil elaborate elements of the system of Valentinian gnosis, named after Valentinus (himself no 'Valentinian') who taught in Rome between *c.* 138 and 158. This means that EvPhil cannot be earlier than the last years of the second century; the date of composition may in fact lie in the third century.

Unfortunately, there are gaps of varying sizes in the upper and lower margins of the papyrus leaves of Nag Hammadi Codex II which contain EvPhil. This makes reconstructions of the text necessary. Our overview, which must confine itself to a few central points, does not usually draw specific attention to these reconstructions, which can be studied in the critical editions of the text.

(2) The contents

– Gentiles, Hebrews and Christians

The opening section shows clearly that there exists a thematic connection between the individual paragraphs, despite the loose construction of the text as a whole and the difficulties involved in understanding its contents. EvPhil begins as follows (§1):

A Hebrew makes another Hebrew, and such a person is called 'proselyte'. But a proselyte does not make another proselyte. Some both exist just as they are and make others like themselves, while others simply exist.

The text begins with a (preliminary) situation of conversion, viz. the conversion to Judaism which makes a Gentile a proselyte. This is the fruit of the missionary endeavour of a Hebrew who – according to the first half of the closing sentence – was born a Hebrew and is therefore able to win (the text says: 'make') others to Judaism. It seems strange that the proselyte should be denied any missionary success (perhaps only for a time?). He must be content to take this step himself (the text says: 'simply exist'). If we bear in mind the rabbinic analogy between a proselyte and a newborn child, we may find an illuminating analogy in §29:

The father makes a son, and the son [i.e. as a child] has not the power to make a son. For he who has been begotten has not the power to beget, but the son gets brothers for himself, not sons.

§2 takes over from §1 the idea of bringing forth or begetting, and relates a parable about a slave, a son and a father, which concerns an inheritance and is reminiscent of Gal 4:1–7 (cf. also § 37). §3 takes up the idea of 'inheritance' and speaks of burying the dead and the living – and this brings us to §4:

A Gentile does not die, for he has never lived in order that he may die. He who has believed in the truth has found life, and this one is in danger of dying, for he is alive ever since Christ came.

It is obvious that 'living' and 'dying' are metaphorical here: a life without faith is no genuine life; and since it does not merit the name of life, it does not know any death. Life in faith was made possible by Christ, who called the dead to life (cf. Lk 7:22; Jn 11:25f.). But this life is exposed to the danger of death – not physical dying, but the spiritual death entailed by falling away from the faith. We see here that the path must lead from being a Gentile, *via* being a proselyte and Hebrew, to being a Christian; and this is explicitly stated in §6 (the references back to the time as 'Hebrews' must surely indicate that the community in which these texts were transmitted had been Jewish and Jewish Christian in one phase of its history):

When we were Hebrews we were orphans and had only our mother, but when we became Christians we had both father and mother.

According to EvPhil, only the Gentiles were bereft of both parents; the Hebrews were half-orphans who at any rate had a mother. This may well refer (following Gal 4:21–31) to the earthly Jerusalem. Christians on the other hand have God as their Father; their mother is either the church or the Holy Spirit (see the discussion of §17, below).

These words lead us naturally to two later interconnected paragraphs. The first of these employs a beautiful parable to describe the imperishable dignity of the children of God (§48):

When the pearl is cast down into the mud it does not become greatly despised, nor if it is anointed with balsam oil will it become more precious. But it always has value in the eyes of its owner. Compare the sons of God, wherever they may be. They still have value in the eyes of their Father.

§49 describes the impact made on the external world, taking up the categories already employed – 'Jews' (= 'Hebrews') and 'Romans' (= 'Gentiles') – and adding a list which recalls Gal 3:28 and Col 3:11:

If you say, 'I am a Jew', no one will be moved. If you say, 'I am a Roman', no one will be disturbed. If you say, 'I am a Greek, a barbarian, a slave, a free man', no one will be troubled. If you say, 'I am a Christian', the world will tremble. Would that I may receive a name like that! This is the person whom the powers will not be able to endure when they hear his name.

We should note the use of the first person singular at the close of this paragraph, where the author (or collector or copyist) of EvPhil addresses the reader and formulates a wish of his own.

– Parables from daily life

'On the surface, EvPhil sometimes seems to be a manual of instructions for interpersonal relationships, interspersed with tips about agriculture and cattle breeding' (Schenke, p. 139). This impression is generated by the metaphors and parables in EvPhil, many of which are drawn from the sphere of farming. The first of these is in §7: 'Those who sow in winter reap in summer.' The agricultural paradigm (cf., e.g. §§40a, 115) is very skilfully interwoven with allusions to the paradise narrative in Gen 2 (cf., e.g. §15; also 84 and 94).

We have already quoted one example of a good parable accompanied by its interpretation, viz. the parable of the pearl in §48. Another fine example is the parable of the ass working at the mill (§52):

An ass which turns a millstone did a hundred miles walking. When it was loosed it found that it was still at the same place. There are men who make many journeys, but make no progress towards a destination. When evening came upon them, they saw neither city nor village, neither creation nor nature, power nor angel. In vain have the wretches laboured.

Another skilful parable based on ancient technology – which has not in fact changed much in the intervening centuries – is found in §51, this time without an interpretation:

Glass decanters and earthenware jugs are both made by means of fire. But if glass decanters break they are done over, for they came into being through a breath. If earthenware jugs break, however, they are destroyed, for they came into being without breath.

Earthenware vessels are fired and hardened in the oven, and this process cannot be reversed; but since glass is melted in the oven, even broken glass can be made into something useful – the glass-blower can use his breath to fashion new vessels out of the liquid mass. It is this breath that gives the glass its special quality, its vitality and durability. Here we should note that the Greek word *pneuma* means 'wind', 'breath' and 'Spirit'. The 'breath' in the metaphor symbolizes the breath of life which changes the body of clay into a living human being (Gen 2:7) and confers on him the potential to be raised to new life (cf. §80: 'The soul of Adam came into being by means of a breath.').

§67a offers a theoretical reflection and justification for EvPhil's obvious delight in metaphorical language:

Truth did not come into the world naked, but it came in types and images. One will not receive truth in any other way.

The reason why EvPhil is so difficult to understand lies not in the metaphors themselves, but rather in the way in which these are employed. This in turn is connected with a general problem which this text has with language, here represented by the 'names'.

– The problem of the names

Sadly, names are not so unambiguous as we tend to think. §§11–13 present very speculative reflections on this problem, beginning with the following premiss (11a):

Names given to worldly things are very deceptive, for they divert our thoughts from what is correct to what is incorrect. Thus one who hears the word 'God' does not perceive what is correct, but perceives what is incorrect. So also with 'the Father' and 'the Son' and 'the Holy Spirit' and 'life' and 'light' and 'resurrection' and 'the church' and all the rest – people do not perceive what is correct, but they perceive what is incorrect ...

Even these theological concepts can be misused by the evil powers in order to lead human beings astray (§13). On the other hand, if one refrains from using them, it is impossible to say anything about God (§12). This is why §19 explains the names 'Jesus', 'Christ', 'Messiah' and 'Nazarene' (cf. also §47).

– On sacrifices

Let us go back to §14 with its polemic against the praxis of killing animals to offer them in sacrifice to idols shaped like animals. The positive counterpoint to this reads: 'As for man, they offered him up to God dead, and he lived.' Conversion, the path from death to life, is interpreted here as a sacrifice: the human person is the sacrificial victim, and God is the one who receives the sacrifice. It is only against this background that we can understand another statement in EvPhil, which is no less shocking in its impact than the metaphor of the man-eating lion in EvThom 7 (§50):

God is a man-eater. For this reason men are sacrificed to him. Before men were sacrificed animals were being sacrificed, since those to whom they were sacrificed were not gods.

The 'man-eating' God does not, however, kill the human beings who are offered to him in sacrifice: on the contrary, he summons them to new life. §93a helps us to understand what is meant here:

This world is a corpse-eater. All the things eaten in it themselves die also. Truth is a life-eater. Therefore no one nourished by truth will die.

The world kills, but the (divine) truth keeps one alive. The sceptical view of the world which can be glimpsed here comes fully into the open in §99a:

The world came about through a mistake. For he who created it wanted to create it imperishable and immortal. He fell short of attaining his desire. For the world never was imperishable, nor, for that matter, was he who made the world.

This understanding of the world as the creation of an incapable demiurge, with the corresponding understanding of the body (cf. §22: the soul 'is a precious thing and it came to be in a contemptible body'), can certainly be called 'gnostic'.

– Virginal conception?

On our way through EvPhil, we pause now at §17a:

Some said, "Mary conceived by the Holy Spirit." They are in error. They do not know what they are saying. When did a woman ever conceive by a woman?

EvPhil takes the opposite position to the church creed ('he was conceived by the Holy Spirit', cf. Lk 1:35) because the word for 'Spirit' is feminine in Hebrew. This means that the Spirit cannot be the power which begets Jesus – at most, the Spirit can be Jesus' heavenly mother, as Mary is his earthly mother. Those who maintain the church doctrine which this paragraph caricatures are called 'Hebrews' and 'apostolic men' in §17b, and the text offers an allegorical interpretation of Mary's virginity: she remained undefiled by the evil powers:

Mary is the virgin whom no power defiled. She is a great anathema to the Hebrews, who are the apostles and the apostolic men. This virgin, whom no power defiled, reveals herself in order that the powers may defile themselves.

This makes Mary the antithesis of Eve, who let herself be seduced by the serpent in paradise: it was not Adam, but the serpent who was the father of Cain (§42). This means that Jesus not only had two mothers – like Adam, who was born of the Spirit and the virginal earth (§83) – but also two fathers, as the introduction to the Lord's Prayer teaches us (§17c):

And the Lord would not have said: 'My Father who is in heaven', unless he had had another father, but he would have said simply 'My father'.

The heavenly father is God, the earthly father is Joseph (see the discussion of §91 below).

– Mary Magdalene

As at Jn 19:25, Mary, the earthly mother of Jesus, is accompanied by Mary the wife of Clopas (here identified with Mary's sister in Jn 19:25) and by Mary Magdalene (§32):

There were three (women) who always walked with the Lord: Mary his mother and her sister and Magdalene, the one who was called his companion [*koinōnos*]. His sister and his mother and companion [*koinōnos*] were each a Mary.

The fact that all three women bore the name 'Mary' suggests an allegorical interpretation: the three Maries who accompanied the earthly Jesus are merely variants of Sophia, the female partner whom the heavenly redeemer needs, if he is to be whole. In the background, we glimpse the idea of the 'syzygies' or mythical pairs which play an important role in Valentinian gnosis; the same idea underlies the continuation of this theme in §55:

As for the Wisdom [*sophia*] who is called 'the barren', she is the mother of the angels. And the companion [*koinōnos*] of the Saviour is Mary Magdalene. But Christ loved her more than all the disciples and used to kiss her often on her mouth. The rest of the disciples [were offended by it and expressed disapproval]. They said to him, 'Why do you love her more than all of us?' The Saviour answered and said to them, 'Why do I not love you like her?'

On the surface, however, this conflict concerns the role of the beloved disciple in the Gospel of John, whom church tradition tended to identify with the apostle John: this role is given here to Mary Magdalene.

– The apostle Philip

Let us remain with the male and female disciples, and look briefly at the only male apostle to be mentioned by name in EvPhil, at §91:

Philip the apostle said, 'Joseph the carpenter planted a garden because he needed wood for his trade. It was he who made the cross from the trees which he planted. His own offspring hung on that which he planted. His offspring was Jesus and the planting was the cross.'

The irony is terribly clear: without realizing what he was doing, Jesus' earthly father himself cultivated the wood and fashioned the cross on which his son hung. Nevertheless, as another 'tree' in §92 shows, all ended well:

But the tree of life is in the middle of the garden. However, it is from the olive tree that we get the chrism, and from the chrism the resurrection.

The word 'resurrection' suggests that we turn back to §21, which begins by speaking of this subject. But first let us consider whether other words in EvPhil may also be spoken by Philip, although he is not mentioned by name. The speaker in §26b may be Jesus, but Philip is certainly also a possibility:

He said on that day in the thanksgiving, 'You who have joined the perfect, the light, with the Holy Spirit, unite the angels with us also, the images.'

This would then be a free insertion by the apostle into the eucharistic prayer of thanksgiving, offering an interpretation of the sacramental action: the syzygy (see above) of the male redeemer and the female Spirit is a model of the union between the heavenly angels and their earthly 'images', i.e. the believers. This longed-for union can already be attained on earth through the eucharist, which is an anticipation of the heavenly wedding feast.

– Death and resurrection

The 'normal' sequence of death and resurrection is reversed by §21. This applies initially to Jesus' resurrection, but a generalizing tendency can be discerned:

Those who say that the Lord died first and (then) rose up are in error, for he rose up first and (then) died. If one does not first attain the resurrection will he not die? As God lives, he would be already dead.

This is later given a general application, towards the end of the work (§90a):

Those who say they will die first and then rise are in error. If they do not first receive the resurrection while they live, when they die they will receive nothing.

We see already in the New Testament that it was possible to conceive of this paradoxical reversal: the author of the Pastoral Letters writes in 2 Tim 2:17f. against Hymenaeus and Alexander, two theologians who hold 'that the resurrection is past already' – not the resurrection of Jesus, but that of the believers. EvPhil affirms that the resurrection must become a spiritual reality during one's lifetime, if we are to survive the physical death which awaits us. The experiential basis of this idea may be conversion, which leads from a state of spiritual death to new life, together with baptism, which sets God's seal upon the path to faith.

Is this idea compatible with the concept of a further resurrection which will take place after our death? This depends on the exegesis of §23, where the author bases his argumentation on 1 Cor 15:20 ('Flesh and blood shall not inherit the kingdom of God.') and begins – as we might expect – by attacking those who profess a resurrection of the flesh, since they are unwilling to put off the 'garment' of the flesh (§23a):

Some are afraid lest they rise naked. Because of this they wish to rise in the flesh, and they do not know that it is those who wear the flesh who are naked. It is those who are able to unclothe themselves who are not naked.

He continues with a surprising attack on the opposite position, although we might suppose that this would be nearer his own (§23c):

I find fault with the others who say that it [i.e. the flesh] will not rise. Then both of them are at fault.

His own solution is to postulate a spiritual or heavenly flesh, distinct from the earthly flesh. It is this heavenly flesh that Jesus bears, and that is present in the eucharist (cf. Jn 6:53b; EvPhil 23b; cf. also §72c). The decisive question then becomes whether the expression 'in the flesh' (§23a) presupposes physical death and resurrection as a precondition for attaining to the spiritual flesh, or whether we can share in the spiritual 'fleshliness' of Jesus even while still in our earthly flesh – e.g. through the eucharist.

– Baptism and anointing

Many of the texts in EvPhil which we have studied so far allude to the sacraments. The clearest passages in the work are those which concern baptism and the post-baptismal anointing which together constitute the initial sacrament marking admission to the community of believers. The metaphor of God as 'dyer' in §43 (cf. Is 1:18) refers to baptism:

God is a dyer. As the good dyes, which are called 'true', dissolve with the things dyed in them, so it is with those whom God has dyed. Since his dyes are immortal, they are immortal by means of his colours. Now God dips what he dips in water.

The metaphor affirms that high-quality colours are durable: they last as long as the cloth which they have coloured. Poorer quality colours, however, are soon washed out. The colour employed by God is of exceptional quality, although it consists, paradoxically, only of the pure water used in baptism. This line of thought leads to the symbolic action which Jesus performs in §54:

The Lord went into the dye works of Levi. He took seventy-two different colours and threw them into the vat. He took them out all white. And he said, 'Even so has the Son of Man come as a dyer.'

We may prescind here from the question whether the number seventy or seventy-two refers to the peoples of the world. The important point is that the Son of Man does exactly the opposite of what we would expect from a dyer – he reduces the bright variety of colours to the uniformity of white, which is not a colour at all. This may be an allusion to the white baptismal garment.

Linguistic reasoning gives the anointing an even higher rank than baptism, according to §95:

The chrism is superior to baptism, for it is from the word 'chrism' [khrisma] that we have been called 'Christians' [*khristianoi*], certainly not because of the word 'baptism'. And it is because of the chrism that 'the Christ' [*Khristos*] has his name. For the Father anointed the Son, and the Son anointed the apostles, and the apostles anointed us. He who has been anointed possesses everything. He possesses the resurrection, the light, the cross, the Holy Spirit.

The three loan-words in the Coptic text are derived from the Greek verb *khrio* ('to anoint'). Through the *khrisma*, Jesus became a *khristos*, i.e. the Lord's Anointed, and the *khrisma* makes us followers of Christ and configures us to him, both linguistically and sacramentally. This is expressed in strong terms – though perhaps no stronger than Paul's words at Gal 2:20, 'It is no longer I who live, but Christ who lives in me' – at the end of §67e, where we are told of the one who has received the anointing: 'this person is no longer a Christian [*khristianos*] but a Christ [*khristos*].'

– The bridal chamber

§68 plays a key role in helping us to understand the teaching about the sacraments in EvPhil:

The Lord did everything in a mystery [*mustērion*], a baptism [*baptisma*] and a chrism [*khrisma*] and a eucharist [*eukharistia*] and a redemption and a bridal chamber [*numphōn*].

It is possible that this text presents a list of the five sacraments which were celebrated ritually by the groups for which EvPhil was written (and only three of which are still known to us), but this is uncertain, since the word 'mystery' is not yet employed here as a technical designation for 'sacraments'. Rather, it is to be understood adverbially: the Lord did everything 'in a hidden manner'. EvPhil tells us remarkably little about the 'redemption' (the only one in the list for which no Greek loan-word is used), but the real problem is posed by the 'bridal chamber', which becomes a main topic in the last third of EvPhil (cf. §§73, 76, 79, 82, 87, 88, 96, 102, 122, 125, 126, 127). The polemic of patristic writers such as Epiphanius of Salamis interpreted the bridal chamber as an act of 'sacred' sexual intercourse, and used this as a weapon against the gnostics. This, however, is a distortion of gnostic thinking and praxis. Let us begin by attempting to clarify what is meant by the temple terminology in §76a:

There were three buildings specifically for sacrifice in Jerusalem. The one facing west was called 'the Holy'. Another facing south was called 'the Holy of the Holy'. The third facing east was called 'the Holy of the Holies', the place where only the high priest enters. Baptism is 'the Holy' building. Redemption is 'the Holy of the Holy'. 'The Holy of the Holies' is the bridal chamber.

The starting-point of this comparison is the existence of precincts in the temple at Jerusalem with differing degrees of holiness: the forecourt of the Israelites, the temple building itself, and the holy of holies inside the temple. 'Initiation', the path from the outside to the inside, begins with baptism. We would have expected to find the anointing mentioned second; here its place is taken by the 'redemption', but this may perhaps be meant as an interpretation of what takes place in the anointing.

The eucharist should have followed as the third sacrament; there is no lack of texts which attest its celebration (cf. §§26b, 53, 98, 100, 108). Are the eucharist and the bridal chamber only two names for the same reality? This is probably suggested by the triad in §76a, when it identifies the holy of holies in the temple with the bridal chamber; cf. also §125a, 'The bridal chamber, however, remains hidden. It is the holy in the holy ...' The use of this image as an interpretation of the eucharistic rite may have been prompted by the idea of the eucharist as an anticipation of the heavenly wedding feast.

How then are we to understand the bridal chamber? Here, it suffices to read §82a:

Is it permitted to utter a mystery [*mustērion*]? The Father of everything united with the virgin who came down, and a fire shone for him on that day. He appeared in the great bridal chamber. Therefore, his body came into being on that very day. It left the bridal chamber.

The bridal chamber is meaningful within the framework of gnostic thinking, where it is connected with the mythical construction of pairs in the heavenly world which lies beyond this earth. §82 tells us how the Father of the universe personally brings about the salvation of Sophia, who has fallen down and sunk into matter. Some scholars interpret the 'body' which comes into being as a result of this union in the bridal chamber as the pre-existent church which is the body of Christ, but it is also possible that the text expresses the particular understanding of the virginal conception which we have already seen in EvPhil 17.

The sacramental dimension of the bridal chamber offers a rite which allows the believers on earth to imitate and share in the mythical event, so that they too may experience even now the longed-for union with their heavenly counterpart. And precisely this is what §26b (see above) affirms about the eucharist.

(3) Conclusions

Much has been said about EvPhil, but just as much had to remain unsaid. One important question concerns the christology of this work. What, for example, are we to make of §26a, which begins as follows: 'Jesus took them all [i.e. all forms] by stealth'? This text seems to speak of the redeemer as polymorphic, one who took on a variety of outward forms. A docetic christology of separation may be indicated by the manner in which Jesus' last words on the cross are presented in §72a:

'My God, my God, why, O Lord, have you forsaken me?' It was on the cross that he said these words, for it was there that he was divided.

Does the word 'divided' mean that he was separated from God, from the body, from the Spirit, from Jesus?

We also find a vision of hell, attributed to an *apostolikos,* i.e. a disciple of the apostles (§65).

A further significant contribution to the doctrine of the sacraments is the affirmation that a hidden spiritual power is at work in the elements of water and the anointing oil. In the water, this power is simply called 'water', while in the oil it is called 'fire' (§§25, 66).

At this point, however, we must call a halt. If we reflect on the texts discussed in the second section above, it becomes easier to grasp why many of the questions which have caused vigorous controversy in the case of EvThom do not occur at all in the case of EvPhil. Its use of the New Testament writings, including the Gospel of John and the letters of Paul, is so obvious that it is impossible to maintain the hypothesis of an independent tradition, and no one attempts to date it even as early as the beginning of the second century. EvPhil is not an independent witness to the tradition about Jesus.

The intellectual world of EvPhil seems very foreign to us, more so than that of EvThom. But even if it is in fact a collection of excerpts from larger works, one cannot deny that EvPhil does possess a coherence and logic of its own. The parables quoted above – e.g. the metaphor of the vessels of glass and clay, or the image of God as dyer – are original, and have a considerable poetic power. It would be well worth investigating the theory of metaphor and language which lies behind EvPhil.

The same is true of its sacramental theology, which is clearly one of the main concerns of EvPhil. This work attempts to steer a precarious middle course between the gnostic rejection of all material things (on the one hand) and ritual praxis, which cannot do without water, oil, wine and bread (on the other hand). The author's solution is to distinguish between the external appearance and the inherent spiritual power, on the analogy of the differentiation he makes between earthly and spiritual flesh in his discussion of the resurrection. There is much here that can invite us to a systematic theological reflection and to the practical question of how far it is possible to develop these ideas and bring them up to date.

Bibliography

W. W. Isenberg, in: NHL, 139–60; H. M. Schenke, in: NTApo I, 179–208; Idem, in: *Nag Hammadi Deutsch* I, 183–213; U. K. Plisch, *Verborgene Worte Jesu,* 153–64; H. M. Schenke, *Das Philippus-Evangelium (Nag Hammadi Codex II,3)* (TU 143), Berlin 1997 (text, translation and detailed commentary; we follow Schenke's enumeration); H. J. Klauck, 'Die dreifache Maria. Zur Rezeption von Joh 19,25 in EvPhil 32,' in: Idem, *Alte Welt und neuer Glaube* (NTOA 29), Freiburg/Switzerland and Göttingen 1994, 145–62; M. L.

Turner, *The Gospel According to Philip: The Sources and Coherence of an Early Christian Collection* (NHMS 38), Leiden 1996.

(c) The Gospel of Truth (EvVer)

(1) Contextual information

The third writing in the first Nag Hammadi codex (NHC I,3) has no title at its head or as a *subscriptio,* but since it begins with the words, 'The Gospel [*euaggelion*] of truth ...', scholars have given it this title, mostly in the Latinized form *Evangelium Veritatis* (following Irenaeus: see below). Although some books were cited by their initial words in classical antiquity (like papal encyclicals even to the present day), it is not certain whether this *incipit* is also meant as a title. The primary message of the phrase 'Gospel of truth' is that this writing deals with the truth and sets out the truth of the one gospel. The genre of EvVer does not in the least resemble that of the canonical gospels; more adequate terms would be homily, meditation, or a phrase such as 'discourse in praise of the truth'.

The first codex from Nag Hammadi, which contains EvVer, is also known as 'Codex Jung', since it was smuggled out of Egypt by a Belgian antiques dealer and was purchased by the Jung Institute in Zurich in 1952 as a present for the great psychologist, who had been interested in gnosis all his life. The individual writings in NHC I were subsequently edited and published in sumptuous large-format volumes; the first of all the Nag Hammadi texts to be printed was EvVer, published in 1956. A small blemish, the omission of two leaves (33–36), was subsequently corrected.

The discussion of the title and author of EvVer must begin with Irenaeus of Lyons, who is familiar with a 'Gospel of Truth' which he considers heretical (*Adversus haereses* 3.11.9):

> But those who are from Valentinus, being altogether reckless, while they put forth their own compositions, boast that they possess more Gospels than there really are. Indeed, they have arrived at such a pitch of audacity as to entitle their comparatively recent writing 'the Gospel of Truth', though it agrees in nothing with the Gospels of the apostles, so that they have really no Gospel which is not full of blasphemy.

Irenaeus attributes the compilation of this Gospel to the *disciples* of Valentinus, not to Valentinus himself, and he interprets its title as implying a particular claim, which he goes on to discuss: viz. that the 'Gospel of Truth' is the only 'true Gospel', the only one to contain the genuine revelation without distortions.

One cannot deny that there are substantial similarities between our EvVer and Valentinian doctrine, and its divergence from the form of the canonical gospels would agree with Irenaeus' observation that the gnostic gospel 'agrees in nothing with the gospels of the apostles'. This makes the identification of the 'Gospel of Truth' in NHC I with the writing mentioned by Irenaeus at any rate understandable; some scholars, however, have taken one step further and identified Valentinus himself as the author of EvVer.

Since we possess only fragments of the writings of this great theological teacher, the discovery of a complete work from his hand would be a very important event. However, this hypothesis dissolves on closer investigation. Quite apart from the question whether EvVer is the same text as the one mentioned in the *Adversus haereses,* we should note that Irenaeus does not claim that Valentinus was its author: he speaks in more general terms of the school of Valentinus, which went beyond its master on a number of points. Secondly, a comparison of EvVer with the surviving fragments of Valentinus discloses not only agreements, but also significant differences. This suggests that EvVer should not be considered an early work of Valentinus, but rather a later reinterpretation of the Valentinian system by an unknown teacher (cf. Markschies).

This has consequences for the dating of EvVer, which cannot be earlier than the second half of the second century. The same applies by analogy to a second version of EvVer which was later discovered in NHC XII,2 (only a few pages in poor condition have survived: 53,19–60,30).

The remarkable cyclical mode of thought and the poetic vigour of its language have rightly prompted many to call EvVer the most impressive of the Nag Hammadi writings. On the other hand, these same features make it almost impossible to discern what may be the underlying structure of the work. (The titles in the next section take up the proposals by Attridge and Layton about the division into various sections.)

(2) The contents

– The prologue

In some texts, the first sentences contain the total substance of the work *in nuce.* This is certainly true of the prologue to EvVer, where we find the great central concepts which will subsequently be elaborated (16,31–17,4):

The gospel of truth is a joy for those who have received from the Father of truth the gift of knowing him, through the power of the Word that came forth from the pleroma – the one who is in the thought and the mind of the Father, that is, the one who is addressed as the Saviour, (that) being the name of the work he is to perform for the redemption of those who were ignorant of the Father, while the name 'gospel' is the proclamation of hope, being discovery for those who search for him.

The note of exultation and joy at the gift of knowing the Father will resound throughout the entire work. This knowledge was communicated through the Word, who appears as a person and accomplishes his work. Redemption means the transformation of ignorance into knowledge: this is what the gospel is about. The last words of the prologue speak of 'finding' and 'seeking', and we naturally ask when we will hear of the 'rest'. We must wait a little (see below, in the discussion of 22,12), but once it is mentioned, the theme of 'rest' becomes a leitmotiv, so that we can find a path through EvVer by following the passages which speak of 'rest' (cf. Heldermann).

– The origin of error

Ignorance gives birth to fear and terror; fear takes solid form as a 'fog' which helps error to gain power. Error now finds matter, which it can shape into the creation, equipping it with a power and beauty which are indeed seductive, yet are nothing more than a wretched substitute for the truth. The Greek loan-word which is used for the personified Error in the Coptic text is *plane* (a feminine term). It takes the place here of the lower Sophia, the fallen Wisdom, in the creation myth of the Valentinians.

– The coming of the Redeemer

Since Jesus brings ignorant human beings the good news, illuminating them and showing them the path, Error takes action to oppose him (18,21–31):

For this reason, Error [*plane*] grew angry at him, persecuted him ... He was nailed to a tree; he became a fruit of the knowledge of the Father, which did not, however, become destructive because it <was> eaten, but to those who ate it gave (cause) to become glad in the discovery. For he discovered them in himself, and they discovered him in themselves.

EvVer does not call into question the real death of Jesus on the cross, but interprets this by superimposing the story of the fall in paradise. There, human beings incurred death when they ate the fruit of the tree of knowledge; now, the process of seeking is brought to its happy conclusion when we eat the fruit of the wood of the cross, i.e. through knowledge. Johannine concepts ('you in me and I in you') are then echoed in the affirmation that this finding is a reciprocal recognition: the redeemed recognize themselves in the Redeemer, and he recognizes himself in them.

The next paragraph too ends with a beautiful reciprocal formulation. This passage, which tells us of Jesus' activity as a teacher, is probably a reminiscence of Lk 2:46–49, and possibly also of narratives such as the Infancy Gospel of Thomas which we discussed in ch. 5b above (19,17–34):

He became a guide, restful and leisurely. He went into the midst of the schools (and) he spoke the word as a teacher. There came the wise men – in their own estimation – putting him to the test. But he confounded them because they were foolish ... After all these, there came the little children also, those to whom the knowledge of the Father belongs ... They knew, they were known; they were glorified, they glorified.

The 'little children' are the gnostics; this designation is born of the experiential fact that little children in families know their father well. Comparisons, metaphors and parables – sometimes hinted at, rather than set out in detail, and always operating in several dimensions – are frequently employed in EvVer to illustrate its doctrine, as in the following text, where the basic metaphor is that of the 'book'.

– The book of revelation

'The living book of the living' is revealed in the hearts of the little ones. This has indeed been ready since the foundation of the world, but the only one who can receive it is 'the one who will be slain' (cf. Rev 5:1–12). Once again, EvVer emphasizes the soteriological importance of the death of Jesus, illustrating this by means of two further metaphors from the world of books, the will and the edict (20,10–28):

For this reason the merciful one, the faithful one, Jesus, was patient in accepting sufferings until he took that book, since he knows that his death is life for many. Just as there lies hidden in a will, before it <is> opened, the fortune of the deceased master of the house, so (it is) with the all, which lay hidden while the Father of the all was invisible ... For this reason Jesus appeared; he put on that book; he was nailed to a tree; he published the edict of the Father on the cross [cf. Col 2:14]. O such great teaching!

The preacher himself is lost in wonder at the message he must proclaim, and this gives a glimpse of the communication-situation in EvVer: such exclamations envisage hearers and readers. In other passages too, the author speaks directly in the first person (27,34f.: 'I do not say, then, that they are nothing.') or weaves addresses in the second person plural into his discourse (on the paraenetic section at 31,31–33,2, see below).

The metaphor of the book, which recurs at 22,28–23,18, frames a programmatic passage which also contains the eagerly-awaited first mention of 'rest' (22,2–15):

Therefore if one has knowledge, he is from above. If he is called, he hears, he answers, and he turns to him who is calling him, and *ascends* to him. And he knows in what manner he is called. Having knowledge, he does the will of the one who called him, he wishes to be pleasing to him, he *receives rest* ... He who is to have knowledge in this manner knows where he comes from and where he is going.

Fundamental questions of gnosis are broached here: whence do we come, whither are we going? The Redeemer's summons, which wakes human beings from their slumber, is the embodiment of the act of salvation: ascent and rest denote its goal.

– A parable of redemption

Unfortunately – as we are almost forced to say – we find such programmatic statements in EvVer at every turn. What, for example, of the 'great wonder' that even those in error were in the Father and came forth from him, although they themselves did not know this (22,27–33)? What of the strange Trinity of Father, Mother and 'Jesus of the infiniteness of gentleness' (24,7–9), where the 'Mother' is the Holy Spirit? And what of this fundamental affirmation, to which we find parallels in the church fathers' reports on gnosis: 'Since the deficiency came into being because the Father was not known, therefore when the Father is known, from that moment on the deficiency will no longer exist' (24,28–32)? We cannot discuss all these texts here; instead, we move on a little further to the parable of the earthenware vessels, which describes some aspects of the process of redemption (25,25–26,15):

(It is) as in the case of some people who moved out of dwellings where there were jars that in spots were not good. They would break them, and the master of the house does not suffer loss. Rather <he> is glad because in place of the bad jars there are full ones which are made perfect. For such is the judgment which has come from above ... It is a drawn sword, with two edges, cutting on either side [cf. Heb 4:12]. When the Word came into the midst, the one that is within the heart of those who utter it – it is not a sound alone but it became a body – a great disturbance took place among the jars because some had been emptied, others filled; that is, some had been supplied, others poured out, some had been purified, still others broken up.

The metaphor speaks of tenants who break some earthenware vessels in the course of vacating a dwelling – but this does not worry the owner of the house, since the vessels that were broken were in any case damaged. He can replace them with new jars. This is what happens when the Redeemer comes. His coming means judgement, separating that which is worthless (and is removed) from that which is valuable. The 'victims' include Error, which is confused and no longer knows what it is supposed to do.

The Redeemer appears as a word and a cry – not only as a linguistic event, but with a body (*sōma*). How realistically is the incarnation meant here? Our answer will depend also on the interpretation of a latter passage, where we are told that the Redeemer 'came by means of fleshly appearance' (31,5f.). Since we find the same concept of 'flesh' (*sarx*) at Jn 1:14, it is difficult to agree with those scholars who attempt to give a completely docetic exegesis of this affirmation in EvVer.

– Unredeemed existence: a nightmare

In a sequence of nightmare power, EvVer describes the unredeemed existence (29,8–28):

as if they were sunk in sleep and found themselves in disturbing dreams. Either (there is) a place to which they are fleeing, or without strength they come (from) having chased after others, or they are involved in striking blows, or they are receiving blows themselves, or they have fallen from high places, or they take off into the air though they do not even have wings. Again, sometimes (it is as) if people were murdering them, though there is no one even pursuing them, or they themselves are killing their neighbours, for they have been stained with their blood. When those who are going through all these things wake up, they see nothing (since there is nothing to see).

The state of ignorance is like a nightmare; the one who comes to knowledge wakes up and comes into the light. Two beatitudes which stand (structurally speaking) at the centre of EvVer take up this image of nocturnal terrors and exclaim: 'Good for the man who will come to and awaken. And blessed is he [i.e. Jesus] who has opened the eyes of the blind' (30,13–16).

– The good shepherd

EvVer consists of an unbroken stream of associations, but it offers another 'resting place' in the parable of Jesus as good shepherd (cf. Jn 10:11), which combines Mt 18:12f. with Mt 12:11f. (31,35–32,22):

He is the shepherd who left behind the ninety-nine sheep which were not lost. He went searching for the one which was lost. He rejoiced when he found it, for 99 is a number that is in the left hand which holds it. But when the one is found, the entire number passes to the right (hand) ... Even on the sabbath, he laboured for the sheep which he found fallen into the pit. He gave life to the sheep, having brought it up from the pit ...

The right hand is always luckier than the left, and 100 is a more perfect number than 99, since it lacks nothing. Besides this, the Romans had a way of counting which allowed them to express numbers with the help of their fingers: when they reached 100, the counting was transferred from the left hand to the right. Our text presupposes this cultural knowledge.

– Works of mercy

A long paraenetic section in the second person plural seems at first sight to recommend traditional works of mercy such as healing the sick and giving food to the hungry; but it soon becomes clear that these works are to be understood metaphorically, as 'first aid' in situations of spiritual need (33,1–9):

Make firm the foot of those who have stumbled and stretch out your hands to those who are ill. Feed those who are hungry and *give repose* to those who are weary, and raise up those who wish to rise, and awaken those who sleep. For you are the understanding ...

The aid that is to be given is intellectual and spiritual, and the author goes on to urge his readers to take care of themselves too.

– The anointing

One of the remarkable features of EvVer is that some themes seem for a time to have disappeared completely, only to re-emerge suddenly later on. For example, we are reminded *en passant* that we are listening to a proclamation of salvation in terms of seeking and finding: 'This <is> the word of the gospel of the discovery of the pleroma for those who await the salvation which is coming from on high' (34,35–35,2). The parable of the earthenware jars is reactivated in order to provide an allusion to the anointing which Christ bestows. The translation consciously avoids adding any interpretative elements, apart from inverted commas (36,19–34):

But those whom he has anointed are the ones who have become perfect. For full jars are the ones that are usually 'anointed'. But when the 'anointing' of one jar is dissolved, it is emptied, and the reason for there being a deficiency is the thing through which its 'ointment' goes. For at that time a breath 'draws' it, one by the power of the one with it. But from him who has no deficiency no seal is removed, nor is anything emptied. But what he lacks the perfect Father fills again.

Since this seems virtually incomprehensible, the reader may be left with the impression that a parable which itself needs exegesis does not really help us to understand what is meant by the 'anointing'. The key is supplied by the word 'seal': the 'anointing' is the sealing of amphoras with hot wax, and an intact seal means that the vessel is full. If the seal breaks, the liquid contents seep out, or else evaporate in the warm air. The application proceeds *e contrario*. One who has received the anointing becomes perfect and suffers no deficiency; he need not fear that he may lose this seal and hence 'seep out' or 'evaporate'.

In EvPhil, the anointing is one of the three fundamental sacraments to which the gnostics attached particular importance. In EvVer, we have only this one allusion to the anointing, and one can read the entire passage as a metaphor: 'anointing' would then refer to the condition of those who are chosen and possess knowledge. It is not, however, completely impossible that the 'anointing' in EvVer, as in EvPhil, should be understood against the background of the concrete praxis in Christian communities.

– The names

In the penultimate section, EvVer elaborates in lofty flights of thought a doctrine about the 'names' which has its origin in Jewish reflections on the ineffable, hidden name of God, and contains elements of a formal theory of language. It can be reduced to a brief formula in the thesis: 'Now the name of the Father is the Son' (38,6f.), which is immediately followed by this explanation (38,7–17):

It is he [i.e. the Father] who first gave a name to the one who came forth from him, who was himself, and he begot him as a son. He gave him his name which belonged to him; he is the one to whom belongs all that exists around him, the Father. His is the name; his is the Son. It is possible for him [i.e., the Son] to be seen. But the name is invisible ...

We may be tempted to speak here of a 'trinitarian theology'; but it is important to note that the author's reflections are presented, not by means of logical argumentation, but by pursuing trains of associations. According to the explanation which he provides, the brief formula 'Now the name of the Father is the Son' can also be reversed: 'He [the Father] gave him [the Son] his [own] name.' Three distinct levels of meaning overlap here. (1) It is possible that 'Father' was employed in the milieu which produced EvVer as a rare and particularly exclusive title of Jesus Christ. (2) The Son does for the Father what a name does for its referent: he names him, designates him, and makes him linguistically present. This is no small claim, when we recall that for Judaism, even the name of God was unutterable. (3) A name can only be heard – not seen. However, we can see the Son in human form, and this means that he makes the Father not only audible, but also visible. Undoubtedly, 'the name is a great thing' (38,24).

– Rest

It is no surprise to see that EvVer ends by speaking of the place of 'fullness' (*plērōma*) and of 'rest', that place from which the Redeemer comes and to which he returns. This place is not a wholly eschatological reality; it is mediated by fellowship with the Father and the Son and enters our present existence (which otherwise must be considered a time of waiting for things to be brought to perfection). This is indicated by the ideal portrait of his addressees which the author sketches at 42,11–38:

This is the manner of those who possess (something) from above of the immeasurable greatness, as they stretch out after the one alone and the perfect one, the one who is there for them. And they do not go down to Hades ... but they rest in him who is at rest ... and the Father is within them and they are in the Father ... being in no way deficient in anything, but they are set at rest, refreshed in the Spirit ... This is the place of the blessed; this is their place.

At this point, the author finally speaks in the first person and explains why his discourse sometimes seems so obsessive: everyone must realise 'that it is not fitting for me, having come to be in the resting-place, to speak of anything else' (42,41–43,2). He is addressing the group of 'the true brothers, those upon whom the love of the Father is poured out' (43,5–6), just as it has been poured out upon him. He speaks out of his own experience and his profound insight.

(3) Summary

Even if Valentinus was not the author of this text, EvVer is still the work of a highly gifted and educated theologian who knows what he is doing and calculates very precisely the effects he wishes to produce. There is something hypnotic about the circular, oscillating (or even undulating) style of the Gospel of Truth; at the same time, however, there is a logical development which never loses sight of its goal, leading us by stages from 'finding' to 'rest'. The parables are based to some extent on precise observations from daily life, and are used in an original manner; the description of a nightmare, with dreams of flying and falling, could find a place in a textbook of psychology. It is a pity that we know nothing about the author of EvVer, and have no other works of his to compare with this single text, for such comparisons would make it easier to understand.

It must indeed be said that EvVer is not easy reading. The general difficulties in understanding it make it hard to grasp exactly the doctrine it teaches. We must look very closely, and possess a certain amount of background information, if we are to detect the gnostic traces in it. These are undeniably present, especially in the case of the personified Error (*planê*), and the importance attached to such themes as the question of knowledge points in a gnostic direction. Nevertheless, most of EvVer sounds completely orthodox to unschooled ears, and it is possible to interpret some key passages in a way that would be acceptable to doctrinal orthodoxy. Two passages can be understood to speak of the incarnation; the author does not eliminate Jesus' death on the cross, but interprets the death of Jesus in soteriological terms as part of his work of redemption for the sake of many. It seems doubtful whether our categories of 'orthodox' and 'heretical' do justice to such a complex work – and that in itself is a point worth pondering.

One question which we have repeatedly posed in the course of this book plays only a marginal role in EvVer, viz. its relationship to the New Testament writings. One reason for this is that it contains neither narratives about Jesus nor brief and pointed logia which would require us to discuss their tradition-historical status. Some images (shepherd, sheep) and titles and terms (Son, anointing, flesh) indicate points of contact. Exegesis was an important activity for the Valentinians, who knew and used a number of New Testament texts. The language of EvVer, with its biblical colouring, probably derives from the context of Valentinian theological activity.

Bibliography

H. W. Attridge and G. W. MacRae, in: NHL, 38–51; H. W. Attridge, (ed.), *Nag Hammadi Codex I (The Jung Codex)* (NHS 22/23), Leiden 1985, I, 55–122; II, 39–135; H. M. Schenke, in: *Nag Hammadi Deutsch* I, 27–44; G. Lüdemann and M. Janssen, *Bibel der Häretiker*, 26–41; B. Layton, *The Gnostic Scriptures*, 250–54; M. Krause, 'The Gospel of Truth', in: W. Foerster, (ed.), *Gnosis*, II: *Coptic and Mandean Sources*, Oxford 1974, 53–70; J. Heldermann, *Die Anapausis im Evangelium Veritatis* (NHS 18), Leiden 1984; Idem,

'Das Evangelium Veritatis in der neueren Forschung', *ANRW* II/25.5 (1988) 4054–106; C. Markschies, *Valentinus Gnosticus? Untersuchungen zur valentinianischen Gnosis. Mit einem Kommentar zu den Fragmenten Valentins* (WUNT 65), Tübingen 1992, 339–56.

8

DIALOGUES WITH THE RISEN JESUS

We have already mentioned several times a literary phenomenon for which scholars have coined the generic term 'dialogue gospels'. These begin with an apparition of the risen Lord in the group of his disciples, followed by conversations and discourses; at the end, the risen Lord bids farewell and ascends definitively to heaven. Precise indications of time are rare, but where these are found, the forty days between Easter and the ascension (cf. Acts 1:3) can be extended almost at will; in the Pistis Sophia, this period lasts for eleven years. The starting point for the development of this genre is the New Testament narratives of the appearances of the risen Jesus, especially where he appears on a mountain in Galilee and sends out the disciples (Mt 28:11–20). This genre was also influenced by models in classical literature, viz. the Platonic dialogues (which were frequently imitated) and a literary genre called *erōtapokriseis*, which imparted instruction and information by means of a series of questions (Greek: *erōtaō*, 'I ask') and answers (Greek: *apokriseis*).

An impressive list of almost twenty works have been categorized by scholars as 'dialogue gospels':

The First Apocalypse of James (NHC V,3)
The Second Apocalypse of James (NHC V,4)
The Apocalypse of Paul (NHC V,2)
The Apocalypse of Peter (NHC VII,3)
The Apocryphon of John (NHC II,1, etc.)
The Letter of Peter to Philip (NHC VIII,2)
The Book of Thomas the Contender (NHC II,7)
The Two Books of Jeū (in the Coptic 'Codex Brucianus', cf. GCS 45)
The Dialogue of the Saviour (NHC III,5)
The Apocryphon of James (NHC I,2)
Epistula Apostolorum (see section b, below)
The Gospel of Mary (BG 8502,1; see section c, below)
The Freer logion (see ch. 1b, nr. 4, above)
The Hypostasis of the Archons (NHC II,4)
Pistis Sophia (in the Coptic 'Codex Askewianus', cf. GCS 45)
The Sophia Jesu Christi (NHC III,4; BG 8502,3)
The Acts of Peter and the Twelve Apostles (NHC VI,1)
The Gospel of Thomas (NHC II,2; see ch. 7a, above)
Zostrianos (NHC VIII,1)

Even a superficial reading of this list will note interesting information. Most of these writings were found at Nag Hammadi, and where this is not the case – as with the Gospel of Mary, the Pistis Sophia, and the Books of Jeū – these are nevertheless unmistakably gnostic works in the Coptic language; the main exception is the non-gnostic Epistula Apostolorum. It is undeniable that gnostic thinkers felt a particular affinity to this literary form, and the reason is obvious: it allowed specifically gnostic material to be presented as a special revelation of the Lord, thereby legitimating it. These writings contain 'the second teaching' (to borrow the appropriate title of Judith Hartenstein's book), which takes up the teaching of the earthly Jesus, both developing it and going beyond it.

The designation 'dialogue gospels' is, however, highly problematic. First, the 'Gospel of Mary' is the only one of these texts to bear this title; the others do not in fact present themselves to the reader as 'gospels'. Secondly, various factors prevent us from seeing all these texts as examples of *one* particular genre. For example, the Apocalypse of Paul, which describes a heavenly journey of the apostle's soul, belongs to the genre of apocalypses; the same can be said of the other 'Apocalypses' in the list, if we understand this term in the broad sense of 'texts containing revelations'. The Acts of Peter and the Twelve Apostles could be associated with the genre of apocryphal Acts of Apostles. Unlike the Epistula Apostolorum, the Letter of Peter to Philip has an elaborate (though possibly secondary) epistolary framework, so that it surely belongs to the genre of letters. Since the Gospel of Thomas is a collection of sayings, with exceedingly little in the way of dialogues and nothing to indicate a post-Easter situation, it does not belong here at all. Such processes of elimination leave us with a list of fewer than ten works, four of which will be discussed in the present chapter.

First, we discuss the Sophia Jesu Christi, probably the oldest surviving example of a dialogue gospel, and the Epistula Apostolorum, an equally indisputable and non-gnostic example. The Gospel of Mary commends itself to our investigation because it both calls itself a gospel and consists primarily of a dialogue on the occasion of an apparition by the risen Lord. Finally, we have the Apocryphon of John with its dialogue framework. This is perhaps the most important of all the gnostic revelatory texts, and its affinities to the writings which we call 'apocrypha' go far beyond its title alone; this makes it difficult to understand why it is only mentioned briefly in the sixth edition of *New Testament Apocrypha,* but not discussed in any detail.

Two other works which are presented in full under the heading of 'dialogue gospels' in *New Testament Apocrypha,* the Book of Thomas and the Dialogue of the Saviour, are treated in the following chapter, for reasons which will be explained there.

Bibliography

H. Koester, *Ancient Christian Gospels*, 173–200; J. Hartenstein, *Die zweite Lehre*; S. Petersen, 'Zerstört die Werke der Weiblichkeit!', 35–93; P. Perkins, *The Gnostic Dialogue: The Early Christian Church and the Crisis of Gnosticism* (Theological Inquiries), New

York 1980; K. Rudolph, 'Der gnostische "Dialog" als literarisches Genus' (1968), in: Idem, *Gnosis und spätantike Religionsgeschichte. Gesammelte Aufsätze* (NHMS 42), Leiden 1996, 103–22.

(a) The Sophia Jesu Christi (SJC)

(1) Contextual information

'The Sophia of Jesus Christ' (SJC) bears this title not only in the *subscriptio*, but also in its first line. The state of transmission resembles that of other works which we have studied above: SJC survives in two Coptic versions, as the third text in the 'Berolinensis Gnosticus' (BG 8502,3: pp. 77,8–127,12) and the fourth writing in the third Nag Hammadi codex (NHC III,4: pp. 90,14–119,18); we also have POxy 1081, a Greek fragment of barely 50 lines. The Coptic manuscripts from the fourth or fifth century are complemented by the Greek papyrus fragment from the third or early fourth century. This makes it certain that the work was written in Greek; a number of considerations indicate a dating in the second century.

We are fortunate to possess not only SJC, but also the work on which it is based, viz. 'Eugnostos the Blessed', which also survives in two versions among the Nag Hammadi documents (NHC III,3 and V,1). This work begins with a typical epistolary greeting: 'Eugnostos the Blessed, to those who are his.' The parallels between SJC and the Letter of Eugnostos, which includes no explicitly Christian affirmations but rather resembles a philosophical treatise from Middle Platonism, are due to SJC's use of Eugnostos. The later author has integrated it into his own text, expanding it in Christian, gnostic and salvation-historical terms and omitting anything that could not be accommodated to this aim.

'Sophia' means 'wisdom', and the genitive construction 'wisdom of Jesus Christ' can be understood in two senses (perhaps intentionally). On the analogy of the deuterocanonical 'Wisdom of Solomon', the title could indicate the sapiential instruction given by Jesus Christ; this is how outsiders, non-initiates, would understand it. In the body of the text itself, we encounter Sophia as a mythical entity, the consort of Jesus who forms a syzygy with him. For those 'in the know', therefore, the title would indicate that the text presented the personified heavenly Wisdom as the female pendant to the Redeemer.

Our quotations refer to pages and lines, and we normally follow the version of SJC in NHC III,4 (the exception concerns the eleventh question: cf. below). Parallel references to BG 8502,3 and a comparison with Eugnostos can be found in the specialised editions of the text.

(2) The contents

At the beginning of SJC, twelve disciples and seven women assemble after the resurrection of Jesus on a mountain in Galilee which bears the promising name 'Place of Harvesting and Joy'. Nevertheless, the first thing the disciples observe is that they are deeply confused. The Saviour (virtually the only name used for Jesus in the narrative) appears to them (91,10–22):

not in his first form, but in the visible spirit. And his form was like a great angel of light. And his likeness I must not describe. No mortal flesh can endure it, but only pure (and) perfect flesh like that which he taught us about on the mountain called 'Of the Olives' in Galilee. And he said: 'Peace to you! My peace I give to you!'

Despite the erroneous location in Galilee, the reference is to the Mount of Olives where the disciples experienced the transfiguration of Jesus; this was already a foretaste of the manner in which the risen Lord would appear. The next passage has a relatively straightforward structure, consisting of thirteen dialogues between Jesus and the group of disciples.

The *first* exchange is prompted by the Saviour himself, who asks: 'What are you thinking about? (Why) are you perplexed? What are you searching for?' (92,1–3). *Philip* replies: 'For the nature of the universe and the plan' (92,4f.). The Saviour now speaks of the human person's vain search for God, illustrating this with the example of the wisest men, viz. the Greek philosophers whose various schools saw the world as a whole, providence or fate as the highest power (the reader thinks spontaneously of the Epicureans, Stoics and Sceptics). It is easy to refute these positions; but if we are to get any further, we need the knowledge which is transmitted through revelation.

The *second* exchange begins with a confession and a request by *Matthew*: 'Lord, no one can find the truth except through you. Therefore teach us the truth' (94,1–4). Jesus' second discourse takes the form of a negative theology, making affirmations about the highest God precisely by refusing to give precise information about him (94,5–95,18):

... Now he is eternal, having no birth ... He is unbegotten, having no beginning ... No one rules over him, since he has no name ... While he is not known, he ever knows himself. He is immeasurable. He is untraceable ... He is called 'the Father of the universe'.

The *third* question is posed by *Philip*: 'Lord, how then was he [i.e. the highest, incomprehensible God] revealed to the perfect ones?' (95,19f.). The answer is relatively brief, but very hard to understand: those who are counted worthy of the self-disclosure of the highest God are not only destined beforehand to receive this; thanks to the immeasurable power of his thought, these persons must also already be present in a kind of pre-existence.

The *fourth* question, posed by *Thomas* (96,15–17), prompts an answer which includes a summons to wake up (97,19–24). This is the first time, but not the last, that we shall hear this summons in SJC; here, it continues with words which some scholars have classified as an agraphon (see ch. 1, above):

He called out, saying, 'Whoever has an ear to hear about boundless things, let him hear,' and 'It is those who are awake I have addressed.'

Mary Magdalene, who poses the *fifth* question, is the only one among the women to speak directly: 'Lord, then how will we know these things?' (98,10f.). The wide-ranging answer of the 'perfect Saviour' describes how the other entities proceed from the highest principle: when the 'beginningless First Father' and 'Lord of the universe' beheld himself in a mirror, his image took independent form, and thus the process of emanations began.

Matthew puts the *sixth* question: 'Lord, Saviour, how was man revealed?' (100,17–19). The answer makes it clear that this refers to a mythical entity, the primal human being, an immortal and androgynous being under the 'First Father'. In order for him to exercise his function as redeemer, another mediatory instance is needed, who has some features in common with the Paraclete of the farewell discourses in John (101,9–16):

... so that through that immortal (primal) man they [i.e. human beings] might attain their salvation and awake from forgetfulness through the interpreter [*hermêneutês*] who was sent, who is with you until the end of the poverty of the robbers. And his consort [*syzygos*] is the great Wisdom [*sophia*] ...

The meaning of 'poverty' in this context is made clear a little later on, when this world is called 'the creation of poverty'. The 'robbers' are the powers which rule this world; they dwell in the lower heavens and seek to 'steal' human souls.

The *seventh* dialogue begins with *Bartholomew's* question: 'How (is it that) <he> was designated in the Gospel "Man" and "Son of Man" ...?' (103,23–104,4). The answer speaks of Sophia as consort of the Saviour, and of the various forms of his name, some of which are masculine and some feminine.

The *disciples* as a group (i.e. the twelve male disciples and the seven women mentioned at the beginning of SJC) formulate the *eighth* question: 'Lord, the one who is called "Man", reveal to us about him, so that we also may know his glory exactly' (105,4–8).

The same group also pose the *ninth* question: 'Tell us clearly how (it happened that) from things invisible they came down from the immortal one to the world, since (here) they die?' (106,10–14). This touches on an important issue: how does the spiritual enter matter? What kind of 'fall' precedes this? The answer, in which Jesus defines his role as gnostic redeemer-figure, is correspondingly important (107,11–25):

But I came from the places above by the will of the great Light, (I) who escaped from that bond [i.e. matter, which threatened him too]. I cut off the thing of the robbers. I wakened it, namely, that drop [i.e. the fallen spark of light from the world of light] that was sent from Sophia, so that it might bear much fruit through me, and be perfected, and not be lacking, but be set apart by me, the great Saviour, in order that his glory might be revealed, so that Sophia might also be justified in regard to that defect [which had led to the imprisonment of souls, etc.] . . .

The *tenth* question is posed by *Thomas:* 'Lord, Saviour, how many are the aeons of those that surpass the heavens?' (108,17–19). 'Aeon' is a temporal concept drawn from apocalyptic, and can also designate spheres; here, it refers to personal powers and forces.

The *eleventh* question, once again posed by the group of *disciples* as a whole, runs as follows: 'How many are the aeons of the immortal ones, counted by those who are infinite?' (This question is found only in BG, p. 107,14–16; at this point, NHC III has a gap of three pages.) The Saviour replies with a list of twelve aeons, which includes the first mention of the concept *ekklēsia* ('church') for the assembly of the many; this is thought of as a pre-existent entity on a level higher than the world.

The *twelfth* question confirms that when *the disciples* pose a question, we are to understand this as referring to the male disciples and the women as a group: here we have a reduction to the *twelve* male disciples, where *'the holy apostles'* act as spokesmen. This is the penultimate question in SJC: 'Lord, Saviour, tell us about those who are in the aeons, since it is necessary for us to ask about them' (NHC III: 112,19–24).

Once more, it is *Mary Magdalene* who takes centre-stage for the *thirteenth* and last question: 'Holy Lord, your disciples, whence came they, and where do they go, and (what) should they do here?' (114,9–12). These are the classical questions of gnosis, familiar to us from the definition of the 'gnosis which sets free' by the gnostic teacher Theodotus (in Clement of Alexandria, *Excerpta ex Theodoto* 78.2):

Who were we? What have we become? Where were we? Whence have we been cast? Whither are we hastening? From what have we been set free? What is birth, what is rebirth?

The Saviour gives Mary a highly detailed reply which includes a synthesis of anthropology. Sophia, the mother of the universe, committed the error of seeking to create human beings without her consort; the result was that a particle (or, to use the term in SJC, a 'drop') from the realm of light and of spirit fell into the lower regions of chaos, where the demiurge and the 'robbing' powers want to hold it captive. The Saviour had to come in order to free this particle. Knowledge is both the instrument and the goal on the path of salvation (117,8–21; square brackets indicate lacunae):

Whoever, then, knows [the Father in pure] knowledge [will depart] to the Father [and repose in] the unbegotten [Father]. But [whoever knows] him [defectively] will depart [and repose] in [the rest of the Eighth. Now] whoever knows [the immortal spirit] of light, in silence, through reflecting and desire, in truth, let him bring me signs of the invisible one, and he will become a light in the spirit of silence.

(The 'Eighth' is a higher heaven or aeon, but not the highest of all.) Rest and silence as the ultimate goal, spirit and light, signs by which one will be recognized and which have a protective function – all these themes are gnostic, and we have encountered them many times in the course of this book, indeed with increasing frequency, e.g. in the Gospel of the Egyptians (NHC; see ch. 4c) or the Gospel of Thomas (see ch. 7a). It is probable that SJC envisages the abolition of gender difference as the ideal of true human existence (an idea which we have seen in EvThom), since the final reply to Mary includes the affirmation that the Saviour came 'so that the two might become one, as it was in the beginning' (according to BG p. 122,6–11; in NHC III, the text resumes here after a further gap of two pages).

The extreme brevity of the *narrative conclusion* indicates that the real interest of this dialogue gospel is not the narrative framework, but the contents of what is said (NHC III: 119,8–17; square brackets indicate lacunae):

These are the things [the] blessed Saviour [said, and he disappeared] from them. Then [all the disciples] were in [great, ineffable joy] in [the spirit from] that day (on). [And his disciples] began to preach [the] Gospel of God, [the] eternal, imperishable [Spirit]. Amen.

(3) Summary

This relatively transparent structure makes the Sophia Jesu Christi the model of a 'dialogue gospel'; its author may even have been the first to develop and employ this genre. Unfortunately, the clarity of the structure is not matched by clear and comprehensible contents. We soon find ourselves in lofty flights of mythological thought, but the basic mythological scheme is always presupposed, never set out or explained. This applies with particular force to the ninth reply, which alludes to the fatal error of Sophia and its consequences for the events which brought salvation.

Of the texts discussed earlier in this book, it is EvEg NHC (see ch. 4b, above) which comes closest to SJC, closer even than EvPhil, although EvEg is not itself a dialogue gospel. EvThom proceeds on a completely different path from SJC. Although Mary Magdalene is not as prominent in SJC as in the 'Gospel of Mary' (see below), she has an important position among the disciples. She is mentioned by name twice when she asks the Saviour questions, and she poses the last question of all, which prompts Jesus to give a particularly lengthy and weighty reply.

The risen Lord appears in SJC as an angel in radiant light, but the concept of 'flesh' is retained, though hedged about with cautionary qualifications when the text speaks of the body of the risen Jesus: this is a pure, immortal, spiritual flesh which it is almost impossible to describe. This is not without significance in view of the next text which we shall study, since the main aim of the Epistula Apostolorum is a determined defence of the 'resurrection of the flesh' in the most literal sense of the term.

Bibliography

D. M. Parrott, in: NHL, 220–43; J. Hartenstein, in: *Nag Hammadi Deutsch* I, 323–79; W. C. Till and H. M. Schenke, *Die gnostischen Schriften des koptischen Papyrus Berolinensis 8502* (TU 60), Berlin 2nd edn. 1972, 52–61, 194–295; D. M. Parrott, *Nag Hammadi Codices III,3–4 and V,1 with Papyrus Berolinensis 1502,2 and Oxyrhynchus Papyrus 1081* (NHS 27), Leiden 1991 (an excellent synopsis of all the texts); D. Lührmann, *Fragmente*, 96–101 (for POxy 1081); G. Lüdemann and M. Janssen, *Bibel der Häretiker*, 256–68; J. Hartenstein, *Die zweite Lehre*, 35–62.

(b) Epistula Apostolorum (EpAp)

(1) Contextual information

The 'Letter of the Apostles', a lengthy work of 51 chapters, took on particular importance in the church of Ethiopia; the complete text survives only in recent Ethiopic manuscripts from the sixteenth to the nineteenth century. An additional problem for scholars is posed by the fact that the translation into Ethiopic was made *via* Coptic and Arabic. Roughly half of EpAp survives in an older Coptic textual witness from the fourth or fifth century, which is a direct translation from the original language, viz. Greek. No trace of the Greek text survives, but a leaf with a textual fragment in Latin from the fifth or sixth century has been discovered in a palimpsest in Vienna (i.e. a parchment manuscript which was 'rubbed out' and reused for another text).

EpAp was completely unknown in the west before it was edited and translated at the beginning of the twentieth century. The title 'Letter of the Apostles' was suggested by the word *epistula* in the upper margin of the Latin fragment, and it finds some support in the introductory scene, where the apostolic college addresses a letter to the churches in the four corners of the world. However, this epistolary fiction is not consistently maintained throughout the text. In ch. 10, the risen Lord appears to them, and the ensuing dialogue determines the form of the work as a whole.

Although it is transmitted only in later textual witnesses, scholars agree in dating EpAp to the second century. Some appeal to the dating of the parousia in ch. 17: it is to occur either 120 years (Coptic version) or 150 years (Ethiopic version) after the appearance of Jesus and the dialogue with the apostles. If we assume that the dialogue is supposed to be taking place *c.* 30, this would bring us to the year 150 or 170. Even apart from this question, however, there is much to be said (despite the recent suggestion of a date at the beginning of the second century) for Carl Schmidt's initial proposal of a date in the 160s. There is no agreement about the place of composition; Egypt, Asia Minor and Syria have been suggested.

SJC has a structure consisting of 13 questions and answers. EpAp has almost 60 questions by the disciples and answers by Jesus. In view of the length of the text and the variety of its contents – sometimes only loosely connected to the context – all that we can do in the next section is to give some samples of its contents. As far as possible, translations follow the Coptic version; where this has not survived, we follow the Ethiopic text in the light of the translations by Wajnberg, Duensing and Müller.

(2) The contents

– Introduction: Revelatory discourse and letter

In the English translation in NTApo, ch. 1 begins as follows: 'What Jesus Christ revealed to his disciples as a *letter,* and how Jesus Christ revealed the *letter* of the council of the apostles.' This prompts the reader to ask why a letter is revealed (its contents are given in the next chapter). If this were the only philologically acceptable translation, we should have to accept it; but this is not the case. There are good reasons for following Wajnberg and translating the Ethiopic term as 'book' instead of 'letter'. This makes much better sense of the introductory lines:

The book of the revelation of Jesus Christ for his disciples. The book with those things that Jesus Christ has revealed for all human beings through the college of the apostles, the disciples of Jesus Christ. It was written because of the false apostles Simon and Cerinthus, so that no one should join their company ...

Since Simon Magus (from Acts 8) and Cerinthus were considered the prototypical heads of gnostic schools in the 2nd century, these words immediately shed light on the polemical position of the author. The echo of Rev 1:1 is surely not accidental: it characterizes the entire work as a revelatory discourse transmitted by means of the apostolic letter (cf. Rev 1:4!) which begins in ch. 2:

We, John and Thomas and Peter and Andrew and James and Philip and Bartholomew and Matthew and Nathanael and Judas Zelotes and Cephas, we write to the churches of the East and West, towards North and South, recounting and *proclaiming* to you concerning our Lord Jesus Christ, how we have written and *heard and felt him* after he had risen from the dead, and how he has revealed to us things great, astonishing, real.

If we compare this list of the apostles, which contains only eleven names, with a list such as Acts 1:13, we notice a number of remarkable features (quite apart from the unusual order of the names). James the son of Alphaeus is missing, while Nathanael has been added;

EpAp does not identify him with Bartholomew, as does the Gospel of Bartholomew (see ch. 6c, above). Simon the Zealot and Judas the son of James have become 'Judas Zelotes', leaving a vacant place for 'Cephas' – the sobriquet for Simon Peter has become a person on its own. Why do all the apostles write, rather than one prominent member of the college such as Thomas, Philip or James? This is because their letter is addressed to the worldwide church: the intention is not to disclose some special gnostic revelation as a private teaching for a few initiates, but to send a message of truly 'catholic' proportions (here as elsewhere, this word means 'all-embracing, universal', and is not to be understood in the modern sense of restriction to one Christian confession).

The words in italics in our quotation are literal echoes of 1 Jn 1:1–3: 'That which was from the beginning, which we have heard, which we have seen with our eyes, which we have looked upon and touched with our hands ... we proclaim also to you.' Clearly, the author intends to fight against a docetic dissolution of Jesus' true human nature and of the reality of his bodily resurrection. Since, however, he sometimes adopts gnostic elements in the course of his battle against gnosis, we may legitimately question the extent to which he succeeds in his aim.

– Allegorical exposition of miracles and a profession of faith

A long profession of faith in God's creative power in ch. 3 ends with the miraculous conception of Jesus and his birth as a true human being: 'He was wrapped (in swaddling clothes) and made known at Bethlehem; and he was reared and grew up, as we saw.' Chapter 4 provides a transition to the adult Jesus by illustrating the miraculous power he possessed as a child; the 'Alpha and Beta' episode with the teacher is familiar from chs. 6 and 14 of the Infancy Gospel of Thomas (see ch. 5b, above). Chapter 5 unfolds a great panorama of Jesus' miracles, presenting in summary or in detail twelve (or fourteen) miracles known from the gospels. Those related in greater detail are selected because of their 'usefulness' in relation to other themes: for example, the episode of the healing of the woman with the flow of blood (Mk 5:25–34) is given so much space because the point is that she *touched* Jesus, just as the apostles will touch the risen Jesus in EpAp 12 (see below). Finally, the multiplication of the loaves and fishes (Mk 6:35–44 and parallels) is given an allegorical exegesis. When the disciples ask Jesus to explain the five loaves, he interprets them as the 'basic nutritional elements' of the faith:

They are a picture of our faith concerning the great Christianity; and i.e. faith in the Father, the ruler of the entire world, and in Jesus Christ our Saviour, and in the Holy Spirit, the Paraclete, and in the holy Church and in the forgiveness of sins.

God the Father, Son and Holy Spirit, the 'catholic' church and the forgiveness of sins: these are the five basic elements of an ancient profession of faith which Jesus here teaches during the period of his earthly ministry. His crucifixion will be related in ch. 9, where we also find the introduction to the narrative of his appearance after the resurrection.

– The narrative of the appearance: no bodiless demon

In ch. 9, three women go to Jesus' tomb in order to anoint his dead body. The risen Lord shows himself to them and charges them to bring the other disciples the news that he has risen. The disciples, however, react by rejecting this message, and their doubts are not dispelled even when Jesus in person appears before them. He must ask them (ch. 11f.):

Why do you still doubt and why are you not believing? I am he who spoke to you concerning my flesh, my death, and my resurrection. That you may know that it is I, put your finger, Peter, in the nailprints of my hands; and you, Thomas, put your finger in the spear-wounds of my side; but you, Andrew, look at my feet and see if they do not touch the ground [*Ethiopic adds:* and leave a footprint. For it is written in the prophet,] 'The foot of a ghost or a demon does not join to the ground'. But we <touched> him that we might truly know whether he <had risen> in the flesh . . .

This text is a variation not only on Jn 20:25–27, but also on Lk 24:39, 'See my hands and my feet, that it is I myself; handle me, and see; for a spirit has not flesh and bones as you see that I have.' The prints left by the Lord's feet in the sand are meant as irrefutable evidence of the reality and bodiliness of his resurrection. Within the text of EpAp, this high point has been prepared by the reception of 1 Jn 1:1 in ch. 2 and of Mk 5:25–34 in ch. 5. The 'quotation from the prophet' at the end of ch. 11 is not found either in the Old Testament or in non-biblical Jewish literature, but the idea that spirits and demons leave no footprints on the earth is relatively widely attested (cf. the caricature in Dan 14:14–22) and may simply have been formulated *ad hoc* by the author, in association with Lk 24:39, as an appropriate 'prophetic' dictum.

– From the incarnation to the parousia

The aim of the ensuing dialogues is to reveal 'what is above heaven and what is in heaven, and your rest that is in the kingdom of heaven' (ch. 12). Jesus begins by speaking of his descent to earth in the form of an angel and of his becoming man. This is indeed interpreted terminologically as an 'incarnation' ('becoming flesh'), but it takes place in a remarkable manner: Jesus himself was the angel Gabriel who appeared to Mary and entered into her on that occasion (ch. 14):

On that day, when I took the form of the angel Gabriel, I appeared to Mary and spoke with her. Her heart received me and she believed [*Ethiopic adds (cf. Gen 18:12–15):* and laughed]. I [*Ethiopic adds:* the Word] formed myself and entered into her womb; I became flesh . . .

The incarnation takes place in view of Jesus' saving death on the cross, and this is why ch. 15 speaks abruptly of the memorial of the death of Jesus, which the apostles are to celebrate every Passover night in an act of worship consisting of eucharist and agape (fellowship meal). Chapter 16 brings us to the expectation of the Lord's return, which ch. 17 calls the parousia of *the Father*. Jesus replies to the disciples' objection with an explanatory formula which recalls the language of immanence in the Gospel of John: 'I am wholly in my Father and my Father is in me' (cf. Jn 17:21). One may, however, wonder whether this language is not excessive: does it truly preserve the distinction between the Persons in the Trinity? The terrifying events which will accompany the parousia and the last judgement are set out in greater detail from ch. 34 onwards.

– Resurrection of the flesh

Clearly, the author found it necessary to place particular emphasis on the resurrection of the flesh, since he discusses it at great length in chs. 20 to 30 – cf. the logion of Jesus in ch. 21: 'As the Father awakened me from the dead, in the same manner you also will arise in the flesh.' It is precisely at this point that the text itself reflects on the literary form of communication. In other words, the conversation–situation itself becomes the theme of the dialogue.

In ch. 22, the apostles ask: 'Is it really in store for the flesh to be judged together with soul and spirit?' (on this threefold anthropological model, cf. 1 Thess 5:23), and Jesus rebukes them: 'How long do you still ask and inquire?' But the apostles persist. They must proclaim and teach this article of faith, and if they are to be good preachers, they themselves must be certain about this matter (ch. 23). Jesus becomes angry and cries out, 'O you of little faith, how long will you keep on asking?' But when the apostles display contrition, they are encouraged to continue with their questions (ch. 25):

Again <we> said to him, 'O Lord, already we are ashamed that we repeatedly question and trouble <you>.' Then <he> answered and said to us, 'I know that in faith and from your whole heart you question me. Therefore I am glad because of you. Truly I say to you: I am <glad>, and my Father who is in me, that <you> question me. For your boldness <affords me> rejoicing and gives yourselves <life>.'

Chapter 26 takes up again the theme of the resurrection of the flesh for judgement, and this paves the way for the description in ch. 27 of Jesus' descent to the fathers and the prophets in the underworld.

– Paul and the first apostles

When the college of apostles act together, as here in Epistula Apostolorum, we cannot avoid the question of the status of Paul, who called himself an 'apostle' and was the great missionary to the Gentiles.

In order to integrate Paul into the narrative, the author employs a clever literary device: 'Christ himself, in the form of a prophecy, presents Paul to the first apostles as their future colleague, and draws on the accounts in the Acts of the Apostles to sketch for the apostles Paul's personality and the course of his life, so that they now possess the relevant information' (Schmidt, p. 186). The shortened version of Paul's conversion in EpAp 31 is easier to understand, if we bear in mind the narrative in Acts 9:

And look; you will meet a man whose name is Saul, which being interpreted means Paul. He is a Jew, circumcised according to the command of the law; and he will hear my voice from heaven with terror, fear and trembling; and his eyes will be darkened and by your hand will be crossed with spittle [cf. Jn 9:6] . . . his eyes will be opened, and he will praise God, my heavenly Father . . . The last of the last [cf. 1 Cor 15:9] will become a preacher to the Gentiles . . . he will be for the salvation of the Gentiles.

It is no longer Ananias (as in Acts 9:17) who heals Saul's blindness, but the first apostles. This reinforces Paul's subordination to them: despite all the friendliness displayed by the apostles in EpAp, he always remains inferior to them. As Schmidt puts it (p. 191), Paul is 'reduced to the eager pupil of the first apostles'. According to EpAp 33, it is these apostles who found the community in Damascus which Saul seeks to persecute, and the text interprets the failure of his attempt to destroy this community as the fulfilment of a prophetic promise:

. . . that the word of the prophet may be fulfilled where it says, 'Behold, out of the land of Syria I will begin to call a new Jerusalem, and I will subdue Zion and it will be captured; and the barren one who has no children will be fruitful and will be called the daughter of my Father, but to me, my bride.'

Once again, we look in vain for the source of this 'prophetic' text. In its own way, it too is 'apocryphal', although it may have been suggested by the use made of Is 54:1 at Gal 4:27.

– The wise and the foolish virgins

The unknown prophet is quoted again in ch. 43, where we are told that the five wise and the five foolish virgins in Mt 25:1–13 are 'those with respect to whom the prophet said: "They are daughters of God".' The free version of the parable, cast in the form of a dialogue, begins in ch. 43 when Jesus charges the apostles: 'Be like the wise virgins who watched and did not sleep.' In Matthew, all the virgins sleep; here, the wise virgins show their wisdom by not sleeping – while the foolish slumber. Nevertheless, the latter too remain 'daughters of God', and the apostles weep for those who have fallen asleep, and expect that the wise virgins will pray for their foolish 'sisters' (!). This means that the controversy illustrated by means of the two groups of virgins is located within the community of believers. It is, in other words, a conflict between Christians.

A new level of understanding is introduced when Jesus offers an allegorical interpretation of the two groups of virgins:

The *five* wise are (1) Faith and (2) Love and (3) Grace, (4) Peace and (5) Hope. Among those who believe they who have these (virtues) will be guides to those who have believed in me and in him who sent me. I am the Lord and I am the bridegroom whom they have received, and they have gone into the house of the <bridegroom> and have laid themselves down with me in my <bride>chamber <and rejoiced>.

The five wise virgins are to be interpreted allegorically as five personified virtues which are particularly necessary for those (such as the apostles) who are leaders among the faithful. EpAp differs from Mt 25, on the metaphorical level, by making the five wise virgins collectively the bride of the Lord. We are familiar with the 'bridal chamber' from the Gospel of Philip (see ch. 7b, above). It is probable that the author of EpAp takes up here a conception of his gnostic opponents and gives it an 'orthodox' application.

The apostles then ask the Lord to explain the meaning of the five foolish virgins:

But we said to him: 'O Lord ... who are the foolish?' He said to us, 'Hear their names. They are (1) Knowledge [*gnōsis*] and (2) Insight, (3) Obedience, (4) Forbearance and (5) Mercy. These are they which slept in those who have believed and acknowledged me.'

This is difficult to understand. Why should these five be excluded from salvation, as ch. 44 so vigorously insists? A negative evaluation of 'gnosis', which heads the list, and perhaps also of 'wisdom', understood as the fallen Sophia of the gnostic myth, might be plausible, but what of obedience, forbearance and mercy? Hills suggests that the word 'These' refers not to the foolish virgins, but to the virtues which have slept *in* the believers, so that their profession of faith is neither genuine nor fruitful. In linguistic and contextual terms, however, it is more likely that all the five terms are meant to be understood as negative qualifications. Obedience would be wrong where 'offices or authoritative positions in the community were occupied' by persons holding the gnostic views which the author of EpAp attacks; true believers ought not to listen to them; and the 'warnings against forbearance and mercy are perhaps intended to underline the seriousness of the conflict' (Hartenstein, p. 105). The polemic would be directed not so much against the spokesmen of the other party, but rather against the lukewarmness, laziness and indecisiveness of members of the community who appealed to the precepts of tolerance and consideration of others as an excuse for their own laissez-faire attitude.

– Jesus departs

Three days after the crucifixion which was mentioned in ch. 9, Jesus takes farewell once and for all. This leaves little time – in reality, only the day of the resurrection itself – for the dialogue between the risen Lord and his disciples. Chapter 51 employs conventional motifs of apparition and ascension to depict his departure:

And after he had said this and had ended the discourse with us, he said again to us, 'Look. After three days and three hours he who sent me will come that I may go with him.' And as he spoke there was thunder and lightning and an earthquake, and the heavens divided and a bright cloud came and took him away. And (we heard) the voice of many angels as they rejoiced and praised and said, 'Assemble us, O priest, in the light of glory.' And when he had come near to the firmament of him, we heard him say, 'Go in peace.'

(3) Summary

Epistula Apostolorum is a little-known work which is remarkably interesting, and not only because it is the one New Testament apocryphon which is still copied and read as an edifying text in the Ethiopian church to the present day. It has a special place among the dialogue gospels: its author has borrowed the genre from his gnostic opponents and turned it into a useful weapon against them. But although polemic is undoubtedly present in EpAp, it does not blind the author to the reality that both parties belong to one single Christendom. When the apostles express their concern about the spiritual well-being of the representatives of the opposing party, this sounds genuine. The primary goal is not the refutation of other views, but the consolidation of the faith held by the author's own group.

Although a modern reader may find some positions unorthodox, we may agree with Carl Schmidt in calling EpAp an 'ancient catholic' text, in view of the openness with which it addresses a wide range of readers and of the most important of its affirmations. The five elements of the profession of faith symbolized by the 'bread', the basic nutrition for the believing soul (ch. 5), the profession of faith in the creator God (ch. 3), the affirmations about the incarnation (ch. 14) and the crucifixion (ch. 9), the expectation of the parousia (ch. 17), and the all-pervasive theme of the resurrection of the flesh offer an outline of the Apostolic Creed.

EpAp frequently speaks of the heavenly realms, thereby introducing apocalyptic traits into the formal structure of the work, but those addressed by Jesus' words never lose contact with ordinary life: catechetical and paraenetic concerns, not the transmission of revealed knowledge, occupy the foreground. This is more appropriate to the epistolary form indicated in ch. 2 – it is this that has given the work its modern name, and we can be glad that it has been discovered and made accessible to us today.

Bibliography

C. D. G. Müller, in NTApo I, C. Schmidt and I. Wajnberg, *Gespräche*

Jesu mit seinen Jüngern nach der Auferstehung. Ein katholisch-apostolisches Sendschreiben des 2. Jahrhunderts (TU 43), Leipzig 1919, reprint 1967; H. Duensing, *Epistula Apostolorum* (KIT 152), Bonn 1925; J. N. Pérès, *L'Epître des Apôtres* (Apocrypha 5), Paris 1994; J. Hartenstein, *Die zweite Lehre*, 97–126; M. Hornschuh, *Studien zur Epistula Apostolorum* (PTS 5), Berlin 1965; J. V. Hills, *Tradition and Composition in the Epistula Apostolorum* (HDR 24), Minneapolis, Minn. 1990.

(c) The Gospel of Mary (EvMar)

(1) Contextual information

The Gospel of Mary is transmitted in a Coptic codex which was purchased from an antiques dealer in Cairo and was acquired by the Egyptian Museum in Berlin in 1896. It was, however, only in 1955, in the aftermath of the Nag Hammadi discoveries, that it was published. The codex contains four writings: first the Gospel of Mary, then the Apocryphon of John, the Sophia Jesu Christi, and a part of the non-gnostic Acts of Peter. Since the first three are Christian gnostic texts, the codex was given the name 'Berolinensis Gnosticus' and the number BG 8502. The Gospel of Mary is found at BG 8502,1: pp. 7,1–19,5.

The Nag Hammadi codices contain three other versions of the Apocryphon of John (NHC II,1; III,1; IV,1) and one version of the Sophia Jesu Christi (NHC III,4; see above). This has led most scholars today to discuss BG 8502 as a whole in the context of the Nag Hammadi writings, although the Gospel of Mary has no parallel in those codices.

The Coptic text of EvMar is in a fragmentary state: pp. 1–6 and 11–14 of the codex are missing. What remains is less than half of the original work. Unfortunately, the discovery of two papyri with sections from EvMar in Greek have not supplied any missing passages, since these papyri, from two different codices, contain only texts already known from the Coptic translation: POxy 3525 overlaps with 9,21–10,14 in BG 8502,1, and PRyl 463 with 17,4–19,5. Some differences in verbal detail are, however, informative (see below), and the two papyri are particularly important for the question of dating. The Coptic codex was written in the fifth century, while the two papyri are from the third century; PRyl 463 may date from the beginning of the third century. This brings us to a second-century date for the composition of EvMar. The contents point to a date in the second half of the century. An early date between 100 and 150 has been proposed by some scholars, but is not convincing.

Since the beginning of the text is missing, we cannot determine whether EvMar originally had a title. The *subscriptio* calls it 'The Gospel according to Mary'. In the Coptic, this personal name is *Mariham* in the body of the text and *Marihamm* in the *subscriptio*, while the Greek has *Mariammē*. Normally, these forms of the name are used only for Mary Magdalene, not for Mary, the mother of the Lord. In other words, this is a Gospel of Mary Magdalene, and the contents of the work confirm this title.

No division of EvMar into paragraphs or verses has been suggested; we quote it by page and line, which is in any case more precise. Since the standard *New Testament Apocrypha* gives only extracts from EvMar, which is not particularly long, we depart from our usual practice here and quote it in full.

(2) The contents

Although the first pages of EvMar are lost, we can reconstruct the scene which must have been set at the beginning: it is clear that the dialogue takes place after Easter. The risen Lord – never called 'Jesus', but always 'Redeemer' or 'Lord', occasionally 'the blessed one' – appears to his male and female disciples and replies to their questions. The dialogue concerns fundamental questions about how the world and the human person are to be understood.

– Matter and sin

The surviving text begins with the last words of a question by the disciples and the Redeemer's answer (7,1–9):

[...] 'will matter then be [destroyed] or not?' The Saviour said, 'All natures, all formations, all creatures exist in and with one another, and they will be resolved again into their own roots. For the nature of matter is resolved into (the roots of) its nature alone. He who has ears to hear, let him hear.'

'Matter' (*hylē*) and 'nature' (*physis*) are categories drawn from the philosophy of nature. 'Root' here denotes 'origin', and the triad of 'all natures, all formations, all creatures' designates the totality of all that exists and has been created, in its present mutually interwoven condition. The message is that all this will pass away. Indeed, we might add that all this *must* perish, in order that the pure spirit alone may remain. The summons to watchfulness – 'He who has ears to hear, let him hear!' – emphasizes that this is the secret instruction which the reader must hear in this difficult text. The point is not to provide neutral cosmological information: Peter's next question makes the transition into the ethical sphere (7,10–20):

Peter said to him, 'Since you have explained everything to us, tell us this also: What is the sin of the world?' The Saviour said, 'There is no sin, but it is you who make sin when you do the things that are like the nature of adultery, which is called "sin". That is why the Good came into your midst, to the essence of every nature, in order to restore it to its root.'

The closing words of Jesus' reply show that the starting point of Peter's question are his preceding reflections on matter, nature and origin; these conceptions are picked up in the word 'root'. The 'sin of the world' about which Peter asks is defined by Jesus in very broad terms and linked to the conduct of human beings: it is 'the nature of adultery' or 'the essence of fornication' (terms which are certainly meant as metaphors). These words allude, within a mythological framework, to the creation of matter as a kind of 'fall' on the part of the heavenly Sophia, which human beings then make their own when they turn to the world and to matter. The Saviour came into the world as 'the Good', in order to correct this situation.

The next paragraph develops this theme and adds a double call to watchfulness in the words italicized below (7,20–8,11):

Then he continued and said, 'That is why you [become sick] and die, for [. . .] of the one who [. . . *He who*] *understands, let him understand.* [Matter gave birth to] a passion that has no equal, which proceeded from (something) contrary to nature. Then there arises a disturbance in the whole body. That is why I said to you, "Be of good courage," and if you are discouraged (be) encouraged in the presence of the different forms of nature. *He who has ears to hear, let him hear.*'

Suffering, death and the vices are the result of a state of servitude to deceitful nature. But (gnostic) believers are not completely defenceless in this situation, as the Redeemer has already told them with such exhortations as: 'Be of good courage!' (Jn 16:33), 'Be consoled!', 'Do not be afraid!' (Jn 6:20). They have the power to resist the world and all its wicked doings.

– Words of farewell

When he bids them farewell at Jn 14:27, Jesus promises the disciples the gift of peace, and his first greeting to them after his resurrection is: 'Peace be with you!' (Jn 20:19). The superimposition of the pre- and post-Easter situations which we find in the Gospel of John is adopted and practised throughout the Gospel of Mary: the hour of farewell is transposed completely into the period after the resurrection, and the departure of the Redeemer no longer signifies his departure in death, but his definitive ascension into heaven (8,12–9,5):

When the blessed one had said this, he greeted them all, saying, 'Peace be with you. Receive my peace to yourselves. Beware that no one lead you astray, saying, "Lo here!" or "Lo there!" For the Son of Man is within you. Follow after him! Those who seek him will find him. Go then and preach the gospel of the kingdom. Do not lay down any rules beyond what I appointed for you, and do not give a law like the lawgiver lest you be constrained by it' [i.e. lest you yourselves be convicted by the law and become subject to its penalties]. When he had said this, he departed.

Like EvThom 3, EvMar has recourse here above all to Lk 17:20–23, where Jesus warns the disciples not to let themselves be led astray by false signals (cf. also Mk 13:5.21). The logion at Lk 17:21, 'The kingdom of God is in the midst of you', is transformed in EvMar into the affirmation that 'the Son of Man is within you'. It is there, within oneself, that one must seek him, and it is there that one will find him (see below, on EvThom 2); only so is it possible to follow after him. This is the gospel that the disciples must proclaim to others. The title 'Son of Man' is stripped of its apocalyptic element (cf. Dan 7:13; Mt 24:30), so that it can be employed as the embodiment of true humanity and as a cipher for the fulfilment of the individual. The warning against a legalistic misunderstanding of the Christian faith fits this context. This may still reflect the earlier debate about the validity of the Jewish law (cf. the letters of Paul), but by now, the opponents are not outsiders, but Christians who hold views at variance with the author's.

– Mary as consoler

The disciples are aware that they will not achieve any great success with this particular message – on the contrary, they will suffer the same fate as the Redeemer himself (9,5–11):

But they were grieved. They wept greatly, saying, 'How shall we go to the Gentiles and preach the gospel of the kingdom of the Son of Man? If they did not spare him, how will they spare us?'

Mary Magdalene now assumes the central position. She does exactly what the Redeemer did before her, embracing the disciples and encouraging them. Not only does she reduplicate what the Lord has done: Jesus has promised his disciples in the farewell discourses that 'another Paraclete' will come to their assistance, and this is precisely the function which Mary assumes here (9,11–22):

Then Mary stood up, greeted [POxy 3525: greeted and kissed] them all, and said to her brethren, 'Do not weep and do not grieve nor be irresolute, for his grace will be entirely with you and will protect you. But rather let us praise his greatness, for he has prepared [POxy 3525: has bound] us (and) made us into human beings.' When Mary said this, she turned their hearts to the Good, and they began to discuss the words of the Redeemer.

Mary's seemingly unremarkable words – 'he has made us into human beings' – must be read in the light of Jesus' affirmation that 'The Son of Man is within you': his saving work has allowed us to discover the path to true human existence and to find within ourselves the Son of Man as our own better 'I'.

– Hidden tradition

Peter concedes that Mary played a special role even before Easter, and he now asks her for a 'hidden revelation' (10,1–8):

Peter said to Mary, 'Sister, we know that the Saviour loved you more than the rest of women. Tell us the words of the Saviour which you remember – which you know (but) we do not nor have we heard them.' Mary answered and said, 'What is hidden from you I will proclaim to you.'

The statement that the Redeemer loved Mary Magdalene 'more than the rest of *women*' sounds like a high compliment, but it does not begin to match the affirmation in EvPhil 55 that he loved her 'more than all the other *disciples*'. Nevertheless, Peter assumes that Mary knows further 'logia' of Jesus – post-Easter, rather than pre-Easter – which she has hitherto withheld from the other disciples. She now declares her willingness to impart this special teaching too; in pragmatic terms, this material is legitimated by appeal to the authority of the Lord himself.

– Mary's vision

Mary owes her privileged knowledge (naturally enough) to a vision, but the status of this vision remains unclear, since several distinct linguistic levels interlock in her words (10,9–16):

And she began to speak to them these words: 'I,' she said, 'I saw the Lord in a vision and I said to him, "Lord, I saw you today in a vision." He answered and said to me, "Blessed are you, that you did not waver at the sight of me. For where the mind is, there is the treasure".'

Our first question must be: when and where did this vision occur? It is possible that it happened before Easter, in a kind of transfiguration-scene. The second question is why Mary confirms in direct speech that she has seen the Lord. The past tense ('I *saw* you today in a vision') would appear to indicate that the ensuing dialogue takes place outside the vision – but what then are the contents of the vision itself? The answer becomes clear as soon as we realise that this passage is based on Jn 20, where Mary tells the *disciples,* 'I have seen the Lord' (v. 18); in EvMar, she addresses these words to the Lord himself. The vision as a whole is based on her encounter with the risen Lord in Jn 20:14–17, where Jesus tells her: 'I have not yet *ascended* to the Father' in heaven, and entrusts her with precisely this message for the disciples: '... and say to them, I *am ascending* to my Father and to your Father' (v. 17). This suggests the ascent of the soul as the theme of the vision which Mary goes on to narrate.

When the Lord sees that Mary reacts fearlessly when she sees him, he pronounces a blessing which reveals her to be a true gnostic; 'standing firm' and 'not wavering' are standard terms in gnostic texts for those who possess knowledge. He also alludes to his logion about the 'treasure' and the 'heart' in Mt 6:21 (par. Lk 12:34), replacing 'heart' with 'mind' and leading into the following anthropological debate (10,16–22):

I said to him, 'Lord, now does he who sees the vision see it <through> the soul <or> through the spirit?' The Saviour answered and said, 'He does not see through the soul nor through the spirit, but the mind which [is] between the two – that is [what] sees the vision and it is [. . .].'

According to this text, the interior dimension of the human person, where he is most truly himself, is divided into three: soul (*psychē*), mind (*nous*) and spirit (*pneuma*). The mind, situated between the two others, is the organ of visionary experience.

– The ascent of the soul

Pages 11–14 of the text are missing. It seems that Mary continues the account of her special vision. She begins to describe the ascent of the soul through the various heavens until it reaches its eternal goal. The use of the past tense in this passage prompts the question whether Mary has experienced a visionary anticipation of the ascent of her own soul, or has accompanied the soul of the Saviour from afar, as it ascended; the answer depends on the interpretation of the final words at 17,7–9 (see below).

Evil powers lie in wait for the soul in the lower heavens and endeavour to block its path. Many such obstacles are mentioned in EvMar. The lacuna prevents us from knowing the nature of the first obstacle; the second barrier is erected by desire (15,1–9):

. . . it. And desire said, 'I did not see you descending, but now I see you ascending. Why do you lie, since you belong to me?' The soul answered and said, 'I saw you. You did not see me nor recognize me. I served you as a garment, and you did not know me.' When it had said this, it went away rejoicing greatly.

In this battle of words, victory and defeat are decided by success or failure in acquiring the correct knowledge. This is the message of the next encounter too, where the representative of the hostile power bears the eloquent name of 'ignorance' (15,10–16,1):

Again it came to the third power, which is called ignorance. [It (the power)] questioned the soul, saying, 'Where are you going? In wickedness are you bound. But you are bound; do not judge!' And the soul said, 'Why do you judge me, although I have not judged? I was bound, though I have not bound. I was not recognized. But I have recognized that the All is being dissolved, both the earthly (things) and the heavenly.'

The fourth and mightiest power, 'wrath', is articulated into seven distinct forms, probably an indication that two models have been super-imposed here, one with four and one with seven lower heavens (16,1–13):

When the soul had overcome the third power, it went upwards and saw the fourth power, (which) took seven forms. The first form is darkness, the second desire, the third ignorance, the fourth is the excitement of death, the fifth is the kingdom of the flesh, the sixth is the foolish wisdom of flesh, the seventh is the wrathful wisdom. These are the seven [powers] of wrath.

The following question, which the seven forms of wrath put to the soul, contains two complicated terms, 'slayer of men' and 'conqueror of space', which require an explanation. The soul has 'murdered' the earthly human being, whom it had to abandon in order to become free, and the place which it 'conquers' or 'destroys' is the material world, to which it was previously bound (16,13–17,7):

They ask the soul, 'Whence do you come, slayer of men, or where are you going, conqueror of space?' The soul answered and said, "What binds me has been slain, and what turns me about has been overcome, and my desire has been ended, and ignorance has died. In a [world] I was released from a world, [and] in a type from a heavenly type, and (from) the fetter of oblivion which is transient. From this time on will I attain to the rest of the time, of the season, of the aeon, in silence.'

The definitive rest (*anapausis*), which is the great goal of the spiritual path in gnosis (though the concept is not exclusive to gnostic writings), means that the dimension of time is abolished; 'silence' is not only a further characteristic of the place of rest, but also another name for it. When Mary falls silent, this does not only mean that the account of the vision is now finished: it means that Mary herself has already attained this silence and made it her own (17,7–9):

When Mary had said this, she fell silent, since it was to this point that the Saviour had spoken with her [*PRyl 463:* as if the Saviour had spoken up to this point].

There is a significant divergence between the Coptic and the Greek at the end of this passage: the Coptic says merely that the Saviour had spoken to Mary in the vision up to this point, whereas the Greek can be understood to mean that it was not in reality *Mary* who spoke, but the *Saviour* who spoke through her. This is probably the original meaning, which was lost in the process of translation into Coptic. Accordingly, the vision is a description of the ascent of the Saviour's own soul to the highest heaven.

– Andrew, Peter and Mary

After the account of the vision is ended, Andrew is the first to speak. He expresses fundamental doubts about what Mary has just said. He is motivated by doctrinal considerations: her words do not agree with the accepted, customary teaching (17,10–15):

But Andrew answered and said to the brethren, 'Say what you (wish to) say about what she has said. I at least do not believe that the Saviour said this. For certainly these teachings are strange ideas.'

His brother Peter comes to his aid, but he transposes the question to another level. Although it was he himself who had asked Mary to reveal her hidden knowledge, he is no longer sure whether such a secret revelation was really entrusted to a woman – for that would give her a privileged position in relation to the male disciples and to office-bearers such as Peter himself (17,15–22):

Peter answered and spoke concerning these same things. He questioned them about the Saviour: 'Did he really speak privately with a woman (and) not openly to us? Are we to turn about and all listen to her? Did he prefer her to us?'

Mary replies directly only to Peter, whom she continues to call 'my brother', but her words indirectly envisage Andrew too, when she rejects the implicit suggestion that she has made all this up and is manipulating the disciples (18,1–5):

Then Mary wept and said to Peter, 'My brother Peter, what do you think? Do you think that I thought this up myself in my heart, or that I am lying about the Saviour?'

Someone must speak an authoritative word at this point, but it is neither Andrew nor Peter who intervenes: it is Levi who now takes Mary's side. (We may recall that Levi appears at the close of the Gospel of Peter after Mary Magdalene and alongside Peter and Andrew: see ch. 6a, above.)

– Levi and Mary

One may be tempted to equate this Levi with the apostle Matthew, but a number of factors argue against this. It is more appropriate to see here two apostles from the college of the twelve, and another disciple of Jesus from *outside* this college: the contrast is between Andrew and Peter on the one hand, and Levi and Mary on the other hand. We are not left in any doubt about where the sympathies of EvMar lie (18,6–19,1f.):

Levi answered and said to Peter, 'Peter, you have always been hot-tempered. Now I see you contending against the woman like the adversaries [*PRyl 463:* like her adversary]. But if the Saviour made her worthy, who are you indeed to reject her? Surely the Saviour knows her very well. That is why he loved her more than us. Rather let us be ashamed and put on the perfect man [*PRyl 463:* and let us do what we have been charged to do], and separate as he commanded us and preach the gospel, not laying down any other rule or other law beyond what the Saviour said.' When [. . .] and they began to go forth [to] proclaim and to preach [*according to PRyl 463, only Levi goes forth to preach*].

Once again, the Greek text claims our interest, since it has the singular 'adversary' rather than the plural in the Coptic text. PRyl 463 does not compare Peter with merely human enemies – i.e. in this context, with those who criticised the active involvement of women in the Christian communities – but with *the* adversary, viz. Satan himself (cf. Mk 8:33). Finally, the Greek text states that Levi is the only one who actually goes off to preach, and this sheds an unfavourable light on the other male disciples. Even in the Coptic text, however, Levi explicitly says that the Lord loved Mary Magdalene 'more than *us*', tacitly correcting the reservation previously expressed by Peter (see above) and agreeing with EvPhil's implicit characterization of Mary as the (female) beloved disciple.

We also note that Levi accepts the directives of the Lord: he summons the other disciples to discover the perfect human being within themselves, to proclaim this as the 'gospel', and not to distort this gospel with a multitude of new laws.

Bibliography

K. L. King *et al.*, in: NHL, 523–27; W. C. Till and H. M. Schenke, *Die gnostischen Schriften des koptischen Papyrus Berolinensis 8502* (TU 60), Berlin 2nd edn. 1972, 24–32, 62–79; H. C. Puech and B. Blatz, in: NTApo I; D. Lührmann, *Fragmente*, 72–93 (Greek text from POxy 3525 and PRyl 463); U. K. Plisch, *Verborgene Worte Jesu*, 137–42; S. Petersen, *'Zerstört die Werke der Weiblichkeit!'*, 55–61, 133–88; J. Hartenstein, *Die zweite Lehre*, 127–60; E. de Boer, *Mary Magdalene: Beyond the Myth*, London 1997, 74–117; F. Stanley Jones, *Which Mary? The Maries of Early Christian Tradition* (SBL Symposium Series 19), Atlanta, GA 2002.

(3) Evaluation

The title 'Gospel of Mary (Magdalene)' awakens high expectations, which unfortunately point in the wrong direction – will we get a glimpse of the secret life of Jesus of Nazareth, which the church deliberately suppressed? Will we perhaps glean intimate information about his 'real' relationship to Mary Magdalene? Not a trace of such matters will be found in EvMar, the only surviving text with this title. Instead, we are confronted with cosmological and ethical speculations, and with a description in mythical language of the ascent of the soul. This means that EvMar provides no historical information whatever, either about Jesus or about Mary Magdalene herself.

It does, however, tell us something about the variety of structures in the post-Easter communities and about controversies concerning those women who occupied positions of responsibility. EvMar is unambiguous on this point: it portrays Mary as the beloved disciple of the pre-Easter Jesus and as the earthly representative of the risen Lord, and it shows her accompanied by Levi, the only male disciple who accepts her special role and himself does what the Lord wants of him. When we attempt to identify the historical *Sitz-im-Leben* of this text, we should pay heed to the assessment by Hartenstein and Petersen: 'We read the Johannine writings as testimonies to a specifically Johannine Christianity. In exactly the same way, EvMar is a rediscovered testimony to an early Christian community which appealed to the authority of Mary Magdalene' (p. 766).

Bibliography

J. Hartenstein and S. Petersen, 'Das Evangelium nach Maria. Maria Magdalena als Lieblingsjüngerin und Stellvertreterin Jesu', in: L. Schottroff and M. T. Wacker (eds.), *Kompendium Feministische Bibelauslegung*, Gütersloh 1998, 757–67.

(d) The Apocryphon of John (AJ)

(1) Contextual information

A writing with the *subscriptio* 'The Apocryphon of John' (AJ), i.e. 'the secret writing of John', is found four times in our sources, as the first work in the second, third and fourth of the Nag Hammadi codices and as the second work (following EvMar) in the 'Berolinensis Gnosticus'. The four textual witnesses constitute two groups: a shorter version in NHC III,1 and BG, and a longer recension in NHC II,1 and IV,1. The two manuscripts with the shorter version contain mutually independent translations from the Greek; the two manuscripts with the longer version must be copies of the same Coptic original, which in turn is a translation from the Greek.

After initial controversies, scholars agree today that the short version is the older text and that the longer version arose through the subsequent insertion of other material. It is also possible that the longer version contains older material at some points, e.g. in the *subscriptio* (see below).

This, however, is not the only literary-critical question posed by AJ. It is relatively easy to detach the dialogue framework, which portrays the apostle John in conversation with what we may cautiously call a celestial being, and a dialogue section in the body of the text itself. We are left with a detailed creation myth: its first half reflects the intellectual world of Middle Platonism, while the second half offers a corrective to the story related in the first chapters of Genesis. There are no explicitly Christian traits here (unless we count the title 'Christ'), and it is probable that a dialogue framework has been added to an earlier text in order to Christianise it more effectively. The relationship between AJ and this underlying text would be similar to that between SJC and the Letter of Eugnostos.

In *Adversus haereses* 1.29.1–4, Irenaeus sketches the mythological model employed by a group of so-called 'Barbelo gnostics'. This excerpt displays such striking similarities to the first part of the creation myth in AJ that there must be direct contact here: it is likely that Irenaeus knew either the underlying text which is supplied with a dialogue framework in AJ, or else a short early version of AJ. This is not unimportant in view of the question of dating the work, since the text which Irenaeus used *c.* 180 must have been composed between *c.* 150 and 160. If, however, AJ's remodelling of the underlying text by means of a dialogue framework presupposes the development of this technique by SJC, a date in the 150s would be too early even for the short version of AJ (from which the longer version was made in the third century). A more probable date for the composition of the short version would be *c.* 200.

Both Coptic translations of the short version have 'The Apocryphon of John' in the *subscriptio,* while the long version has: 'According to John, an apocryphal work'; the name 'John' appears in the Greek accusative form, which the Coptic text does not use elsewhere. This emphasizes the similarity to the titles of the canonical Gospels ('. . . according to Mark', etc.), and it is possible that AJ in its original Greek form was characterized as 'The secret (Gospel) according to John' (see Hartenstein).

The importance of AJ is confirmed not only by its multiple textual attestation, but also by its position at the beginning of three codices (and it has been suggested that it also headed Codex XIII, of which only a few leaves remain). If we accept as a working hypothesis the proposal of Williams that each codex had the function of 'sacred Scripture' in the group for which it was written and which used it, then AJ would have the position of the Old Testament in Codex II, followed immediately by the Gospel: the second writing in that codex is the Gospel of Thomas.

The following survey, which pays particular attention to the narrative framework, is based primarily on the short version in BG 8502,2 (pp. 19,6–77,8).

(2) The contents

– Debate and heavenly apparition

'One day' after the death of Jesus, John, the brother of James and son of Zebedee, goes to the temple, where he encounters a Pharisee named Arimanius and engages in a debate with him. The Pharisee asks: 'Where is your master whom you followed?' When John replies: 'He has gone to the place from which he came,' the Pharisee rejoins: 'This Nazarene has deceived you [*pl.*] and filled your ears with lies . . . he has turned you from the traditions of your fathers' (19,13–20,3). John becomes dejected, and leaves the temple. He goes to a mountain in the desert, which will replace the temple as the place of revelation. But first, he himself asks a number of questions (20,8–19):

How then was the Saviour chosen? And why was he sent into the world by the Father? And who is his Father? And of what sort is that aeon to which we shall go? He told us, 'This aeon to which you will go is of the type of the imperishable aeon.' But he did not teach us concerning that one, of what sort it is.

The Johannine echoes – in John's answer to the Pharisee, and the concept of being 'sent' in this passage – presuppose knowledge of the Gospel of John, and this also accounts for the choice of John (instead of another apostle such as Thomas or Philip) as the one who receives revelation: the authority which John's writings enjoyed in some groups is meant to rub off on AJ. The subsequent cosmological reflections are prepared here by the question about the place and nature of the 'imperishable aeon'. While John is still pondering these matters, something happens (20,19–21,6):

All at once, while I was contemplating these things, behold the heavens opened and the whole creation ... shone and the world was shaken. And I was afraid, and behold I saw in the light a youth who stood by me. While I looked at him he became like an old man.

These transformations, which manifest the *polymorphia*, the 'plurality of forms' of the Redeemer, continue. Many forms appear in the light, until an apparition with three faces tells John that he need not be afraid, assuring him in language typical of the dialogues in apparition narratives: 'I am the one who is with you [*pl.*] for ever' (cf. Mt 28:20), and identifying himself as the Father, the Mother and the Son (21,14–21). Later, John addresses the one who appears as 'Christ' (according to BG; the other versions call him 'Redeemer'). He has come in order to teach John about 'what is and what was and what will come to pass' (22,3–5; cf. Rev 1:19). This entails a task which John must accomplish for believers like himself (22,10–16):

Now then, lift up your face, that you may receive the things which I shall tell you today, and that you may tell them to your fellow spirits who are from the unwavering race of the perfect Man.

The race of those who are perfect, those who stand firm and do not waver, is found as a gnostic self-description in other writings. We note the contrast between the gnostics and the world, which had begun to shake a short time earlier, when John's vision began.

This has set the scene for the lengthy revelatory discourses in the body of AJ, which now begin.

– The kingdom of light

Initially, these discourses take us on a long journey into the heavenly world, into the kingdom of pure light and pure spirit. They begin with the highest God, about whom only negative affirmations can be made (23,19–24,6):

He is immeasurable because there was no one prior to him to measure him. He is invisible because no one saw him ... He is ineffable because no one could comprehend him to speak about him. He is unnameable because there is no one prior to him to name him.

Nevertheless, the highest God does not remain alone: his perfection is reflected in his own light, and a second being with female traits appears, named 'Barbelo'. (This artificial term has not yet been satisfactorily explained. At any rate, she represents the first, higher part of the figure of Wisdom, while the second, lower part is detached and appears only later: see below.) Barbelo asks permission to emanate another entity, 'first knowledge'. Gradually, the kingdom of light is populated, always preserving perfect harmony and beautiful order, and 'Christ' and 'Adam' already find their transcendental places here.

– The god of the world

All this changes in one of the lower hierarchies, when Sophia appears on the scene and takes an unwelcome initiative (from 36,16 onwards). Without the permission of the highest God, and without the consent of her consort in her syzygy, she generates a being which – thanks to the irregular conditions of his coming into existence – can only be misshapen, with fiery eyes and the appearance of serpents and lions. Sophia hides her child in a cloud of light with a throne, and gives him the name 'Yaltabaoth', which can be explained as a parody of divine predicates in the Bible (Yahweh, El and Sabaoth).

When he is expelled, Yaltabaoth takes with him 'great power from his mother', i.e. light from the kingdom of light and particles of spirit from the realm of spirit. This enables him to become the creator of his own world, to which he gives a structure of various sections ('aeons' and heavens), filling it with beings of various kinds such as angels, powers, and authorities. Their appearance is strange, as are their names (though reminiscent of the Old Testament): 'Yao, the serpent's face', 'Eloaiou, the donkey's face', 'Adonaios, the dragon's face', 'Adoni, the monkey's face' ... (41,18–42,7). Yaltabaoth does not, however, communicate any of his spiritual power to his creatures; he keeps this for himself. Finally, he leans back in satisfaction and says, 'I am a jealous God, and there is no other God besides me' (44,14f.; cf. Ex 20:5; Is 45:5f.). We shall evaluate below this view of the creation of the world and this way of using the Old Testament.

– The countermeasure

When Sophia realizes what she has done, she repents in shame and does not dare to return 'above', but wanders about in the darkness. Her 'brothers' intercede for her, her consort comes to her aid, and the perfect spirit 'nods in consent'. But Sophia is granted only a time of probation: she is not allowed to return to the tenth and highest heaven, but must remain in the ninth until the consequences of her error are overcome.

This requires a trick, which is put into practice in a complicated manner: the highest God sends his reflection into the depths of the water in the form of a human being. Yaltabaoth's creatures are delighted when they see this, and resolve: 'Come, let us create a man according to the image and likeness of God' (48,16–18; cf. Gen 1:27). Working together (cf. the plural in Gen 1:26), they produce the *soul* of a human being, which they call 'Adam'; all the creatures make their own contributions to his composition. However, this soul lacks the life-force and lies immobile on the ground. Emissaries from the kingdom of light come unrecognized to Yaltabaoth and give him this counsel (51,15–20):

'Blow into his face something of your spirit, and his body will arise.' And he blew into his body something of the *spirit* which is the power of his mother, and it moved

(cf. Gen 2:7). Only now do we see the meaning of the whole stratagem. The kingdom of light wants to regain possession of the treasure which Yaltabaoth has guarded jealously hitherto. Now that he has handed over a portion of this treasure, the kingdom of light hopes that its lost treasure can be restored, *via* the human being, to its proper place.

However, there is still a long way to go. As a spiritual soul, Adam proves far superior to the powers which created him. These powers react by mixing together something of the four elements as clothing for Adam: 'This is the fetters, this is the tomb of the bodily structure with which the human being was clothed, as fetters (consisting) of matter' (55,9–13). In classical Platonist terms, the *body* of the human being serves as the fetters and tomb of the soul, and the human being as a whole consists (less Platonically) of three parts, viz. *body, soul* and *spirit*.

– A new reading of the first chapters of Genesis

We return to dialogues at 58,1 (or earlier in the text, at 45,6). These correct a number of affirmations in the first chapters of the Bible. John asks, 'Christ, was it not the serpent that taught her (Eve)?', and Christ replies: 'The serpent taught her the sexual desire which leads to stain and corruption.' This negative evaluation of sexuality is continued in the ensuing exegesis of Gen 2–7. For example, in a later passage, Yaltabaoth violates Eve, whom he has still to create (see below), and begets Cain and Abel with her; the episode of the fall of the angels in Gen 6:1–4 is related in great detail. However, a being from the kingdom of light called 'Insight' (*epinoia*) succeeds in freeing the first human couple from their ignorance, and helps them to attain the saving knowledge by eating from the fruit of the tree of knowledge.

With Epinoia's aid, this saving knowledge is also gained by another, related route. In his zealous endeavour to regain possession of his particles of light, Yaltabaoth brings forth Eve from Adam's side; he hopes that she will be a better instrument for the realization of his goal. The initial result, however, is the opposite of what he had intended: as soon as he sees Eve, Adam sobers up, wakes up, and begins to know (the text plays on the various meanings of the biblical 'knowing'). The child of Adam and Eve is Seth, who does not resemble Cain and Abel in any way, since he bears in himself the genuine image and spirit of the God of light (we may compare the role of Seth in the Nag Hammadi Gospel of the Egyptians: see ch. 4b, above).

When he sees his utter failure, Yaltabaoth finally repents of having created human beings (from 72,12 onwards; cf. Gen 6:6) and seeks to destroy them with a great flood which comes out of the darkness; but Noah is saved, as the representative of 'the immovable race' (73,9f.).

In a dialogue inserted into this 'midrash' on Gen 1–7, John several times asks about the fate of the souls (from 76,13 onwards): will they be saved or perish? Why do they perish, and what happens to them then? This passage expresses both pastoral concern and a paraenetic intention: in a situation where those addressed by AJ are under attack (cf. the controversy between John and the Pharisee at the beginning of the work), the author wishes to strengthen their assurance of salvation.

– The commission

This brings us to the closing framework of AJ, which takes up expressions from the opening framework such as 'kindred spirits' (which means more than 'like-minded' persons, since it refers to their sharing in the one *Pneuma*) and 'the immovable race'. John is charged to write these things down, and a conditional curse is formulated (76,7–15):

'I am saying this to you, in order that you may write it down and give it secretly to your kindred spirits, for this mystery belongs to the immovable race ... I have given this to you, so that you may write it down and keep it in a safe place.' Then he said to me, 'Cursed be all those who exchange this for a present or for food or drink or clothing or for any other such thing.'

The secret message is destined for others (i.e. for a select circle of believers), but it would be a grave sin to communicate it for the sake of material gain. The fact that this warning was necessary indicates that the temptation did in fact exist; and in view of the modest reward (food and clothing) which made it attractive to betray the secret, we may infer that those for whom AJ was written were not particularly well off.

(3) Evaluation

If we review the text of AJ as a whole, we note that the train of thought suddenly breaks off: we reach only the half-way point, and nothing is said about the second half of the trajectory which involves the definitive return into the heavenly homeland. This could be read as corroborating the suggestion (mentioned above) that AJ represents only the first part of a Bible, which must be followed by a Gospel (e.g. EvThom). This argument would not apply to BG, however, since a Gospel – EvMar – *precedes* AJ in that codex. On the other hand, AJ is followed in BG by SJC, which is a 'dialogue gospel', but contains paraenetic material and could therefore be considered a representative of the epistles (especially since it is based on the Letter of Eugnostos). The fourth text in BG, a section from the Acts of Peter, would represent the Acts of the Apostles. All that would be missing is a 'secret revelation' written by an author named John ...

Irenaeus of Lyons uses the basic text of AJ (or a short version of it) as one of his main sources when he relates the gnostic myth. This is precisely the function which AJ has for us too, after the rediscovery of its four textual witnesses in the twentieth century. Where other texts discussed in this book have only allusions, obliging us to assume things we cannot actually prove, AJ presents the gnostic system with all desirable clarity. It is, however, not easy to identify the gnostic school which produced AJ (most scholars assign it to 'Sethians'); ultimately, however, this is not so important.

The exegetical treatment of the first chapters of Genesis and the reception of the Wisdom myth point to a hellenistic Jewish environment, rather than to a Christian and gnostic background. The astonishing 'defamiliarization' which this entails is based on a far-reaching strategy which is ultimately born of an overlapping of biblical thinking and Platonism. AJ splits the biblical image of God into two halves (cf. M. Waldstein, *RGG* 4th edn. I [1998], 605). On the one hand, we have the creator God who adopts the role of the Platonic demiurge and is at the same time degraded to a power outside the realm of light (no doubt thanks to negative experiences in the encounter with this world). On the other hand, the transcendental God moves further and further away from this world into the realm of pure idea, where no anthropomorphic language can take hold of him; he resembles the primal ground of all things in Platonism, though without completely sloughing off his 'past' as the God of Israel.

This constellation may contain some basic information about how what we call 'gnosis' came into being, and this gives AJ an importance which goes far beyond the role it plays as one of the 'ancient Christian apocrypha'. In view of its title and its form as a dialogue gospel, however, it cannot be denied that precisely this is the category to which it properly belongs.

Bibliography

M. Waldstein and F. Wisse, *The Apocryphon of John: Synopsis of Nag Hammadi Codices II,1; III,1; and IV,1 with BG 8502,2* (NHMS 33), Leiden 1995 (indispensable); F. Wisse, in NHL, 104–23; M. Waldstein, in: *Nag Hammadi Deutsch* I, 95–150; W. C. Till and H. M. Schenke, *Die gnostischen Schriften des koptischen Papyrus Berolinensis 8502* (TU 60), Berlin 2nd edn. 1972, 35–51, 78–195; J. Hartenstein, *Die zweite Lehre*, 63–95; T. Onuki, *Gnosis und Stoa. Eine Untersuchung zum Apokryphon des Johannes* (NTOA 9), Freiburg (Switzerland) and Göttingen 1989; M. A. Williams, *Rethinking 'Gnosticism'. An Argument for Dismantling a Dubious Category*, Princeton, N.J. 1996, 8–18, 235–62.

9

NON-LOCALIZED DIALOGUES WITH JESUS

Two other writings from Nag Hammadi, the 'Dialogue of the Saviour' (Dial) and the 'Book of Thomas' (LibThom, an abbreviation for 'Liber Thomae'), are often included in the list of dialogue gospels. Quite apart from the fact that Dial contains the decisive word in its title, both these works do indeed consist mostly of dialogues (although those in LibThom are conversations of a very particular kind). Nevertheless, important elements of this genre are either missing or else only weakly represented in LibThom and Dial; above all, there are no framework passages, a constitutive element of the genre 'dialogue gospel', and it is a matter of conjecture whether these works intend to relate conversations with the *risen* Jesus. At most, the mention of the ascension in LibThom points in this direction; in Dial, on the other hand, a number of elements suggest rather that the conversations take place during the life of the earthly Jesus. It is, however, also possible that Dial ultimately aims at the kind of supra-temporal quality which is typical of EvThom.

The controversy about the correct genre should not prevent us from paying these two works the attention they deserve. LibThom gives us a further insight into the rich Syriac tradition about Thomas, which includes both EvThom and the apocryphal Acts of Thomas, while the title alone compels us to discuss Dial within the broader context of the dialogue gospels. These works, like a number of other writings, are perhaps best grouped together in a new category: 'non-localized dialogues'.

(a) The Book of Thomas (LibThom)

(1) Contextual information

The 'Book of Thomas' – to use the correct title of the work which we shall now discuss – is often called 'The Book of Thomas the *Contender* (or *Athlete*)' in the secondary literature. No title is found at the head of this work in the codex, but two titles are given in the *subscriptio:* 'The Book of Thomas. The Contender writing to the Perfect.' These are two syntactically independent units, which ought not to be fused into one single title, even if we admit the probability that the last hand to work on this text equated 'Thomas' and the 'Contender'.

This brings us to the question of the composition of LibThom, which in its present form is a dialogue between Jesus and Thomas. It is usually supposed that the *risen* Jesus speaks to Thomas, and that the dialogue takes place during an apparition; one indicator in favour of this hypothesis is Thomas' request to Jesus, 'Therefore I beg you to tell me what I ask *before your ascension*' (138,22f.). However, we are not told explicitly that Jesus 'appears', nor does the text end with his 'departure'. Besides this, the dialogue is surely rather odd – it has been correctly observed that in the dialogue section, Thomas and Jesus usually talk past one another, while the dialogue peters out completely in the final third of the text, which takes the form of a lengthy monologue on the part of Jesus, resembling a collection of aphorisms. At one point, we are told that Thomas says something that he could not really have said to Jesus; the same is true of one of the affirmations placed on the lips of Jesus.

Hans-Martin Schenke has proposed a plausible hypothesis about the genesis of LibThom, which starts from the two titles and seeks to make sense of a number of internal inconsistencies which can be observed in the text. First comes an older work to which the second title in the *subscriptio* belongs: 'The Contender writing to the Perfect'. This title is a typical epistolary *praescriptio,* and the 'Letter of the Contender' (as we may call it) was not a dialogue, but a letter which was subsequently reworked (with a varying measure of success) into a dialogue between Jesus and Thomas, borrowing, albeit inconsistently, the form of the dialogue gospels. An analogous case would be SJC, which reworked the older Letter of Eugnostos into a dialogue (see above). While we possess the underlying text of SJC, however, we can propose only a hypothetical reconstruction of the 'Letter of the Contender'. (For Schenke's proposal, cf. TU 138, pp. 198–202. Turner has suggested an alternative reconstruction: a dialogue was added to the first, longer main section of LibThom, and a homiletic collection of aphorisms was added to the second, shorter section.)

What is signified by the term 'contender' or 'athlete'? When we bear in mind the character of the underlying work – a Jewish sapiential text with a strong tendency to sexual asceticism – we see that the *athlete* is the *ascetic.* This word denotes more than mere renunciation: it means a continuous struggle, an unbroken endeavour and toil aimed at achieving perfection. In the Jewish tradition, the model 'athlete' in this sense was Jacob, primarily because of the nocturnal struggle related at Gen 32:23–32.

This helps us identify the provenance of LibThom. The choice of the apostle Thomas points to the east Syriac sphere, where the rest of the Thomas-literature originated. The Platonizing, Hellenistic Jewish orientation of the underlying sapiential text, which perhaps takes Jacob as a model, suggests rather a provenance in Alexandria. (In his commentary, Schenke quotes a great number of illuminating parallels in the works of the Jewish philosopher of religion Philo of Alexandria.)

When was LibThom composed? Let us begin by looking at the external transmission of this text. LibThom is the seventh and last work in the second Nag Hammadi codex (NHC II, pp. 138,1–145,19), which also contains EvThom. This unique textual witness to LibThom was written in the fourth century; this, of course, indicates only the date when the last copy was made. There are no papyrus fragments which would help us further. Since LibThom presupposes EvThom, to which it refers in its opening lines (see below), it must have been composed at a later date than EvThom itself – although this does not help us much, since the dating of EvThom is a matter of great debate. A cautious hypothesis dates the Greek original of the Coptic LibThom to the early third century (Turner); accordingly, the 'Letter of the Contender' must have been written in the second century. The presence at each stage of Jewish, Christian and gnostic traits must be evaluated on a case-by-case basis.

(2) The contents

– A new authoritative narrator

Apart from the *subscriptio* in two parts, which we have just discussed, the work also has an introduction, which is linked to the first part of the *subscriptio*, viz. 'The Book of Thomas' (138,1–4):

The secret words that the Saviour spoke to Judas Thomas which I, even I Mathaias, wrote down – I was walking, listening to them speak with one another.

These lines take up the fictitious situation indicated at the beginning of EvThom, where the 'living Jesus' reveals 'hidden words' to Thomas. In the Gospel of Thomas, it is the one addressed who writes down these words; here, another person is the author. The text calls him 'Mathaias', a name similar to Matthew or Matthias. At any rate, he too is one of the twelve apostles, and he is directly linked, as narrator, to the trans-formation of an underlying monologue into a dialogue: not only does he hear what 'the Saviour spoke to Judas Thomas', but he also hears them 'speak with one another'. Purely by chance, he overhears their dialogue and bears witness to it.

– The twin brother

Immediately after these opening words, 'the Saviour' begins to speak, addressing Thomas as 'brother' – indeed, as 'twin brother' (138,7–10):

Now since it has been said that you are my twin and true companion, examine yourself that you may understand who you are, in what way you exist, and how you will come to be.

We have already spoken, in our discussion of EvThom 1 (see above), of 'twin' as a translation of the Aramaic 'Thomas' and Greek 'Didymos'. The emphasis on the unique friendship between Jesus and Thomas may be meant to portray Thomas as the 'beloved disciple' from John's Gospel.

The summons to self-knowledge need not automatically be inter-preted in gnostic terms, since Jesus goes on to tell Thomas, 'And you will be called "the one who knows himself"' (138,15f.). These words recall the famous maxim, 'Know yourself!', which stood above the entrance to the temple of the oracular god Apollo at Delphi. This was adopted by the Socratic-Platonic tradition and became a commonplace, not only in the general culture of educated persons in classical antiquity, but also in the Hellenistic Jewish sapiential tradition within which the author of LibThom stands.

– The principal theme of the text

Thomas' first two questions concern the hidden truth. After reproaching his hearers (the plural is used, in keeping with the style of an exhortatory discourse) for their lack of understanding, the Saviour reveals a portion of the truth. The lower third of the manuscript pages is badly damaged, and the square brackets in the translation of the first lines in the following section show that extensive reconstructions of the text are necessary (138,39–139,9):

[All] bodies [of men and] beasts are begotten [irrational ...] ... since that body is bestial. So just as the body of the beasts perishes, so also will these formations (i.e., the human body) perish. Do they not derive from intercourse like that of the beasts?

This brings us to the true subject of the dialogue, viz. sexuality and procreation, which are seen as a prominent symptom of the imperfection, fragility and mortality of existence. The valuable part of the human person, his soul, must free itself from this dimension if it is to reach its own true home, which lies 'above' (in Middle Platonism, this was pictured in very concrete terms, between the earth and the moon and between the moon and the sun).

– The light of the sun

The next passage goes far beyond the normal measure of intellectual slowness and incomprehension to which a work like Mark's Gospel has accustomed us (139,12–16):

And Thomas answered, 'Therefore I say to you, Lord, that those who speak about things that are invisible and difficult to explain are like those who shoot their arrows at a target at night ...'

As Schenke writes, 'Thomas' "answer" at this point is unexpectedly appropriate and prudent. It has only one thing against it: it is completely impossible for Thomas to have said these words!' (TU 138, p. 87). This is because Thomas' intention is to teach (or even rebuke) Jesus by means of a parable, although 'In all the relevant literature, it is Jesus alone who has the right to formulate parables' (Schenke, *ibid.*). LibThom corrects this impression only with some difficulty at the end of Thomas' words, when he confesses, as the spokesman of his group, that the Lord is the light of the world: 'And you, *our* light, enlighten, Lord' (139,20). At any rate, the metaphor of light makes it possible to give a practical application of the parable of the archer in the night: if we wish to hit the goal, rather than merely shooting arrows pointlessly, we need light. This makes a smooth transition to the following passage, which concerns the sun (139,24–31):

The Saviour said, 'O blessed Thomas, of course this visible light shone on your behalf – not in order [that] you remain here, but rather that you come forth – and whenever all the elect abandon bestiality, then this light will withdraw up to its essence, and its essence will welcome it since it is a good servant.'

The 'visible light' is the earthly sun, which carries out its task as a 'good servant' of the highest God. This entails activity 'here' (i.e. shining on this earth), but the true home of the sun is in heavens which lie still higher up. The sun seeks to motivate the elect (more precisely, the souls of these persons) to set out on the journey to the higher realms. They must depart from 'here' and leave the bestial body, like the rays of the sun which depart from the sun in the morning and return to it in the evening. To understand these affirmations correctly, it is important to note that in Middle Platonism, e.g. in Plutarch of Chaironeia, the sun will be the final home of the highest part of the soul, which coalesces with the sun.

– The fire of the passions

The metaphor now changes from light to the fire which symbolises the 'fiery' form of the passions. The Saviour continues (139,33–42):

O bitterness of the fire that burns in the bodies of men and in their marrow, burning in them night and day, burning in the limbs of men and [making] their minds drunk and their souls deranged [and moving] them within males and females [by day and] night and moving them [with] a [movement that moves] secretly and visibly. For the males [move; they move upon the females] and the females upon [the males].

The text itself needs no explanation; what requires explanation is the obsession with eros which this text so clearly evidences. LibThom now attempts to demonstrate by means of a new parable how one can escape from eros: one must take 'refuge' with the genuine Wisdom, rather than with the false Wisdom (cf. Prov 9:1–18). This lends wings to the soul (an image older than Plato's *Phaedrus,* and certainly not confined to Platonism, as we see e.g., in Joseph von Eichendorff's poem, 'And my soul spread wide its wings . . .'), with which it can fly away and escape from lust. This flight leads the soul on to the path of perfection, for otherwise one will succumb to the fire of lust, which employs deceitful cunning to destroy the soul *via* the body (140,21–31):

For the fire will give them an illusion of truth, [and] will shine on them with a [perishable] beauty, and it will imprison them in a dark sweetness and captivate them with fragrant pleasure. And it will blind them with insatiable lust and burn their souls and become for them like a stake stuck in their heart which they can never dislodge. And like a bit in the mouth it leads them according to its own desire.

The 'stake' in the heart may remind us of the 'arrows' of eros (which likewise possesses wings, in its mythical form), and the 'bit' which leads a horse may remind us of the charioteer in Plato's model of the soul. The difference is that here it is not the reason which governs the two other powers of the soul, but unfettered lust which has taken over control.

– Seeking and finding

The frightened hearers need a pause for encouragement and consolation, and this is achieved by a beatitude inserted as a response of the Lord between two brief questions by Thomas (140,41–141,2):

[Blessed is] the wise man who [sought after the truth, and] when he found it, he rested upon it forever and was unafraid of those who wanted to disturb him.

Seeking, finding, rest as reward, safety from all those influences and forces that create confusion – these concepts bring us into familiar sapiential and later gnostic territory. In LibThom, this goal will be attained only in the promise with which the book closes (see below); before that, we encounter massive threats of punishment.

– The fire of punishment and torment

The metaphor of 'fire' proves universally applicable as a weapon: now it is transformed into an instrument of punishment for those whose souls are too closely bound to the flesh. It seems that a transmigration of the soul is envisaged in the case of former believers who have fallen away from their 'first love': 'On account of love for the faith they formerly possessed, they will be gathered back to that which is visible' (141,10f.). At the end, however, the visible world will perish completely in the fire (exactly like the conflagration which Stoics believed would destroy the world). A terrible fate awaits the unredeemed souls, who will no longer have a body (141,15–18):

Then shapeless (*morphē*) shades (*eidōlon*) will emerge and in the midst of tombs they will forever dwell upon the corpses in pain and corruption of soul.

Plato too speaks in the *Phaedo* of 'dark apparitions (*phantasmata*) of souls' wandering around beside the graves, 'shadowy images' (*eidôla*) which have been completely detached from matter (81D). In LibThom, these ghosts are the tormented souls themselves, who roam about near the graves and find no rest.

– Human beings and animals

When Thomas asks what they as teachers and preachers ought to say to blind human beings, the Saviour denies outright that such persons are human beings at all: he calls them 'beasts'. When human beings turn into animals, this has societal consequences (cf. Gal 5:15), as we read at 141,25–31:

The Saviour said, 'Truly, as for [those], do not esteem them as men, but regard them [as] beasts, for just as beasts devour one another, so also men of this sort devour one another. On the contrary, they are deprived of [the kingdom] since they love the sweetness of the fire and are servants of death and rush to the works of corruption ...'

The word-pair 'sweetness of the fire' brings us back to fire as a metaphor for lust. The mention of the 'kingdom' develops the blessing uttered earlier on the wise person who seeks truth and finds rest, illuminating it by means of a contrast. It was a commonplace of popular hellenistic philosophy that only the wise man is a true king, and rules as king. 'Naturally, one who himself becomes an animal – instead of living like a wise man, the king who rules over the animals – has forfeited his kingship' (Schenke, TU 138, p. 139).

– The penalty for mockers

Thomas speaks again, voicing his concern for all who will meet such a fate. The Saviour's reply is based on the principles that 'A man will reap what he sows' (cf. Gal 6:7f.) and 'A bad tree bears bad fruit' (cf. Mt 7:17–20), and Thomas must concede that judgment and punishment are necessary. The text allows him only one further question: he evaluates the situation correctly and expresses the fear that those who hear the demand for radical continence, which must now be preached, will react with mockery and contempt (142,19–26a):

Thomas replied, 'You have certainly persuaded us, Lord. We realize in our heart and it is obvious that this is so, and that your word is sufficient. But these words that you speak to us are ridiculous and contemptible to the world since they are misunderstood. So how can we go to preach them, since we are [not] esteemed in the world?'

The closing monologue by the Lord begins at 142,26b and is interrupted only by brief 'stage directions' such as: 'Then the Saviour continued, saying' or: 'Then Jesus continued and said'. His first observation is that those who do what Thomas fears – viz. turn away their faces or sneer – will be handed over to judgement and thrown into Tartarus, where they will be subject to an angel of the underworld named 'Tartarouchos'. Once again, fire is employed as a means of punishment (142,40–143,5):

[The Rulers who will] pursue you [will] deliver [them over to the] angel Tartarouchos [and he will take whips of] fire, pursuing them [with] fiery scourges that cast a shower of sparks into the face of the one who is pursued. If he flees westward, he finds the fire. If he turns southward, he finds it there as well. If he turns northward, the threat of seething fire meets him again.

It seems that there is an exit to the east, which could provide an escape-route, viz. a narrow bridge spanning the stream of fire, or a slit in the fiery wall. But these persons cannot reach this exit.

– Twelve cries of woe

There follows a series of twelve cries of woe, varying in length. Like the concluding beatitudes, these belong to the sapiential genre. We mention only a few examples here: the second woe is pronounced upon those 'who hope in the flesh and in the prison that will perish!' (143,11), employing the classical Platonic theme of the body (*sōma*) as prison or tomb (*sēma*) of the soul. The third, fourth and fifth woes employ the images of fire and the revolving wheel (143,15–19):

Woe to you for the fire that burns in you, for it is insatiable! Woe to you because of the wheel that turns in your minds! Woe to you because of the burning that is in you!

In Greek mythology, Ixion was punished for killing his father-in-law by being lashed to a fiery (!) wheel which turned perpetually. The ceaseless turning of the wheel is a metaphor for the wearying circular motion of the world and of time, which always brings back the same things (cf. the expression 'the wheel of birth' at Jas 3:6).

The sixth and eleventh cries of woe are expanded into little treatises which we cannot discuss in detail here. The beginning of the sixth woe is doubtless a reminiscence of Plato's parable of the cave: 'Woe to you, captives, for you are bound in caverns!' (143,21–23). The eighth woe tells us clearly why fire, smoke and darkness are repeatedly specified as instruments of punishment: 'Woe to you who love intimacy with womankind and polluted intercourse with it!' (144,8–10). The tenth cry of woe is the shortest: 'Woe to you because of the forces of the evil demons!' (144,12f.).

– Three beatitudes and the conclusion

Three beatitudes offer a contrast to the final cry of woe (145,1–7). They praise those to whom the discourse is addressed, (1) because they recognize and escape from the snares that are laid out to entrap them; (2) because they are 'reviled and not esteemed'; and (3) because they 'weep and are oppressed'. The text closes with the appeal: 'Watch and pray that you may not come to be in the flesh, but rather that you come forth from the bondage of the bitterness of this life' (145,8–10). The heavenly goal, seen on the horizon, is the place of rest and participation in kingly rule, as in EvThom (see ch. 7a, above) and the agraphon from EvHeb (see ch. 3a, nr. 1, above).

(3) Summary

LibThom is a timely reminder that we must be extremely cautious in using the label 'gnostic'. Scholars were too quick in applying the term to LibThom in the first period after its publication. There are indeed many points of contact with gnostic thinking here, and the demand for strict sexual continence was made in many gnostic circles, especially in eastern Syria. But LibThom contains none of the elements which are specific to gnosis (e.g. the myth of the fall of Sophia) and occur only in gnostic writings.

The Christian dimension of LibThom seems somewhat skin-deep. Formally speaking, it is limited to the mention of the name of one apostle (or two, if we include 'Mathaias', who writes the words down) and to the presence of Jesus as redeemer-figure; when we bear this in mind, the mention of his ascension seems even more isolated. Reasons internal to the text itself suggest why the author of LibThom made only a superficial attempt at employing the dialogue form when he reworked the older 'Letter of the Contender'. This does not detract in any way from the fact LibThom would have found a ready audience in Christian groups with encratite leanings (on this subject, see ch. 4a, above).

We encounter an extraordinary number of Platonic commonplaces in LibThom. These are, however, not the fruit of a direct and intensive study of Platonism, but have been mediated by the Jewish sapiential tradition. However, the world of LibThom is no longer the down-to-earth, practical wisdom of the Book of Proverbs, but the Platonizing, hellenistic variant of this wisdom. The slight tendency to a 'flight from the world' which we often notice in Philo of Alexandria has been radicalized in LibThom and concentrated almost exclusively on the sphere of sexuality. This makes it easy to understand how this exhortation, undergirded as it is by massive eschatological threats, could be prized as spiritual nourishment by monks in Syria and Egypt. This may indeed be the reason why LibThom survived at all.

Bibliography

J. D. Turner, in: NHL, 199–207; H. M. Schenke, in: NTApo I, 232–40; Idem, in: *Nag Hammadi Deutsch* I, 279–91; U. K. Plisch, *Verborgene Worte Jesu*, 123–33; H. M. Schenke, *Das Thomas-Buch (Nag-Hammadi-Codex II,7)* (TU 138), Berlin 1989; J. D. Turner, *The Book of Thomas the Contender from Nag Hammadi (CG II,7)* (SBL.DS 23), Missoula, Mont. 1975; C. Scholten, *Martyrium und Sophiamythos im Gnostizismus nach den Texten von Nag Hammadi* (JAC.E 14), Münster 1987, 133–49.

(b) The Dialogue of the Saviour (Dial)

(1) Contextual information

The 'Dialogue of the Saviour' is the fifth writing in the third Nag Hammadi codex (NHC III,5: pp. 120,1–147,23). The title is found both at the beginning and as a *subscriptio*. Unfortunately, the papyrus leaves in this codex are very heavily damaged towards the end, and sometimes almost half a page is missing. This makes it extremely difficult to study the contents of Dial.

It is, however, possible to discern a number of fundamental characteristics. The dialogue sections which have given the work its title predominate, but these are continually interrupted by textual units belonging to other genres, such as a creation myth, the narrative of a vision, and a list of the four elements with a 'natural-philosophical' (i.e. sapiential) orientation. This fact, along with the shift between 'Saviour' and 'Lord' as designations for Jesus, has been understood by scholars as indicating that Dial has been put together from four or five separate sources. It is at any rate certain that the work in its present form is the result of a complicated composition process. In our discussion, we make use of such observations only to the extent that they help to identify a basic structure in a writing which – thanks to its poor state of preservation – is particularly opaque.

The Coptic copy of Dial was written in the fourth century; we cannot date the Greek original more precisely than to the second half of the second century. Koester's thesis – that the work in its present form comes from the early second century and is based on a first-century writing which cannot be later than the Gospel of John – is untenable as it stands. The same applies to the affirmation (linked to this hypothesis) that Dial betrays no knowledge of New Testament literature. At least one passage is clearly dependent on Matthew's Gospel (see discussion of § 53, below); other echoes are not so certain.

Dial has also a number of points of contact with EvThom (Koester provides a synoptic list of parallels). This may be due to use of similar traditional material, but it may also indicate that Dial knew and used EvThom. The frequent variations on the themes of seeking, finding and rest sound like an exegetical meditation on EvThom 2 (and parallels).

The standard critical edition by Emmel introduces a subdivision of the text into paragraphs, and since this has been adopted by the sixth edition of NTApo, we too follow it here.

(2) The contents

– Introduction

The kinship between Dial and EvThom is obvious from the very first lines in § 1:

The Saviour said to his disciples, 'Already the time has come, brothers, that we should leave behind our labour and stand in the *rest;* for he who stands in the *rest* will *rest* forever … But when I came, I opened the way; I taught them the passage through which will pass the elect and the *solitary ones.*'

The appropriate reaction of the disciples is thanksgiving, and a suitable prayer is provided in § 2, introduced by a kind of liturgical rubric: 'when you give glory, do so in this way …'. Unfortunately, there is a lacuna in the text of § 3, which seems to describe the ascent of the soul past the tyrannical powers and terrible places, a journey which the disciples have still to take.

– Dialogue (beginning)

In § 4, 'Matthew' puts the first question. He will put six questions in all; 'Judas' (probably Judas Thomas) joins him in § 6, and puts sixteen questions. The third questioner is 'Mary' (according to the form of her name in Coptic, this is Mary Magdalene), who puts thirteen questions. Sometimes 'the disciples' speak as a group; only in § 1 do we find the 'twelve disciples'. Judas Thomas (as in EvThom) and Mary Magdalene (as in EvMar) take the first places in the group of disciples, together with Matthew (the 'writer' in LibThom and questioner in SJC). The lacunae in § 7 make it impossible to say who is described there as the 'consort' (*suzugos*) of whom. The threat at the end of § 14, '[there will] be the weeping and [the gnashing] of teeth at the end of [all] these things', refers to the dissolution of matter, which causes the powers of darkness to mourn.

– Creation myth (first part)

In § 15, Judas Thomas asks, 'Tell [us], Lord, before [the heaven and] the earth were, what was it that [existed]?' The Lord replies with a little excursus into creation history, beginning with Gen 1:2, 'It was darkness and water and a spirit that was upon a [water].' Only fragments of his words survive, e.g. 'you seek after', 'the power', 'spirit', 'the wickedness', 'the mind', 'fire [of the] spirit', and finally in § 18: '[If] a man [establishes his soul (?)] in the height, then [he will] be exalted.' This passage shows how difficult it is to reconstruct a plausible narrative sequence from such fragments.

– Dialogue (first continuation)

In a brief dialogue section which helps knit together the dialogue and the myth, the Saviour gives Matthew an important answer in § 20: 'And he who [knows, let him] *seek and find* and [rejoice].'

– Creation myth (second part)

A new question from Judas Thomas (§ 21) elicits a continuation of the creation narrative. The Saviour relates in § 22 that a wall of fire separates the earth from the water (cf. Gen 2:5). Once this separation is overcome, paradisiac conditions ensue (cf. Gen 2:10). The subject of the first verb may be 'the creative Word':

Then [he] cast forth from himself [springs] of milk, and springs [of] honey, and oil, and [wine], and good fruits, and a sweet taste, and good roots, [in order that] it might not be in want from generation [to] generation and from age [to] age.

In § 23, it seems that unidentifiable beings take some of the fire and throw it in all directions. This results in 'works'; it is not easy to make sense of the fragmentary text, but this may be an allusion to the creation of the lower, material world.

– Dialogue (second continuation)

From § 25 onwards, questions are posed by Mary, who greets her 'brothers' and is addressed by the Lord as 'sister', by Matthew and by Judas Thomas. Matthew is told: 'You cannot see' the longed-for place of life 'as long as you wear the flesh' (§ 28), and when he persists with his questioning, he is instructed about the necessity of correct self-knowledge: 'Every one [of you] who has known himself has seen it; everything that is fitting for him to do, [he does] it ...' (§ 30).

– 'Natural history' list

Most scholars hold that the instruction based on natural-historical considerations begins in § 35, but it is also arguable that it begins in § 31, when Judas Thomas asks about the forces that cause an earthquake and the Lord replies with a symbolic action (§§ 32–34), taking a stone in his hand and speaking about the powers which sustain heaven and earth. The point of his words is anthropological: those whom he addresses have a stable standpoint, because they come from above and return thither.

The list in § 35 is based on the doctrine of the four elements water, fire, air and earth, but replaces the earth with the human body. The line of argument runs as follows: one must understand the inner principle of these elements in order to be able to use them to one's own profit, instead of perishing along with them. Otherwise, there is no point in letting oneself be baptised with water. The problem of understanding is emphasized at the end of this passage:

He who will not understand how he came will not understand how he will go, and is not a [stranger] to this world which [will perish and] which will be humbled.

This means that it is absolutely necessary to be a foreigner in this world, if one is to succeed in returning to one's heavenly origin. In other words, the cosmological reflections in §§ 31–34 are all concerned with the same theme. Their common starting point is the dilemma generated by the existential disjuncture between knowledge on the one hand, and the continuing necessity of living under the conditions of this world on the other.

– Apocalyptic vision

In § 36, the Lord takes Judas Thomas, Matthew and Mary to the 'edge of heaven and earth'. Judas Thomas (who may have been the only one to receive this vision in the first version of the text) looks up into infinite heights and down into a profound abyss where a mighty fire burns. This abyss is the world itself. From it there emerges 'a word' which puts a question to Judas Thomas: 'Why have you [singular] come down?' It is 'the Son of Man' who replies in § 37; this is not Jesus, but an interpreting angel who sketches briefly one basic component of the gnostic worldview: the creation came into being because of a cosmic accident ('the greatness' designates the highest God):

A grain from a power was deficient and went down below to [the] pit of the earth. And the greatness remembered, and sent the word to it. He brought it up to [his presence], because the first word was abrogated.

All the disciples wonder at this message, believe in it and join in a prayer of thanksgiving.

– Dialogue (third continuation and conclusion)

The long closing section in the form of a dialogue, which amounts to about one third of the text, is connected thematically to the preceding vision by the distinction which the Saviour makes in §§ 42–44 between a 'great, eternal vision' and a 'vision which will cease'. The disciples and Mary must realize that they are still seeking: even a vision must be considered something transitory, not something eternal.

In § 49, Judas Thomas voices his concern about the 'archons' in the lower heavens who rule over human beings on earth. Jesus promises the sovereignty which follows 'seeking and finding' in EvHeb's variant on EvThom 2 (§ 50):

The Lord said, 'You will rule over them. But when you remove envy from you, then you will clothe yourselves with the light and enter into the *bridal chamber*.'

The 'bridal chamber', a concept in Valentinian gnosis (see the discussion of EvPhil, above), is introduced more or less *en passant* here. The next paragraphs elaborate the metaphor of 'clothing' and make an important affirmation about Mary (§§ 52f.):

The Lord said, '... But they gave the garments of life to the man, for he knows the way on which he will go. For indeed it is a burden to me as well to reach it.' Mary said, 'Thus about "The wickedness of each day," and "The labourer being worthy of his food," and "The disciple resembling his teacher".' This word she spoke as a woman who knew the All.

It is difficult even for Jesus to find the path which leads to life (a statement which he repeats in § 96); it seems that even he has not yet reached the state of perfection. This may be an indication that his passion still lies in the future; it seems unlikely that the ascent of his soul after the resurrection would be so arduous. Mary refers to a sequence of logia of Jesus (Mt 6:34, 10:10, and 10:24f.; cf. Jn 13:16), with an extreme concision which assumes that those addressed by Dial know the contents and contexts of these words. The logion about the right of missionaries to receive material help ('The labourer is worthy of his food') is presented in a form which exegetes see as a redactional recasting by the evangelist. It follows that Dial has employed the Gospel of Matthew. The choice of Matthew as one of the three prominent disciples fits this pattern: as Petersen has argued, Dial attempts in this way to claim a share of the authority which was enjoyed precisely by Matthew and his gospel in the universal church.

Why is Mary singled out in the narrative commentary for praise of her complete understanding? Probably, this is because she knows how to penetrate to the very depths of the words she cites from Matthew's Gospel – and this in turn means that she applies these words to the Master and the disciples. In § 61, the Lord himself praises her for this very reason: 'You reveal the greatness of the revealer' (or: 'the interpreter, the explainer', i.e. of Jesus himself).

A central theme of the entire work is cast in the form of a question by Matthew in § 65: 'Why do we not rest at once?' Jesus replies (§ 66): '(You will) when you lay down these burdens' – which include the body. The disciples have not yet reached the place of rest nor begun to rule; they must still seek, and will at most have the proleptic experience of finding something or other.

The human body is described, not only as a 'burden', but also as clothes that are laid aside. This is the teaching of §§ 84–85, which have a parallel in EvThom 34:

Judas said to Matthew (!), 'We wish to know with what kind [of] garments we will be clothed, when we come forth from the corruption of the [flesh].' The Lord said, 'The archons [and] the governors have garments that are given to them for a time, which do not abide. As for you, however, since you are sons of the truth, it is not with these temporary garments that you will clothe yourselves. Rather, I say to you that you will be blessed when you strip yourselves.'

Finally, let us look more closely at some connected paragraphs in the closing section, which ends with § 104. An unmistakable tension is introduced here into the picture of women presented by Dial – a tension that we have seen in other works:

(§ 89) The Lord said, 'When [the] Father established the world for himself, he left behind many things from the Mother of the All. Because of this he speaks and acts.' (§ 90) Judas said, 'You have said this [to] us from the mind of truth. When we pray, how should we pray?' (§ 91) The Lord said, 'Pray in the place where there is no woman.' (§ 92) Matthew said, 'He says to us, "Pray in the place where there is [no] woman," and "Destroy the works of femaleness," not because she is another [...], but so that they will cease [...].' (§ 93) Mary said, 'Will they never be destroyed?' (§ 94) The Lord said, '[...] is the one who knows that [the works] of [femaleness] will dissolve and ...'

At this point, the text once again becomes fragmentary, and we can only guess that Dial continues to struggle with the theme of 'destroying'. The contrast is very sharp: in the presence of Mary, who has appeared up to now to be fully integrated into the group of disciples, the Lord recommends that they pray only in places where no women are present. This would forbid women from worshipping together with men. Matthew is aware of the difficulty, and offers an interpretation of the Lord's words: what he really meant to say was: 'Destroy the works of femaleness!' And this in turn meant that women should cease bearing children.

This puts us on the track of the correct interpretation, and all we can do here is repeat what we said in our discussion of the Greek Gospel of the Egyptians, where we found almost exactly the same logion: 'I am come to undo the works of the female' (see ch. 4a, above). Another parallel in the same text helps: when Salome asks, 'How long will death have power?', the Lord replies: 'So long as you women bear children.' He uses similar words at Dial § 59: 'He who is from the woman dies.' The cycle of coming into being and passing out of existence, the sign of a world that has succumbed to death, can be brought to a halt only if we succeed in stopping human reproduction. Sexual continence is the most certain (though not the only) way to achieve this goal. Only thus can we overcome the gender differentiation which was the first result of a fatal separation. According to EvThom 114, a woman who collaborates in this project 'makes herself male' and becomes 'a living spirit'.

As we noted above, this final logion in EvThom does not offer a value-free description of the abolition of gender difference; it depends on a culturally-determined view of sexuality and birth as matters concerning the 'weaker' female sex. It is possible that Mary Magdalene is making a quiet protest against this view when she realistically observes in Dial that this hybrid goal will never wholly succeed, and that the 'works of femaleness' will never completely be destroyed. It appears, however, that she personally has paid the price for a harmonious integration into the group of disciples, where all the others are men. As Petersen puts it, 'Mary Magdalene is such a prominent female disciple precisely because she has transcended her inferior femaleness' (p. 298).

(3) Summary

As we have seen in the first section of this chapter, LibThom is not a gnostic work; but the closeness of Dial to the world of gnosis can scarcely be denied. Although it does not seek to narrate or interpret the gnostic myth, numerous individual components of this myth are present, and surface at various points in the text. It suffices to recall the idea that the creation is the result of an error, the liberation and ascent of the soul, and the view that the gender polarity of human beings is a form of separation which must be overcome. These nodal points draw other ideas (themselves neutral) into the sphere of gnosis: seeking and finding, rest and ruling, the isolation and foreignness of the individual, knowledge of oneself and of others, and the bridal chamber.

Dial is particularly interested in the question how it is possible under these intellectual presuppositions for believers to lead a meaningful life under the burdensome conditions of the present time. Its answer: now is the time for seeking, not for rest. A transient visionary experience may be bestowed, but not the perfect vision; as yet, the body is a burden which prevents us from putting on the heavenly garment of light. Nevertheless, one should not doubt that redemption has already taken place, and that salvation becomes a reality even here on earth. This gives the text as a whole a function of consolation and exhortation, as we see in one last example, from one of the many small dialogues. When Mary asks whether there is a place 'that is deprived of the truth', the Lord replies: 'The place where I [am] not' (§ 63). We may infer from this that true believers, those who possess knowledge, will be with their Lord at all times and places, whether they live or die (1 Thess 5:10).

Bibliography

S. Emmel *et al.*, in: NHL, 244–55; S. Petersen and H. G. Bethge, in: *Nag Hammadi Deutsch* I, 381–97; B. Blatz, in: NTApo I, 300–12; U. K. Plisch, *Verborgene Worte Jesu*, 143–52; S. Emmel (ed.), *Nag Hammadi Codex III,5: The Dialogue of the Saviour* (NHS 26), Leiden 1984; H. Koester, *Ancient Christian Gospels*, 173–87; S. Petersen, *'Zerstört die Werke der Weiblichkeit!'*, 79–90, 111–17; A. Marjanen, *The Woman Jesus Loved. Mary Magdalene in the Nag Hammadi Library and Related Documents* (NHMS 40), Leiden 1996, 75–93.

10

LEGENDS ABOUT THE DEATH OF MARY

(a) Typology and topology

The beginning and the end of a biography lend themselves to the composition of apocrypha, as we have seen in the case of the traditions about Jesus. Infancy and Easter gospels were the most popular genres, thanks to the desire to know more about what happened both before the canonical narratives begin and after they end.

We have already seen that the composition of apocrypha also encompassed the 'prehistory' of Mary, the mother of the Lord. The Protevangelium is basically a detailed narrative of Mary's infancy; only in the last third of the text does the author take up the narrative cycle concerning the conception and birth of Jesus.

The logic of this development would lead to a similar creation of stories about the end of Mary's life, but this was more problematic. It was not difficult to work backwards from Mt 1–2 and Lk 1–2, but the New Testament offered no points of departure for the end of Mary's life. Even as late as the fourth century, Epiphanius of Salamis discusses various possibilities: Mary may have died and been buried; or she may have died a victim of violence (cf. Lk 2:35), and now has her resting place among the martyrs; 'or she may still be alive [!], since God is not unable to do whatever he wills'. He concludes with the lapidary observation: 'No one knows how her life ended' (*Panarion* 78.23.8). On the other hand, the sixth-century *Decretum Gelasianum,* which we quoted in the Introduction, rejects a 'Book which is called The Home-going of the holy Mary'.

A great number of narratives about the end of Mary's life do in fact exist. In his thorough and authoritative study of this whole complex, Simon Claude Mimouni lists 62 texts in eight different languages (Greek, Latin, Syriac, Coptic, Arabic, Georgian, Armenian and Ethiopic) and divides them into typological and topological categories.

The starting point is provided by the terminology. If we restrict our attention to the Latin texts alone, we find a strange oscillation between *dormitio* ('falling asleep'), *transitus* ('passing') and *assumptio* ('being taken up'). Despite the confusion which prevails even in our sources on this point, these terms indicate distinct models, which can be set out in a temporal and substantial sequence:

1. At the beginning, we find the *dormitio* in the strict sense of the term: Mary 'falls asleep' and her soul is received by Christ and brought to heaven. Her body, which is preserved from corruption, is initially buried in a tomb, but after three days it is taken to

paradise (which is distinct from heaven) or to an unnamed place. For Mary as for others, soul and body will be united only at the resurrection of all the dead at the end of time.

2. In Coptic and Ethiopic texts, the period of separation of Mary's soul and body is extended to 206 days. After this, they are reunited. This can be considered a 'resurrection'.

3. *Assumptio* in the pure form is found in texts where Mary does not die, but is brought with soul and body into heaven. Here, the model of rapture (as in the cases of Enoch and Elijah) is applied to her.

4. The attempt is made to integrate elements of the older *dormitio* into this new conception, by insisting on Mary's physical death. For three days, her soul and body are separated, then they are reunited and Mary as an entire human being is brought into heaven.

All four models have their *Sitz-im-Leben* in the liturgy: these texts were destined for use on Marian feasts in the churches where these feasts were celebrated. This makes the topographical question interesting, since the house where Mary dies 'wanders' along with the feasts. Initially, this house was localized in Bethlehem (more precisely, following Protev 17, half-way between Jerusalem and Bethlehem at 'Kathisma', a name meaning 'place of rest'). Subsequently, the house was located in Jerusalem, but outside the walls at Gethsemane; later, it was placed within the old city walls, on Mount Zion, while Gethsemane remained the place where Mary was buried. There is no ancient tradition which identifies Ephesus as the place where Mary died and was buried. The choice of this city depends (apart from the visions of Anna Katharina Emmerich in the nineteenth century) on two factors: the apostle John, to whose care Mary was entrusted (Jn 19:27), lived there, and there was probably a tomb of Mary Magdalene there too – as so often, she was confused with Mary, the mother of Jesus.

How old are these various models? The first (and earliest) model is found in texts no earlier than the late fifth century; it is impossible to determine whether these may be based on traditions going back to the late fourth century. It is hard to accept the hypotheses of even earlier versions in the third or even second century, which a few scholars propose, since both the *dormitio* and the *assumptio* presuppose a systematic mariological and christological development which is not anterior to the councils of Ephesus (431) and Chalcedon (451).

Obviously, we cannot discuss here the dogma of the assumption of Mary into heaven with body and soul, promulgated by Pope Pius XII in 1950. We observe only that this definition does not explicitly state whether Mary passed through physical death (which would correspond most closely to the fourth model), or was taken up into heaven without dying (third model). This doctrinal development has rendered the older models (1 and 2) obsolete; this was already the case, when the newer models (3 and 4) emerged, and this is why the *Decretum Gelasianum* rejects as 'apocryphal' a 'Book which is called The Home-going of the holy Mary'.

The sheer quantity of the texts – Mimouni has 62, van Esbroeck 76 – makes it impossible to offer even a rough overview of the relevant material. Instead, we shall present one important witness in full.

(a) A textual example

The oldest Greek narrative of the end of Mary's life (according to Mimouni; Clayton disagrees) is entitled: 'The discourse of St John the Theologian about the falling-asleep of the holy Mother of God'; only a few Syriac texts are older. The author, whom we shall call Ps.-John, identifies himself as the apostle and evangelist John, thus claiming to be an especially reliable witness to the events he relates. This text was composed towards the end of the fifth century in Jerusalem, where it was used as a liturgical reading on 15 August. The Greek text is printed by Tischendorf, who divided it into 50 paragraphs. Since he erroneously used the number 15 twice, the translation below has a § 15 and a § 15a. The translation is taken from Elliott (pp. 701–8):

Visit to the sepulchre

1. When the all-holy glorious mother of God and ever-virgin Mary, according to her custom, went to the holy sepulchre of our Lord to burn incense, and bowed her holy knees, she besought Christ our God who was born of her to come and abide with her.

2. And when the Jews saw her resorting to the holy sepulchre they came to the chief priests saying, 'Mary goes every day to the sepulchre.' And the chief priests called the watchmen who were charged by them not to allow anybody to pray at the holy sepulchre, and enquired of them if it were so in truth. But the watch answered and said that they saw no such thing; for God did not allow them to see her venerable presence.

3. Now on one day, which was Friday, the holy Mary came as usual to the sepulchre, and as she prayed the heavens were opened and the archangel Gabriel came down to her and said, 'Hail, you who bore Christ our God; your prayer has passed through the heavens to him who was born of you and has been accepted, and henceforth according to your petition you shall leave the world and come to the heavenly places to your Son, to the true life that has no end.'

Prayer for the arrival of the apostles

4. And when she heard that from the holy archangel she returned to

Bethlehem the holy, having with her three virgins who ministered to her. And when she had rested a little she sat up and said to the virgins, 'Bring me a censer that I may pray.' And they brought it as it was commanded them.

5. And she prayed saying, 'My Lord Jesus Christ, who vouchsafed of your excellent goodness to be born of me, hear my voice and send to me your apostle John, that seeing him I may have the first fruits of joy; and send to me also the rest of your apostles, both those who have already come to dwell with you and those who are in this present world, in whatever land they may be, by your holy commandment, that I may behold them and bless your name that is greatly extolled, for I have confidence that you hear your handmaid in everything.'

John arrives

6. And as she prayed I, John, came to her, for the Holy Ghost caught me up by a cloud from Ephesus and set me in the place where the mother of my Lord lay. And I entered and gave glory to him who was born of her and said, 'Hail, mother of my Lord, who bore Christ our God: rejoice, for you depart out of this life with great glory.'

7. And the holy mother of God glorified God that I, John, came to her, remembering the word of the Lord which he spoke, 'Behold your mother, and behold your son.' And the three virgins came and worshipped.

8. And the holy mother of God said to me, 'Pray and put on incense.' And I prayed thus, 'O Lord Jesus Christ who do marvellous things, do now marvellous things before her who bore you, and let your mother depart out of this life, and let those who crucified you and did not believe in you be troubled.'

9. And after I had finished the prayer the holy Mary said to me, 'Bring me the censer.' And she cast in incense and said, 'Glory be to you, my God and my Lord, because in me are fulfilled all things that you promised me before you ascended into the heavens, that whenever I should depart out of this world you would come to me in glory, you and the multitude of your angels.'

10. And I, John, said to her, 'Our Lord and our God Jesus Christ comes, and you behold him as he promised you.' And the holy mother of God answered and said to me, 'The Jews have sworn that when my end comes they will burn my body.' And I answered and said to her, 'Your holy and precious body shall not see corruption' (Ps 16:10). And she answered and said to me, 'Bring a censer and put incense in it and pray.' And there came a voice from heaven and said the Amen.

11. And I, John, listened to that voice, and the Holy Ghost said to me, 'John, did you hear this voice which was uttered in heaven after

the ending of the prayer?' And I answered and said, 'Yes, I heard it.' And the Holy Ghost said to me, 'This voice which you heard signifies the coming of your brethren the apostles and of the holy powers, which is to be; for today they are coming here.'

The arrival of the other apostles

12. And thereupon I, John, fell to prayer. And the Holy Ghost said to the apostles, 'All of you mount up upon clouds from the ends of the world and gather at the same time at Bethlehem the holy because of the mother of our Lord Jesus Christ.' Peter came from Rome, Paul from Tiberia, Thomas out of the inmost Indies, James from Jerusalem.

13. Andrew the brother of Peter, and Philip, Luke, and Simon the Canaanite, and Thaddaeus, who had fallen asleep, were raised up by the Holy Ghost out of their sepulchres. The Holy Ghost said to them, 'Do not think that the resurrection has occurred. The reason why you have been raised from your graves is so that you may go to greet with an honour and wonderful sign the mother of your Lord and Saviour Jesus Christ. For the day of her departure has arrived, and she is going to abide in heaven.'

14. And Mark, who was still alive, came from Alexandria with the rest, as has been said, from their several countries.

15. But Peter, when he was lifted up by the cloud, stood between the heaven and the earth, for the Holy Ghost sustained him, and looked while the rest of the apostles also were caught up in the clouds to be present with Peter. And so all came together by the means of the Holy Ghost, as has been said.

15a. And we approached the mother of our Lord and God and worshipped her and said, 'Fear not, neither be grieved; the Lord God who was born of you shall bring you out of this world with glory.' And she, rejoicing in God her Saviour (cf. Lk 1:47), sat up in bed and said to the apostles, 'Now I believe that our teacher and our God comes from heaven, and I shall behold him, and so depart out of this life, just as I have seen you come to me. And I wish that you would tell me how you knew that I was departing and came to me, and from what lands and how far you have come hither, that you have been so quick to visit me; for neither has he who was born of me, our Lord Jesus Christ, hidden it from me. For I have believed now also that he is the Son of the Most High.'

The accounts of the apostles

16. And Peter answered and said to the apostles, 'Let each one certify to the mother of our Lord in what manner the Holy Ghost announced it to us and charged us.'

17. And I, John, answered and said, 'When I was entering the holy altar in Ephesus to minister, the Holy Ghost said to me, "The time of the departure of the mother of your Lord has come near; go to Bethlehem to greet her." And a cloud of light caught me up and set me at the door of the house where you lie.'

18. And Peter also answered, 'I was in Rome, and about dawn I heard a voice by the Holy Ghost saying to me, "The mother of your Lord must depart, for the time has come: go to Bethlehem to greet her", and lo, a cloud of light caught me up, and I beheld the rest of the apostles coming to me upon clouds, and a voice saying to me, "Go all of you to Bethlehem".'

19. Paul answered and said, 'I also was abiding in a city not very far off from Rome; and the place is called Tiberia. And I heard the Holy Ghost saying to me, "The mother of your Lord leaves this world to go to the heavenly places, and ends her course by departure: but go to Bethlehem to greet her." And lo, a cloud of light caught me up and set me where it set you also.'

20. Thomas also answered and said, 'I had passed through the land of the Indians, and my preaching was increased in strength by the grace of Christ, and the son of the king's sister, by name Labdanes, was about to be sealed by me in the palace, and suddenly the Holy Ghost said to me, "You also, Thomas, go to Bethlehem to greet the mother of your Lord, for she is departing to heaven." And a cloud of light caught me up and set me with you.'

21. And Mark also answered and said, 'As I was finishing the service of the third hour in the city of Alexandria, while I prayed, the Holy Ghost caught me up and brought me to you.'

22. And James also answered and said, 'While I was in Jerusalem the Holy Ghost admonished me, saying, "Be present in Bethlehem, for the mother of your Lord makes her departure." And lo, a cloud of light caught me up and brought me to you.'

23. And Matthew also answered and said, 'I glorified and do glorify God, for as I was in a ship and it was tossed, the sea boisterous with waves, suddenly a cloud of light overshadowed us, and overcame the billows of the tempest and made them calm, and it caught me up and brought me to you.'

24. Likewise those who had departed this life before told how they came. And Bartholomew said, 'I was preaching the word in the country of Thebes, and lo, the Holy Ghost said to me, "The mother of your Lord makes her departure: go therefore to greet her at Bethlehem." And lo, a cloud of light caught me up and brought me to you.'

25. All these things the apostles said to the holy mother of God, telling how and in what fashion they came. And she spread forth her hands to heaven and prayed, saying, 'I worship and praise and glorify your name, which is greatly extolled, O Lord, because you have regarded the lowliness of your handmaiden, and you who are

mighty have magnified me, and behold all generations shall call me blessed' (cf. Lk 1:48f.).

Premonitory signs and wonders

26. And after the prayer she said to the apostles, 'Cast on incense and pray.' And when they had prayed there came a thunder from heaven and a terrible sound as of chariots, and lo, a multitude of the host of angels and powers, and a voice as of the Son of Man (Dan 7:13) was heard, and the Seraphim came round about the house in which the holy and spotless mother of God, the virgin, lay; so that all who were in Bethlehem beheld the marvellous sights, and went to Jerusalem and declared all the wonderful things that had happened.

27. And it came to pass after that sound that the sun and the moon appeared about the house, and an assembly of the first-begotten saints came to the house where the mother of the Lord lay for her honour and glory. And I saw many signs come to pass, blind receiving sight, deaf hearing, lame walking, lepers cleansed, and those who were possessed of unclean spirits, healed (cf. Lk 7:21f.). And every one with sickness or disease came and touched the wall where she lay, and cried, 'Holy Mary, you who bore Christ our God, have mercy on us.' And immediately they were cured.

28. And many multitudes who were dwelling in Jerusalem out of every country because of a vow, when they heard the signs that were being done in Bethlehem by means of the Lord's mother, came to the place, seeking to be healed of various diseases; and they obtained health. And there was unspeakable joy on that day among the multitude of those who were healed, and among the onlookers, glorifying Christ our God and his mother. And all Jerusalem returned from Bethlehem, keeping a holy day with singing of psalms and spiritual songs.

Jewish opposition (first scene)

29. But the priests of the Jews, together with their people, were amazed at that which was done, and were taken with bitter envy, and with vain thoughts they gathered a council and decided (cf. Mk 15:1) to send men against the holy mother of God and the holy apostles who were there at Bethelem. And when the multitude of the Jews was on its way to Bethlehem, about a mile away, it came to pass that they saw a terrible vision, and their feet were bound; and they departed to their fellow-countrymen and declared the fearful vision to the chief priests.

30. But they, being yet more inflamed in the spirit, went to the governor, crying out and saying, 'The nation of the Jews is destroyed because of this woman; drive her away from Bethlehem

and from the province of Jerusalem.' But the governor was astonished at the wonders and said to them, 'I will not drive her out
from Bethlehem nor from any other place.' But the Jews continued
crying out and urged him by the authority of Tiberius Caesar that
he should lead the apostles out of Bethlehem, 'If you do not do it
we will report it to Caesar' (cf. Jn 20:12). And, being now
compelled, he sent a captain of a thousand against the apostles to
Bethlehem.

31. But the Holy Ghost said to the apostles and the mother of the
Lord, 'Behold, the governor has sent a captain of a thousand
against you, because the Jews have made a tumult. Go therefore
from Bethlehem, and fear not; for behold, I will bring you by a
cloud to Jerusalem; for the power of the Father and of the Son and
of the Holy Ghost is with you.'

32. The apostles therefore rose up straightaway and went out of the
house, bearing the bed of their lady the mother of God, and went
forward towards Jerusalem; and immediately, just as the Holy
Ghost said, they were lifted up by a cloud and were found at
Jerusalem in the house of their lady. And we stood up and for five
days we sang praise without ceasing.

33. But when the captain came to Bethlehem and did not find there
the mother of the Lord nor the apostles, he laid hold upon the
Bethlehemites, saying to them, 'Did you not come and tell
the governor and the priests all the signs and wonders that
happened, and how the apostles came out of every land? Where
then are they? Come to Jerusalem to the governor.' For the captain
did not know of the departure of the apostles and the mother of
the Lord to Jerusalem. So the captain took the Bethlehemites and
went to the governor, saying that he had found no man.

Jewish opposition (second scene)

34. Now after five days it was made known to the governor and to the
priests and to all in the city that the mother of the Lord was in her
own house in Jerusalem with the apostles, because of the signs and
wondrous things that came to pass there; and a multitude of men
and women were assembled, crying out, 'O holy virgin who bore
Christ our God, forget not the race of men.'

35. And because of this the people of the Jews, moved even more with
envy, together with the priests, took wood and fire and came,
desiring to burn the house where the mother of the Lord lay,
together with the apostles. But the governor stood observing the
sight afar off. And when the people of the Jews had come to
the door of the house, behold, suddenly a force of fire came from
within it by means of an angel and burnt a great multitude of the
Jews, and there was great fear throughout all the city and they
glorified God who was born of her.

36.   But when the governor saw what was done, he cried aloud before all the people saying, 'Of a truth he is the Son of God, who was born of the virgin whom you thought to drive out; for these signs are of a true God.' And there was a division among the Jews (cf. Jn 10:19), and many believed in the name of our Lord Jesus Christ because of the signs which came to pass.

The arrival of the Lord

37.   Now after all these wonders occurred because of Mary the mother of God and ever-virgin, the mother of the Lord, while we, the apostles, were with her in Jerusalem, the Holy Ghost said to us, 'You know that on the Lord's day the good tidings were told to the Virgin Mary by the archangel Gabriel, and on the Lord's day the Saviour was born in Bethlehem, and on the Lord's day the childen of Jerusalem went forth with palm-branches to meet him, saying, "Hosanna in the highest: blessed is he who comes in the name of the Lord" (cf. Mt 21:9). And on the Lord's day he rose from the dead, and on the Lord's day he shall come to judge the living and the dead, and on the Lord's day he shall come from heaven for the glory and honour of the departure of the holy and glorious virgin who bore him.'

38.   And upon the same Lord's day the mother of the Lord said to the apostles, 'Cast on incense, for Christ comes with a host of angels; and behold, Christ comes sitting upon the throne of the cherubim.' And as we all prayed there appeared innumerable multitudes of angels, and the Lord riding upon the Cherubim in great power. And lo, an appearance of light going before him and lighting upon the holy virgin because of the coming of her only-begotten son; and all the powers of the heavens fell down and worshipped him.

39.   And the Lord called to his mother and said, 'Mary.' And she answered and said, 'Behold, here am I, Lord' (cf. Lk 1:38; Jn 20:16). And the Lord said to her, 'Be not grieved, but let your heart rejoice and be glad; for you have found grace to behold the glory of my Father that was given me.' And the holy mother of God looked up and saw in him glory which the mouth of man cannot utter nor comprehend. And the Lord stayed by her, saying, 'Behold, henceforth shall your precious body be translated to paradise, and your holy soul shall be in the heavens in the treasuries of my Father in surpassing brightness, where there is continual peace and rejoicing of the holy angels.'

Mary's prayer of intercession

40.   And the mother of the Lord answered and said to him, 'Lay your right hand upon me, Lord, and bless me.' And the Lord spread out

his unstained right hand and blessed her; and she, holding his unstained right hand, kissed it, saying, 'I worship this right hand which made the heaven and the earth; and I beseech your name which is greatly extolled, O Christ, God, King of the ages, only-begotten of the Father, receive your handmaid, you who vouchsafed to be born of me, the lowly one, to save mankind by your unutterable dispensation. To every man who calls on or entreats or names the name of your handmaid grant your help.'

41.   And as she thus spoke, the apostles came near to her feet and worshipped the Lord and said, 'O mother of the Lord, leave to the world a blessing, for you depart out of it; for you blessed it and raised it up from destruction when you bore the light of the world' (Jn 8:12). And the mother of the Lord prayed, and thus she said in her prayer, 'O God, who of your great goodness sent your only-begotten Son to dwell in my lowly body, who vouchsafed to be born of me, the lowly one, have mercy upon the world and upon every soul who calls upon your name.'

42.   And again she prayed and said, 'O Lord, King of the heavens, son of the living God, accept every man who calls upon your name, that your birth may be glorified.' And again she prayed and said, 'O Lord Jesus Christ, who have all power in heaven and on earth, I entreat your holy name with this supplication: At every time and in every place where there is a memorial of my name, sanctify that place, and glorify those who glorify you through my name, accepting every offering and every supplication and every prayer.'

43.   And when she had thus prayed, the Lord said to his own mother, 'Let your heart be glad and rejoice; for every grace and every gift has been given you of my Father who is in heaven and of me and of the Holy Ghost. Every soul who calls upon your name shall not be put to shame, but shall find mercy and consolation and succour and confidence, both in this world and in that which is to come, before my Father who is in heaven.'

Mary departs

44.   And the Lord turned and said to Peter, 'The time has come to begin the song of praise.' And when Peter began the song of praise, all the powers of the heavens answered 'Alleluia.' And then the countenance of the mother of the Lord shone above the light. And she rose up and with her own hand blessed every one of the apostles, and all of them gave glory to God; and the Lord spread forth his unstained hands and received her holy and spotless soul.

45.   And at the going forth of her spotless soul the place was filled with sweet odour and light unspeakable, and lo, a voice from heaven was heard, saying, 'Blessed are you among women' (Lk 1:42; 11:27). And Peter ran, and I, John, and Paul, and Thomas, and embraced her precious feet to receive sanctification; and the twelve

apostles laid her honourable and holy body upon a bed and carried it out.

Jewish opposition (third scene)

46. And behold, as they carried her, a certain Hebrew named Jephonias, mighty of body, ran forth and attacked the bed as the apostles carried it, and lo, an angel of the Lord with invisible power struck his two hands from off his shoulders with a sword of fire and left them hanging in the air beside the bed.

47. And when this miracle came to pass, all the people of the Jews who beheld it cried out, 'Verily he is true God who was born of you, Mary, mother of God, ever-virgin.' And Jephonias himself, being commanded by Peter that the wonderful works of God might be shown, stood up behind the bed and cried, 'Holy Mary, who bore Christ who is God, have mercy on me.' And Peter turned and said to him, 'In the name of him who was born of her, your hands which were taken from you shall be joined back on.' And immediately at the word of Peter the hands that were hanging beside the bed of our lady went back and joined Jephonias; and he also believed and glorified Christ, the God, who was born of her.

Conclusion

48. And after this miracle the apostles carried the bed and laid her precious and holy body in Gethsemane in a new tomb. And lo, an odour of sweet savour came out of the holy sepulchre of our lady the mother of God; and until three days were past the voices of invisible angels were heard glorifying Christ our God that was born of her. And when the third day was fulfilled the voices were no more heard, and thereafter we all perceived that her spotless and precious body was translated into paradise.

49. Now after it was translated, lo, we beheld Elizabeth, the mother of the holy John the Baptist, and Anna the mother of our lady, and Abraham and Isaac and Jacob, and David singing 'Alleluia', and all the choirs of the saints worshipping the precious body of the mother of the Lord, and we saw a place of light, than which light nothing is brighter, and a great fragrance came from that place to which her precious and holy body was translated in paradise, and a melody of those who praised him who was born of her; and to virgins only is it given to hear that sweet melody wherewith no man can be sated.

50. We, therefore, the apostles, while we beheld the sudden translation of her holy body, glorified God who had shown to us his wonders at the departure of the mother of our Lord Jesus Christ, by the prayer and intercession of whom may we all be accounted worthy

to come into her protection and succour and guardianship, both in this world and in that which is to come; at all times and in all places glorifying her only-begotten Son, with the Father and the Holy Ghost, world without end. Amen.

The genuine beauty of this narrative emerges only when it is read independently of dogmatic – and *a fortiori* of historical – questions. The eyewitness-perspective of the narrator (the apostle John as 'I') is not maintained with complete consistency, but it is handled with a certain measure of skill. The narrative is brought to life by the extensive sections in direct speech; there are only a few comments by the narrator himself (e.g. in § 33).

Many details show that the text is thoroughly steeped in the liturgy: the incense which is continually scattered and lit, the light and the oil, the many prayers which expand almost into litanies, the mention of the altar (§ 17) and of the canonical hours of prayer (§ 21), as well as the hymnic style with its piling-up of stereotypical attributes (Ps.-John is so carried away by his zeal that he has the *Holy Spirit* call Mary 'the mother of *our* Lord Jesus Christ' in § 12). In the categories of rhetoric, this is an epideictic (i.e. solemn declamatory) discourse, with similarities to a funeral discourse (*epitaphios logos*).

The text sometimes reminds us of the biblical genre of farewell discourses (cf. Jn 13–17), but the main New Testament sources are the infancy narrative in Luke and the accounts of the passion. There is nothing surprising in the occurrence of parallels to Lk 1–2, such as the appearance of Gabriel and his words in § 2, or the many allusions to the Magnificat; but one would not necessarily expect to find elements from the narrative of Jesus' suffering. These owe their presence in the text to the desire to show traces of a 'passion' in Mary's death too – this is the reason for the verbal onslaughts by Jewish authorities, the Jewish crowd or an individual representative of Judaism such as Jephonias in §§ 46f. (in addition to the three sections to which we have given the title 'Jewish opposition', cf. also §§ 2, 8 and 10). The non-Jewish governor cuts a better figure, and even makes a profession of faith in § 36; he is not named, but he reminds the reader strongly of Pilate. Here too we note the tendency to shift responsibility of the suffering of the Lord and of his disciples on to the Jews; it is only a weak consolation that Jephonias and the whole people of Israel ultimately come to faith (§ 47).

The lists of apostles are strange, since they are incomplete and include not only Paul, but also the evangelists Luke (§ 13) and Mark (§ 14), perhaps a gesture of homage to the literary models on which the author draws. The portraits which the text draws of the individual apostles, by attributing fields of activity to them and placing self-descriptions on their lips, presuppose the existence of well-known legends about the apostles. This brings us close to the genre of apocryphal apostolic Acts.

Among the apostles, the prominent positions are occupied by Peter as spokesman and John as narrator; John owes his central role to his special closeness to Mary, and § 7 specifically quotes Jn 19:26f.

What of the mariology of the text? Ps.-John maintains in its pure form the oldest of the four models set out above: Mary dies, and her son immediately receives her soul (§ 44) and brings it into the heavenly 'treasuries' (§ 39), while her incorruptible body (cf. the quotation from Ps 16:10 in § 10) lies in the grave for three days and then arrives in paradise (§ 48), where the dwellers in paradise venerate it as a 'relic' (§ 49). The author, who lived in Jerusalem, offers a compromise on the topological question: Mary had two houses, one in Bethlehem (§ 4) and one in Jerusalem (§ 32). These are already becoming places of Marian pilgrimage, where streams of sick persons come in search of healing; it suffices to touch the outer wall (§§ 27f.). Mary's principal task is not, however, healing, but intercession. She is gradually taking on the role of *mediatrix* (cf. esp. §§ 40–42).

Can such a text (and all the related narratives) still be classified among the 'New Testament apocrypha' or 'ancient Christian apocrypha'? It is undeniable that Ps.-John's text is closely related to the genres of hagiography, homily and liturgy, and the boundaries are not water-tight; we find repeated overlappings. On the other hand, however, we may justifiably ask whether NTApo is right to exclude all the narratives of Mary's departure from this world from the corpus of apocryphal texts.

Bibliography

J. K. Elliott, *The Apocryphal New Testament*, 689–723; S. C. Mimouni, in: *Ecrits apocryphes chrétiens*, 163–88; C. von Tischendorf, *Apocalypses Apocryphae*, Leipzig 1866, reprint Hildesheim 1966, 95–136; M. Haibach-Reinisch, *Ein neuer 'Transitus Mariae' des Pseudo-Melito . . .* (BABVM 5), Rome 1962; F. Manns, *Le récit de la dormition de Marie (Vatican grec 1982): Contribution à l'étude des origines de l'exégèse chrétienne* (SBF.CM 33), Jerusalem 1989; S. C. Mimouni, *Dormition et Assomption de Marie. Histoire des traditions anciennes* (ThH 98), Paris 1995; M. van Esbroeck, *Aux origines de la Dormition de la Vierge* (Collected Studies Series CS 472), Aldershot 1995; M. Clayton, 'The *Transitus Mariae*: The Tradition and Its Origin', *Apocrypha* 10 (1999) 74–98; S. J. Shoemaker, *Ancient Traditions of the Virgin Mary's Dormition and Assumption* (Oxford Early Christian Studies) Oxford 2002 (this excellent book came to my notice too late to be discussed in more detail).

11

LOST GOSPELS

– The *Decretum Gelasianum*

In the Introduction, the *Decretum Gelasianum* was quoted as an example of the lists of canonical and non-canonical writings which were drawn up in the patristic period. It is worth looking back at this list to see which of the writings rejected as 'apocryphal' have been discussed in the course of this book, and which have not been mentioned. For the sake of simplicity, we assume that texts with identical titles always designate identical writings (although this is not always certain). We have discussed the following six texts:

Gospel under the name of the apostle Peter – Gospel of Peter (ch. 6a)
Gospel under the name of Thomas, which the Manichaeans use – Gospel of Thomas (ch. 7a)
Gospel under the name of Bartholomew (ch. 6c)
Book about the childhood of the Redeemer – Infancy Gospel of Thomas (ch. 5b)
Book about the birth of the Redeemer and about Mary or the midwife – Protevangelium (ch. 6a)
Book which is called the Home-going of the holy Mary (ch. 10)

We have not discussed six other gospel texts in the list:

Gospel under the name of Matthias
Gospel under the name of Barnabas
Gospel under the name of James the younger
Gospel under the name of Andrew
Gospels which Lucian has forged
Gospels which Hesychius has forged

These six titles cover very disparate material (cf. von Dobschütz). The 'forged gospels' of Lucian and Hesychius are editions of the canonical gospels in a textual form which had already provoked criticism on the part of Jerome. The Gospel of Andrew, otherwise unattested, may be the fruit of a misunderstanding: originally, *Acts* of Andrew were meant. The 'Gospel under the name of James the younger' can only be the Protevangelium of James, which accordingly is listed twice in the *Decretum*, under different names. In the case of the Gospel of Barnabas, von Dobschütz suspects a confusion with the well known *Letter* of Barnabas, which is included among the 'apostolic fathers'; we shall discuss a more recent writing with the same name later in this chapter.

– The Gospel of Matthias

This leaves us only with the 'Gospel under the name of Matthias', a work which deserves closer consideration because it is mentioned in other sources (e.g. Origen and Eusebius), though with no literal quotations. The one possible exception is Clement of Alexandria, who quotes several times from the 'Traditions of Matthias'. The first fragment is particularly interesting here, because it is found in the context of the logion (from EvHeb or EvThom 2) about seeking, being astonished and finding, to which it is thematically connected (*Stromateis* 2.45.4):

> The beginning (of the knowledge of the truth) is astonishment at things, as Plato says in the *Theaetetus* and *Matthias* exorts in the *Traditions*: 'Be astonished at that which is present.' Matthias thereby affirms that this is the first step towards knowledge of that which lies beyond the world.

Doubts have been expressed about the customary equation of the *Gospel* and the *Traditions* of Matthias (Lührmann, p. 140: 'it is difficult to see' the Traditions of Matthias 'as belonging to the sphere of gospel tradition'). It has also been suggested that a variant form of the pericope about the chief tax-collector Zacchaeus (Lk 19:10) found at *Stromateis* 4.35.2 comes from the Gospel of Matthias, but in this case it suffices to postulate use of Luke's Gospel.

We note in passing that this book – thanks above all to the writings discovered at Nag Hammadi, but also to the Jewish-Christian Gospels – has presented a much greater quantity of material than the *Decretum Gelasianum*.

– An expanded catalogue

Naturally, the *Decretum Gelasianum* is not the only source on which we can draw for knowledge of early Christian apocrypha. If we assemble all the relevant data, we can in fact draw up lengthy lists; the standard work mentions the following texts:

The Gospel of the Four Heavenly Realms (NTApo I, 356f.)
The Gospel of Perfection (NTApo I, 357f.)
The Gospel of Eve (NTApo I, 350–360)
The Gospel of the Twelve (NTApo I, 374–376)
The Memoria Apostolorum (NTApo I, 376–379)
The Gospel of the Seventy (NTApo I, 380f.)
The Gospel of Judas (NTApo I, 386f.)
The Gospel of Cerinthus (NTApo I, 397)
The Gospel of Basilides (NTApo I, 397–399)
The Gospel of Marcion (NTApo I, 399)
The Gospel of Appelles (NTApo I, 399f.)
The Gospel of Bardesanes (NTApo I, 400)
The Gospel of Mani (NTApo I, 401–413)

Such a catalogue may awaken high expectations, but closer examination dooms these to disappointment. This is not simply because of the poor state of transmission of these texts. In the case of the 'Gospel of Marcion', the name is misleading, because the work in question is the purged version of Luke's Gospel which Marcion used, and we may well wonder whether the other Gospels attributed to 'heresiarchs' ever existed in reality. In other cases, we know nothing beyond the mere name.

– The Gospel of Eve

Two of the titles in this list are surprising – what might a 'Gospel of Eve' be? How could his ancestress be presented as a witness to the life of Jesus? Our only source is Epiphanius, who quotes from it in the *Panarion* (26.3.1; the attribution of a second quotation, at 26.5.1, is disputed). This gospel was an account of a vision in which someone (perhaps Eve) saw a revealer on a high mountain. He comes in two forms and says:

I am you and you are I, and where you are there am I, and I am sown in all things; and from wherever you will, you gather me. But when you gather me, you gather yourself.

This has an unmistakably gnostic ring, and Epiphanius attributes this gospel to gnostics when he mentions its title at 26.2.6. We have no further textual witnesses, but we may presume that the 'good news' which Eve is charged to proclaim is connected with the gnostic *relecture* of the paradise narrative in Genesis, according to which the serpent helped Eve to discover the true gnosis by eating from the tree of knowledge in paradise. A comparable text would be the Apocryphon of John (see ch. 8d, above).

– The Gospel of Judas

Irenaeus writes about a group who clearly took a subversive delight in their choice of heroes, since they venerated Old Testament figures with a bad reputation – Cain, Esau, Korah and the men of Sodom. According to this group, Judas 'alone recognized the truth and perfected the mystery of betrayal; he separated all that is earthly from all that is heavenly' (*Adversus haereses* 1.31.1).

Judas here takes on a highly positive role in the drama of redemption. His betrayal was necessary, for only so could the process of salvation start, overcoming the massive resistance of the powers which ruled the world and did all they could to prevent salvation from being achieved. Judas was able to assume this role because he alone – as the archetypal gnostic – possessed the necessary knowledge.

It is clear that the Gospel of Judas (a title found also in Epiphanius, *Panarion* 37.1.5) related the individual details of this narrative. This text may have offered a consistent *relecture* of the passion accounts 'against the grain', but we have no literal quotations to confirm this hypothesis. We return to the subject of Judas in our next text, and in the final chapter of this book.

Bibliography

H. C. Puech and B. Blatz, in: NTApo I, 354,410; D. Lührmann, *Fragmente,* 140f. (on the Gospel of Matthias); J. K. Elliott, *Apocryphal New Testament,* 19–25; A. De Santos Otero, *Evangelios Apócrifos,* 58–75; E. von Dobschütz, *Das Decretum Gelasianum de libris recipiendis et non recipiendis* (TU 38,4), Leipzig 1912; H. J. Klauck, *Judas – ein Jünger des Herrn* (QD 111), Freiburg i.Br. 1987, 19–21 (on the Gospel of Judas).

The Gospel of Barnabas

In this book, we have with good reason restricted our discussion to the apocryphal writings from the earliest centuries of the church, but we must make an exception in the case of the Gospel of Barnabas. Let us begin by clearing up any possible risk of confusion: this text has nothing to do with the 'Gospel under the name of Barnabas' in the *Decretum Gelasianum.* It was written in Italian or Spanish in the period between the fourteenth and sixteenth centuries. (The Italian manuscript is in the Austrian National Library in Vienna; one of the two known Spanish manuscripts is now lost, but the second – an incomplete text – has turned up again in Sydney.)

What we know, or rather suspect, about the author sounds like the synopsis of a novel. According to the prologue to the Spanish version, a Franciscan named Fra Marino discovered the Gospel of Barnabas in the library of Pope Sixtus V (1585–1590) and stole it. As soon as he had read it, he converted to Islam and fled to Istanbul. This is likely to be an editorial fiction which conceals the true author, perhaps a Spanish Jew who had been forced to convert to Christianity, but later became a Muslim and sought to avenge himself on Christianity with this work. As far as I can see, however, there is no actual evidence to support this hypothesis. There exists a vague possibility – nothing stronger – that the unknown author had genuine access to ancient but otherwise unattested traditions.

The Gospel of Barnabas is a very lengthy work, with 222 chapters. Its title calls it *vero euangelio,* the only true gospel of the prophet Jesus, written down by his apostle Barnabas. The identification of Barnabas with Matthias, who took Judas Iscariot's place, led the Pseudo-Clementines too to number him among the apostles. In the prologue to the Italian version of the Gospel of Barnabas, 'Barnabas' at once attacks Paul as the source of the erroneous views held by many Christians: they call Jesus the Son of God (although he understood himself only as a prophet), they no longer practise circumcision, and they make no dietary distinctions, but eat all impure foods. In an author of the first centuries of the Common Era, we would call such a position 'Jewish-Christian'.

Otherwise, the Gospel of Barnabas is a detailed paraphrase of the tradition about Jesus which we find in the canonical gospels. We present here one relatively innocuous example, ch. 71, which combines Mk 2:1–12 with Lk 7:16. This passage is representative of the style of the work as a whole, and also shows something of its special christology (translation published by the Sabr Foundation, slightly modernized here):

Jesus having arrived in his own country, it was spread through all the region of Galilee how that Jesus the prophet was come to Nazareth. Whereupon with diligence sought they the sick and brought them to him, beseeching him that he would touch them with his hands. And so great was the multitude that a certain rich man, sick of the palsy, not being able to get himself carried through the door, had himself carried up to the roof of the house in which Jesus was, and having caused the roof to be uncovered, had himself let down by sheets in front of Jesus. Jesus stood for a moment in hesitation, and then he said: 'Fear not, brother, for your sins are forgiven you.'

Everyone was offended hearing this, and they said: 'And who is this who forgives sins?'

Then said Jesus: 'As God lives, I am not able to forgive sins, nor is any man, but God alone forgives. But as servant of God I can beseech him for the sins of others: and so I have besought him for this sick man, and I am sure that God has heard my prayer. Wherefore, that you may know the truth, I say to this sick man: "In the name of the God of our fathers, the God of Abraham and his sons, rise up healed!"' And when Jesus had said this the sick man rose up healed, and glorified God.

Then the common people besought Jesus that he would beseech God for the sick who stood outside. Whereupon Jesus went out to them, and, having lifted up his hands, said: 'Lord God of hosts, the living God, the true God, the holy God, that will never die; have mercy upon them!' Whereupon every one answered: 'Amen.' And this having been said, Jesus laid his hands upon the sick folk, and they all received their health.

Thereupon they magnified God, saying: 'God has visited us by his prophet, and a great prophet has God sent unto us.'

Two further points in the Gospel of Barnabas are particularly important. (1) Judas is changed by God into the form of Jesus, and dies instead of him (an ancient gnostic motif which may possibly be read out of an obscure passage in the Koran). (2) Jesus frequently prophesies the coming of Muhammad, whom he calls the last prophet and saviour. In ch. 44, Jesus says: 'O Muhammad, God be with you, and may he make me worthy to untie your shoelatchet, for obtaining this I shall be a great prophet and holy one of God.'

Is it correct to describe this work as a 'forgery'? That depends on how we evaluate the intention of the author and the use made of his work. It is possible that the author was well aware that he was writing at a later time, and merely wanted to achieve a synthesis that would present Islam as the fulfilment of Judaism and Christianity, clothing his work in language which he expected his readers to understand as fiction. On the other hand, the English translation is presented on the internet as an original first-century document which at long last lets us see through and correct Paul's distortion of the true gospel; and this assessment of the Gospel of Barnabas is surely representative of its reception in the Islamic world. We may therefore say that the way in which it is employed as a weapon against Christianity makes it a forgery.

The Gospel of Barnabas regularly portrays Paul as the villain who created the form of Christianity typical of the west, with its emphasis on Jesus' death on the cross and its theology of sacrifice. It is astonishing that (as far as I can see) the secondary literature on this work fails to cite the testimony of Friedrich Nietzsche, who thought the same – not that the appeal to Nietzsche would do anything to confirm this view.

Bibliography

S. M. Linges, *Das Barnabas-Evangelium. Wahres Evangelium Jesu, genannt Christus, eines neuen Propheten, von Gott der Welt gesandt gemäss dem Bericht des Barnabas, seines Apostels*, Bondorf 1994; J. E. Fletcher, 'The Spanish Gospel of Barnabas', NT 18 (1977) 314–20; B. Kollmann, *Joseph Barnabas. Leben und Wirkungsgeschichte* (SBS 175), Stuttgart 1998, 69–71.

Further bibliography on the present state of discussion of the Gospel of Barnabas: L. Cirillo and M. Frémaux, *Evangile de Barnabé. Recherche sur la composition et l'origine/Texte et Traduction*, Paris 1977 (598 pp., with facsimile and French translation; very 'friendly' towards Barnabas); D. Sox, *The Gospel of Barnabas*, London 1984; M. A. Yusseff, *The Dead Sea Scrolls, the Gospel of Barnabas and the New Testament*, Indianapolis, Ind. 1985 (from an Islamic perspective; but what is one to make of a book which finds the allegedly Essene Gospel of Barnabas mentioned in a *Decretum Gelasianum* [p. 101; *sic*]?); E. Guistolisi and G. Rizzardi, *Il vangelo di Barnaba: Un vangelo per i musulmani?*, Milan 1997 (805 pp., but mostly a presentation of the text); C. Schirrmacher, *Mit den Waffen des Gegners. Christlich-muslimische Kontroversen im 19. und 20. Jahrhundert* ... (IKU 162), Berlin 1992, 241–425 (presents a considerable amount of material, tends towards Christian apologetic); L. F. Bernabé Pons, *El texto morisco del Evangelio di San Bernabé* (Biblioteca *Chronica nova* de estudios históricos 57), Granada 1998 (reconstruction of the Spanish version); O. Leirvik, 'History as a Literary Weapon: The Gospel of Barnabas in Muslim-Christian Polemics', StTh 56 (2002) 123–34; http://www.islaminstitut.de/artikel/barnabas3.htm (Christian perspective); http://barnabas.net/ (Islamic perspective). The first edition, with an English translation by Laura and Lonsdale Ragg (Oxford 1907) is cited everywhere in the secondary literature; German libraries are unable to supply it, but I have found a copy of the original edition and a reprint (Karachi 1973) in the Regenstein Library of the University of Chicago.

AN ANTI-GOSPEL: THE TOLEDOTH YESHU

The final work which this book will present is certainly not one of the 'ancient *Christian* apocrypha', since it is a *Jewish* text which criticises Christianity, and it is a matter of dispute whether its origins can be dated to antiquity. If, however, our starting point is the genre 'apocryphal *gospels*', the Toledoth Yeshu is certainly important, since it has more in common with the gospel form than do many other texts which we have studied under this general heading. Christian readers will indubitably find the text offensive, since it is a contradictory antithesis of the Christian gospel; but the correct perspective for study is to understand it as a form of protest by the oppressed and persecuted – as Riccardo Di Segni puts it, this work is a 'gospel from the ghetto'.

(1) Contextual information

Toledoth Yeshu literally means something like 'origins' or 'beginnings' of Jesus (in the Old Testament, *toledoth* designates genealogies and family registers). The Jewish work which bears this title retells the history of Jesus from his birth to his death, while going beyond these boundary-points to narrate how Jesus came to be conceived and what happened to his disciples after his death: we might describe this as a gospel expanded by means of a Protevangelium and Acts of the Apostles. The contents of the Toledoth Yeshu caricature and satirise what the Christian gospels (both canonical and apocryphal) relate, turning everything on its head so that Jesus appears as the villain and Judas as the hero.

A fixed, as it were canonical or authorized version of the Toledoth Yeshu to which we could refer here, never existed; the transmission of the work was always fluid. We do not even possess reliable ancient manuscripts, but must work with manuscripts and printed sources from the modern period. This is connected with the samizdat nature of the work: for obvious reasons, Christians were not to be told of its existence, and it circulated only from hand to hand.

This makes the origins of the Toledoth Yeshu notoriously hard to date; proposals range from the first century (Voltaire) to the eleventh. It is certain that the first century is far too early; this owes more to the pleasure Voltaire took at seeing a critique of Christianity at such an early period than to sober historical observation. On the other hand, if we are to date it to the tenth century, the Toledoth Yeshu would no longer form part of the ancient traditions about Jesus, and would accordingly be out of place in this book.

The following consideration takes us a little further: Celsus, the second-century polemicist against Christianity, makes a number of acute points against the portrait of Jesus in the gospels. He appeals here to a (probably fictitious) Jew as his source. The Protevangelium is already a tacit response to these suspicions (see ch. 5a, above). The individual points from this catalogue – Jesus' illegitimate birth, his study of the magician's trade in Egypt, etc. – are found in the Toledoth Yeshu too, and it may be here that the roots of this work lie. This would mean that its earliest forms took shape in the period of the ancient church, perhaps in the fourth century.

In his book (title in English: *A Jewish 'Life of Jesus'*), Günter Schlichting has presented and translated a printed edition of the Toledoth Yeshu which bears the title *Tam ū-mū'ād,* a formula from rabbinical civil law which means 'completely attested'. According to Schlichting, this is 'probably the most distinctive elaboration of the Toledoth Yeshu, succeeding in uniting' the tone of mockery and sarcasm 'to a cultivated verbal form and serious theological reflection' (p. 6). Numerous doublets in the course of the narrative – Yeshu proposes at least twice to go to Egypt, he is taken captive twice or three times, etc. – are to be seen as literary-critical seams (Schlichting finds 23 such repetitions in the text) which point to a lengthy transmission-history of this version and make it seem an attempt to integrate as many details as possible. In view of the fluid state of the text, we need a fixed point of reference, and our discussion follows Schlichting's text and division into paragraphs.

(2) The contents

– Before the birth of Yeshu

One should not necessarily expect historical precision from a popular work. § 1 begins in the year 3708 after the creation of the world, i.e. 52 BCE (other versions of the Toledoth Yeshu have different datings, some more acceptable). Queen Helene of the Hasmonaean dynasty rules in Jerusalem; she is a composite of Salome, the widow of Alexander Jannaeus, and Helena, the mother of the emperor Constantine and main character in the tradition about the finding of the cross.

At this time, a young man named Joseph Panderi (cf. 'Panthera' in Celsus) falls in love with the virgin Miriam. She, however, refuses his advances, especially since she is already engaged to the pious Yohanan. When Joseph's jealousy makes him sick to the point of death, his family advise him to use ruthless means to achieve his sinful goal. He follows their advice, and starts on his devious course, winning Yohanan's trust – though Miriam strongly disapproves of this, when she sees it – and making him drunk one night. He is given shelter in Miriam's house, since a storm is just beginning; Miriam thinks he is her bridegroom. Although she draws attention to her menstruation, which according to the law makes her impure, sexual intercourse takes place and Miriam becomes pregnant.

Next day, when Miriam reproaches Yohanan for his conduct, the conversation gradually reveals the truth to her. Nevertheless, she continues to tell others that Yohanan had slept with her. He hastens to his teacher, rabbi Simeon ben Shetah, who advises him to keep watch on Miriam's house in order to seize the seducer. In the ensuing period, however, Joseph prudently keeps his distance. When Miriam's pregnancy becomes visible, Yohanan flees to Babylon in order to study the law. Upon this, Miriam not only sleeps with Joseph – she becomes a prostitute.

– The child is born and receives his name

Nine months later, Miriam gives birth to her son in Bethlehem and 'spread a rumour to the effect that she had given birth to a son without intercourse with a man. But only naïve persons will believe her' (§ 56).

An unfriendly interpretation of the child's name is offered: 'But the name Yeshu means: "May his name be blotted out, and his memory too!"' (§ 58). The three letters of which the name Jesus in Hebrew consists, *yod, sîn* and *wāw*, function here as an acrostic, forming the initial letters of the three words which make up this sentence.

– Jesus' deeds as a child

Miriam brings the child to the schoolhouse of Rabbi Jehoshua (in Greek: Jesus) ben Perahia. After only a few days, Yeshu excels all the other pupils in hard work and learning, but he also dares to act as teacher when the master is absent, and to expound the law. For this reason, he falls into disfavour for a time, but he always succeeds in regaining the master's approval through diligent studying. Nevertheless, he remains a problem child. On the sabbath, he throws a ball further than four cubits (something that is forbidden), and he refuses to greet older learned men with respect. Worst of all: while his teacher is praying, he cries out: 'May it be acceptable that they make me God!' (§ 74).

Up to now, Miriam had maintained the fiction that Yeshu was the son of Yohanan; even the child himself did not know the truth. However, the Sanhedrin, the supreme court of justice whose members include Rabbi Jehoshua and the learned men whom Yeshu had refused to greet, examine the negative evidence against him and conclude from his conduct that he must be 'a bastard and the son of a menstruating woman' (§ 82). Miriam is forced to make a confession, and the full truth comes to light, both publicly before the Sanhedrin and then at home, where Jesus forcibly drags it out of her. After this, Yeshu flees to Alexandria in Egypt, where he 'employs sorcery to place one layer of bricks upon another' (§ 101). According to Schlichting, this episode 'has not yet been explained satisfactorily' (p. 197). Let us mention one possibility: it is meant as an aetiological explanation of how the Egyptian pyramids were built.

– The secret name of God

After his secret return from Egypt, Yeshu enters the inner room of the temple in Jerusalem, where a mysterious stone called 'Shetijah' lies (§ 104):

The name of God was cut into this stone. The one who learned this name and knew its mystery, who knew how to write the name in the correct order on a suitable parchment and bore the name on his breast, had the ability to overthrow the existing order, to raise up the dead and to do whatever his heart desired.

The learned men in Israel had indeed devised protective measures to prevent anyone from learning the secret name of God in an improper manner, but Yeshu succeeds in circumventing these, so that he acquires possession of the name. Now he can perform signs and wonders, seducing many people in Israel and gathering them around his own person. Above all, it is now that he makes a claim which runs directly counter to his real social origins (§ 108):

How corrupt is the wisdom of the learned men who told me I was a bastard and the son of a menstruating women, that my soul would not find redemption, and that the name of my father was Joseph Panderi … God said to me, 'You are my son' (Ps 2:7). My mother gave birth to me without intercourse with a man, and it was about me that the prophet predicted: 'Behold, a virgin is pregnant and bears a son' (Is 7:14). Thus did king David prophesy about me: 'The Lord said to me: You are my son, today I have begotten you' (Ps 2:7).

The christological reception of these quotations from the Old Testament is subverted by the simple device of putting them on the lips of an unreliable witness. After further wonders – the healing of a lame man and the cleansing of a leper – Jesus' affirmations about himself bear fruit (§ 112):

Then all who despised the law and had gathered around him began with one voice to cry out to him: 'You are the Son of God!' And they fell on their faces, knelt down and worshipped him.

The dispute about who possesses Scripture and who expounds it correctly is continued in the presence of queen Helene. The learned men accuse Yeshu of sorcery and demand his death. Yeshu refuses to accept the truth (§ 117):

But the fool repeated his folly. He became impudent and said: 'It was about me that Isaiah prophesied, "A shoot shall come forth from the stump of Jesse, and a branch shall grow out of his roots" (Is 11:1), while king David said about me: "Blessed is the man who does not walk in the counsel of sinners" ' (Ps 1:1).

The learned men counter with a quotation from Deut 18:20 which is prefixed to the book as a whole and is repeated at its close: 'But the prophet who presumes to speak a word in my name which I have not commanded him to speak, or who speaks in the name of other gods, that same prophet shall die' (§ 119). However, when Yeshu raises the dead, the queen takes his side and dismisses the learned men from her presence.

– Other miracles

An outright civil war threatens in Israel, and the opposing parties are already confronting one another with drawn swords, when Yeshu makes a suggestion: he will confirm by a series of miracles 'that I am the one whom my Father in heaven has sent' (§ 136). He forms birds of clay and gives them life, so that they fly away (cf. IGThom 2). He crosses the lake on a heavy millstone, as if it were a raft of light wood (cf. Mk 6:48–51).

These actions make a deep impression on the queen, which the learned men now attempt to correct with the help of Deut 13:2–6: it is precisely the false prophet who is able to perform signs and wonders. In the presence of the queen, Yeshu attacks their two principal arguments, viz. the passages from Deut 18:20 and 13:2–6, by applying to himself an adjacent verse, Deut 18:15: 'The Lord your God will raise up for you a prophet like me from among you, from your brethren – him shall you heed', and Jer 1:5, 'Before I formed you in the womb I knew you ...'

– The antagonist

The learned men recognize that they need weapons of a different calibre, and choose one of them, a righteous man named Rabbi Yehuda 'ish Bartōtā (a name based on 'Judas Iscariot'), and allow him too to learn the secret name of God.

Yeshu, embittered at the stubbornness of the learned men, announces: 'Before your very eyes, I shall ascend to my Father in heaven' (§ 157), and he launches forth into a successful flight. Yehuda flies after him, and they fight in the air. The struggle is decided only when Yehuda spills his sperm on to Yeshu: this at once renders him impure, and deprives him of his miraculous power, so that he falls to earth. He has lost the power to work miracles. The learned men mock him before queen Helene (§ 164; this text is based on Mk 14:65, and echoes of the passion narrative begin at this point in the Toledoth Yeshu). The queen hands him over to them for execution.

– Delaying factors

A number of factors delay the end. Yeshu at first collapses in utter despair in the prison, but he escapes twice. After his first liberation, he orders his followers to dress alike in hooded garments which cover them from head to foot and make them unrecognizable. In this disguise, the whole group enter the temple for the slaughter of the passover lambs, and the authorities are helpless, since they cannot discover which of these hooded men is Yeshu. Gaissa, one of his followers who has begun to doubt Yeshu, betrays him to the watchmen and identifies him by bowing his head before him in homage. During the ensuing trial, Yeshu once again strikes a pose (§ 195):

Then he began to speak in a loud voice, so that all the renegades might hear what he said: 'I shall rejoice with exultation and be glad, because I shall find a grave. My power will be even greater then than it is now, for my divinity and my kingdom will be manifest in all the world. And this will be the sign for you of these things: three days after my burial, you will all come to my grave, but you will not find me, since I shall ascend to heaven and take my place at the right hand of my Father.'

Once again, his followers succeed in freeing him, and they flee with him out of the city. Yeshu immerses himself in the Jordan, thereby ending his impurity and regaining his magical powers. He makes a millstone which was large enough only for three persons capable of transporting the entire crowd of his followers – many hundreds of persons – across the water. He whispers a magical spell, and the fish assemble, spring out of the water and provide food for the crowd (cf. Jn 21:1–14). He also makes other food and drink and fine clothing materialize, so that his disciples have as much as they desire (motif of 'the land of plenty').

– Yeshu is captured and executed

In this emergency, Rabbi Yehuda is forced to intervene once more. He makes himself a linen garment like those worn by Yeshu's followers, and spends a number of days undetected in their company, until he discovers a little tag on Yeshu's garment which identifies him. The learned men write two friendly letters to Yeshu, in which they admit that he has got the better of them and invite him to come to Jerusalem; he accepts this invitation. It is at this point that there occurs what Christian tradition calls 'the betrayal by Judas' (§§ 229f.):

When all the members of that evil crowd arrived with Yeshu at the foot of the mountain, Yehuda flung his arms around his neck and cried with a loud voice: 'This is the Messiah. Let us worship him, and let us be afraid in his presence! He is our father and our king.' Then he embraced Yeshu and kissed him. All the learned men of Israel saw this and heard Yehuda's cry that *this* man was Yeshu. Then those who lay in ambush behind the mountain rose up and fell on him. In their terrible anger, they beat him vigorously – displaying the cruelty they felt towards a god like Yeshu.

Yeshu is put on trial before the queen, who ultimately turns away from him, and the learned men send out a herald who cries daily for forty days: 'Yeshu the Nazarene will be led out to be stoned, since he has engaged in sorcery and seduced Israel into falling away from God. If anyone knows anything that can be said in his favour, let him come and present his evidence' (§ 245). No witness comes forward to exculpate Yeshu, and he is stoned to death.

After this, his corpse is to be hanged on the wood of a tree, in keeping

with the regulation at Deut 21:21–23; but as if he had had a premo-
nition of this while still alive, Yeshu had adjured all the trees by the
name of God 'that they were not to accept him for hanging' (§ 250).
Rabbi Yehuda brings a huge cabbage stalk, thick and strong as a tree.
Since Yeshu had overlooked this possibility, the hanging succeeds, and
he is buried at sunset (cf. Deut 21:23, 'His body shall not remain all
night upon the tree').

– The empty tomb

Rabbi Yehuda remembers Yeshu's prediction that he would come forth
from his grave after three days and ascend to heaven. In order to prevent
this, he steals the body before the three days have passed (cf. Mt
28:13–15). He manages to get hold of the body without drawing
attention to himself, and conceals it in his own garden in a pit beneath
the water-canal. He tells no one what he has done (not even his wife and
his children), and goes on a journey to the surrounding towns.

The empty tomb is discovered in the city. The followers of Jesus
rejoice and see this as the fulfilment of his prophecy. The queen
demands that the learned men produce the corpse of Jesus within seven
days, or else they must all die. After a slight delay, Rabbi Yehuda hears
of this, and he rejoices (§ 269: 'For this is a day of good news') and
explains the preventive measures he had taken. The learned men fetch
the corpse from its hiding place, tie it by its hair to the tail of a horse,
and drag it through the city to the house of the queen. This has consequences, not only for the corpse itself, but also for the appearance of
Jesus' disciples in later generations, as we see in the sarcastic aetiology
at § 276:

After the corpse had been dragged by the horse, nothing remained of the hair on its
head – it was completely bald. This is why the priests of Yeshu up to the present day
cut their hair and have bald heads.

Finally, the queen concedes that the learned men are right, and orders
the execution of Yeshu's followers. She justifies this by a quotation from
scripture: 'Purge the evil from the midst of you' (Deut 13:5, quoted at §
282).

– Preview of church history

One might think that the bloody history would end here, but the
Toledoth Yeshu also relates in a kind of 'Acts of the Apostles' what the
twelve surviving disciples of Yeshu, who now call themselves 'apostles'
(§ 287), go on to do.

The Christians grow in strength continually, and sow division among
the people of Israel. The learned men entrust a commission to the
Roman rabbi Yohanan (in other versions of the Toledoth, Elijahu), who
combines traits of John the Baptist (above all because of the bath of

immersion which he takes in § 296) – the 'forerunner' is now an 'imitator' – with traits of John the apostle and evangelist. Yohanan is to join the Christians and 'lead them completely out of the custom of the faith of Israel' (§ 292). Thanks to Yohanan, the Christians reject Torah completely, replace the celebration of the sabbath with the first day of the week, and avoid entering the Jewish houses of prayer and study.

Paul, Nestorius and Simon Cephas also appear in the text. Paul and Peter, just like Yohanan, are fifth columnists for the Jews among the Christians, who perceive nothing, but even make Peter their head and build him a tower (i.e. St Peter's in Rome, built by Constantine) where he can study the law in peace and lead a kosher life. Paul and Peter put the coping stone on this process of separation, which the Jewish party sees as desirable and necessary.

It is surprising to see a fifth-century figure in the same context. The Toledoth Yeshu views Nestorius from the perspective of his opponents in the worldwide church: allegedly, he wanted to reintroduce Jewish rites and denied the divinity of Christ. At § 336, Nestorius says:

And how can you believe that Yeshu is God? How can our understanding tolerate the proposition that God is born of a woman and must die like human beings and animals, whereas he himself said that he was only a prophet!?

This does not lead the Toledoth Yeshu to formulate a positive verdict on Nestorius. On the contrary, his actions threaten to reverse the separation which has been established at such high cost, and this is why he is not mentioned in the concluding paragraph (§ 366), where Yehuda, Yohanan, Paul and Peter are praised as saviours of Israel and a blessing is invoked on their memory. The mention of Nestorius may however say something about the history of the composition of the Toledoth Yeshu; this would be another indicator of a date in the period of the early church, in addition to the points of contact with Celsus' polemic which we have noted above (Krauss dates the Toledoth to the fifth century: p. 246).

(3) Evaluation

It may seem an advantage to retain the name 'Yeshu' in our description of the Toledoth, rather than 'Jesus'. The literary effect of distance which this achieves may not actually make the scandal entailed by this portrait of Jesus more bearable for the Christian reader, but perhaps it makes it easier to go on reading the text. Nevertheless, this literary distance is ultimately deceptive, since the name 'Jesus', which we use as a matter of course, is only the Greek translation of his name, found in the Greek New Testament. We may be certain that his contemporaries did not employ this form of his name when they addressed Jesus; they would have called him 'Joshua' (or something similar). The Toledoth does not allow us to forget that Jesus himself was a Jew – indeed, a highly controversial Jew – and that this is how his people still see him.

We may not like the way in which the Jewish writer employs the person of Jesus to engage in debate with Christianity; and other versions of the Toledoth Yeshu, which are much cruder, would provoke even stronger disagreement. The delight in scoring points off one's opponents and in turning their own weapons against them keeps on surfacing in the Toledoth, which portrays the Christians as so stupid that they do not recognise the presence of Jewish secret agents in their own ranks. Sometimes folkloristic motifs take on a life of their own, thanks to the pleasure the author takes in telling his story.

Despite all this, we should not forget (as we said above) that the voice which speaks here is the voice of the persecuted. The social, religious and political pressure exercised by the Christian majority provoked these reactions in the oppressed minority, who mock what their opponents hold sacred.

Nor should we forget the serious theological and hermeneutical questions in the background. Let us mention only two problematic areas:

First, it is not at all easy to explain how a gradual separation between Judaism and Christianity took place in the first and second centuries (here, we should recall the Jewish Christianity which we encountered in ch. 3 of this book). For a long time, this was not felt by Christians to be problematic at all; but the Holocaust in the twentieth century led the Christian churches to reflect anew on their Jewish roots. The Toledoth Yeshu informs us that the Jewish side experienced this separation as the fulfilment of their own wishes, and that they were sceptical about movements 'back to the roots'. Does this mean that we suddenly discover ourselves to be unwanted guests?

Secondly, Israel's Bible is also the Bible of Christians. However, that is as far as the common ground goes: how the Bible is to be understood is a matter of dispute, even in the Toledoth Yeshu, where one scriptural text is set against another on the narrative level, Deut 18:15 against Deut 18:20. One subtext of the Toledoth is a commentary from the Jewish perspective on the way in which Christians interpret Scripture in the light of Jesus. Christian exegetes too have learned by now that they must respect the Scripture of the first covenant as something valuable in its own right and as the foundations of Jewish faith and life up to the present day. This does not, however, allow us to say that all the problems of methodology have been cleared up.

It may seem something of a detour to study the Toledoth Yeshu, but every apocryphal writing represents something of a detour. And sometimes one learns more if one does not keep to the main road, but looks on at the flow of traffic from the sidelines.

Bibliography

S. Krauss, *Das Leben Jesu nach jüdischen Quellen*, Berlin 1902, reprint Hildesheim 1977, 2nd edn. 1994; G. Schlichting, *Ein jüdisches Leben*

Jesu. Die verschollene Toledot-Jeschu-Fassung Tam ū–mū'ād (WUNT 24), Tübingen 1982; R. Di Segni, *Il Vangelo del Ghetto. Le 'storie di Gesù': leggende e documenti della tradizione medievale ebraica* (Magia e religioni 8), Rome 1985; H. J. Klauck, *Judas – ein Jünger des Herrn* (QD 111), Freiburg i.Br. 1987, 21–23; E. Bammel, *Judaica et Paulina. Kleine Schriften*, II (WUNT 91), Tübingen 1997, 3–63.

CONCLUSION

The Introduction to this book began with the question: what are 'apocryphal' gospels? To answer this, we must first ascertain what a 'gospel' is, and this problem – despite the matter-of-course manner in which we tend to use this concept – is scarcely less thorny. Martin Luther eloquently evoked the linguistic usage of the early Christians when he observed that it is incorrect 'to count four evangelists and four gospels', since there is in fact only one single gospel. He defined the contents of this gospel as follows in the prologue to his exposition of the First Letter of Peter (Weimarer edn., 12 [1891] 259):

> 'Gospel' means quite simply a sermon which cries out in a loud voice about the grace and mercy of God, merited and won by the Lord Christ with his death. The gospel is not what we find in books, encompassed in letters, but rather an oral sermon and a living word, and a voice which resounds in all the world and is shouted out in public, in such a way that it is heard everywhere.

The development from the oral preaching, with the gospel as its contents, to a literary genre with the word 'gospel' in its title, was not by any means smooth, and one must be on one's guard against the assumption that the gospel texts simply suppressed the kerygmatic concept of 'gospel' (i.e. the gospel as oral proclamation), since these remained inter-related. The first verse of Mark's Gospel marks an important stage in this process: 'Beginning of the gospel of Jesus Christ' (Mk 1:1). The message of God's kingdom which Jesus himself had proclaimed, and the good news about what God has done in and by means of Jesus of Nazareth, are transposed by Mark into a narrative which begins with the appearance of John the Baptist, relates what Jesus said and did, tells the story of his suffering and death and ends with the announcement of his resurrection. This created the fundamental type of document which even today goes by the name of 'gospel'.

To speak of a fundamental type which became an established genre does not mean that this was the only way to give the one gospel a written form. The materials which were incorporated into Mark's text were already in their own way 'gospel': the passion narrative, small collections of logia and parables of the Lord, cycles of miracle stories and apophthegmata. The kerygmatic concept of gospel did not lose its own autonomy, and it was capable of being linked to other literary forms – it suffices here to recall the 'Gospel of Truth', which is a theological meditation (see ch. 7c). One may of course object that the term 'gospel' is employed here in an inauthentic and only analogous sense, and this observation is not completely wrong; nevertheless, one does not thereby dispose of all the problems.

The dialectic between the oral and the written dimensions is inherent in the gospel from the very outset, so we should not be troubled by the fact that the literary recording of one particular stage of transmission and of specific forms could not put a halt to further development; indeed, this was not the writers' intention. The written texts were primarily destined for use in worship and in the community assemblies. In this way, they entered the collective memory of the hearers and could be further transmitted to other persons.

Another factor at work here is the basic distrust of the written dimension in classical antiquity, which already found eloquent expression in Plato. It might be necessary to write things down as an *aide-mémoire*, but this was not intended to suppress the *viva vox*, the 'living voice' which (in Martin Luther's phrase) 'resounds in all the world'. Even as late as the end of the second century, Irenaeus of Lyons, a resolute defender of the collection of four gospels, attributes higher authority to logia of the Lord which may have their origin in (primary or secondary) oral tradition. This is one reason why it makes sense in our context not to overlook the 'scattered words of the Lord'.

By the time of Irenaeus at the latest, however, it is clear that the one gospel in its fourfold version has become part of the canon of the early church. This does not mean that the canon had assumed its definitive form by the year 200; it was still taking shape, and this process must be distinguished from the history of the collection of four gospels and of the authority attributed to this collection. Recent scholarship inclines to the older view that the collection of four gospels with canonical status existed by the mid-second century at the latest. Like the emergence of the canon as a whole, the emergence of this collection is an historical fact which historians must take seriously and attempt to evaluate: the plea that one should ignore the boundaries of the canon as a matter of principle, for the sake of free historical research, is itself in danger of putting forward an ahistorical argument.

For obvious reasons, it is not easy to identify the place of the apocryphal gospels in this many-layered process. Very broad definitions are needed, if one is to include as many of these writings as possible: they are theological texts employed by early Christians (not by 'the early church' as such) with a form, contents or terminology which display affinities to those writings which were included as 'gospels' in the canon. This formulation has the advantage of leaving it open whether these texts were composed independently of the texts which became canonical, or were consciously intended as competitors to these texts; we cannot, however, overlook the fact that the four gospels which were to enter the canon very quickly became points of reference, and that attempts were made to harmonize them, to amplify them with extra material, and to continue their narratives. We see at once that the apocrypha – both the fragments and the texts transmitted in full – like to take the beginning and the close of the gospel narratives (the childhood of Jesus and his passion and resurrection) as their own starting-points. And it is at these borders of the gospel narratives that the apocrypha find the supporting characters whose biographies they then fill out.

Walter Bauer's observations about the motives that led to the creation of such 'amplifying' apocrypha have lost nothing of their validity: 'a pious yearning to know more, a naïve curiosity, delight in colourful pictures and folktales – these are the less harmful motifs of this kind which take hold of the story of Jesus' life' (*Leben Jesu,* p. 521). We need only add that such motifs take hold of other life-stories too – those of Mary his mother, of Joseph his father, of John the Baptist and Joseph of Arimathaea, of Nicodemus, Bartholomew/Nathanael, Pilate and many others.

This curiosity and yearning for more information did not suddenly come to a halt at the end of the patristic period. New apocrypha were composed throughout the entire middle ages, to some extent by reusing and expanding existing material. This literature was meant as edifying reading for Christian believers. One particularly fine example is the Irish church with its rich treasure of mediaeval apocrypha, some of which are still unpublished. There we find otherwise unattested texts such as the lamentations sung by four mothers after the killing of the Holy Innocents, and the passion of the soldier Longinus (cf. McNamara). In this late period, the problem of demarcation takes a very different form: what distinguishes such apocryphal writings from legends about the saints? Should these apocrypha ultimately be classified under the broad genre of hagiography?

One cannot maintain that all the apocrypha produced in the middle ages may still be excused by what Bauer called 'naïve curiosity'. We must reckon with the possibility of conscious forgery precisely in this late period, as we have seen in the cases of the Secret Gospel of Mark and the Gospel of Barnabas. This dark shadow will lie henceforth over the composition of new apocrypha.

From the perspective of an Irenaeus or an Origen, the motivation behind the composition of another group of apocryphal gospels is far from 'harmless'. It has long been known from patristic testimony that Christians with gnostic tendencies created their own standard texts; in particular, Epiphanius of Salamis provides a wealth of detail on this subject. The discoveries at Nag Hammadi have immensely expanded our knowledge of this literature; the most obvious point of intersection between the patristic writers and Nag Hammadi is the Gospel of Thomas, because Greek papyri with fragments of this collection of logia had already been discovered. More characteristic forms in this library are the dialogue gospels, texts containing heavenly revelations, theological treatises of all kind, and not least expositions of the first chapters in Genesis. Sometimes it appears that a deliberate decision has been taken to latch on to the four gospels which were to become canonical, either by using the term 'gospel' itself, or by appealing such figures of authority as Thomas, Philip and John or – gnosticism's great surprise – Mary Magdalene. In future, it will be even more important for students of the apocrypha to study gnosis; similarly, students of gnosis will be more dependent than ever on the study of the apocrypha.

This may be a positive side-effect of the present book, which demonstrates that it is impossible to present the apocrypha without also giving basic information about the Nag Hammadi writings and early Christian gnosis.

When we review the texts studied here, one painful gap is obvious, viz. the absence of authentic Jewish-Christian gospels. The few fragments which we possess (thanks to quotations by patristic writers who sometimes seem not really to have understood them) make this lack even more regrettable – especially since the very fact that these texts did not survive indicates that the separation between Judaism and Christianity was far from a peaceful process. This is why we have consciously chosen to include a Jewish response in the form of an 'anti-gospel'.

This brings us back to Walter Bauer. In addition to his book about 'The life of Jesus in the age of the New Testament apocrypha', which was an admirable achievement for its period and continues to be extremely instructive, he wrote a book entitled 'Orthodoxy and Heresy in Earliest Christianity' in which he affirms that heresy was chronologically anterior to orthodoxy. In support of this thesis, he refers to apocryphal writings such as the Greek Gospel of the Egyptians as the basic text of Gentile Christians in Egypt and the Gospel of the Hebrews as the basic text of the Jewish Christians in that country. Bauer's proposal remains both stimulating and controversial. We have offered a somewhat different assessment of his two principal witnesses (in chs. 3 and 4, above), and the boundaries which he drew cannot be maintained with the same sharpness, since there is in fact no clear-cut chronological sequence in which 'orthodoxy' replaces 'heresy'. Rather, these coexisted for a long time, with oscillating boundaries, so that it is difficult to assign an exact classification to many texts, both those which became 'apocrypha' and those which entered the canon. The controversies about the allegedly gnostic character of John's Gospel are an eloquent reminder of this problem.

Let us then close with an apocryphal text which is highly suitable as a point of integration. Its roots lie in the Jewish sapiential tradition, it has echoes in the synoptic tradition about Jesus, it is attested in the Gospel of the Hebrews and in the Gospel of Thomas, and its basic motif of seeking, finding and resting resonates through many other texts discussed in this book (see Index of Matters and Persons). Last but not least, it is directly related to the secret heart of many apocryphal gospels, viz. the search for the interpretation and significance of the word, work and person of Jesus of Nazareth (EvThom 2):

Let him who seeks continue seeking until he finds.
When he finds, he will become troubled.
When he becomes troubled, he will be astonished.
When he began to be astonished, he will rule.
When he began to rule, he will find rest.

Bibliography

W. Bauer, *Leben Jesu*; W. Bauer, *Rechtgläubigkeit und Ketzerei im
ältesten Christentum* (BHTh 10), Tübingen 1934, 2nd edn. 1964; S.
Byrskog, *Story as History*; D. Dormeyer, *Evangelium als literarische
und theologische Gattung* (EdF 263), Darmstadt 1989; H.
Frankemölle, *Evangelium: Begriff und Gattung. Ein
Forschungsbericht* (SBB 15), Stuttgart 2nd edn. 1994; T. K. Heckel,
Vom Evangelium des Markus zum viergestaltigen Evangelium
(WUNT 120), Tübingen 1999; M. Hengel, *The Four Gospels and the
One Gospel of Jesus Christ: An Investigation of the Collection and
Origin of the Canonical Gospels*, London 2000; M. McNamara, *The
Apocrypha in the Irish Church*, Dublin 1975.

GENERAL BIBLIOGRAPHY

The abbreviations follow S. Schwertner, *Internationales Abkürzungsverzeichnis für Theologie und Grenzgebiete*, Berlin 2nd edn. 1992 (used in the TRE). In the bibliographies for individual sections of this book, works mentioned here are indicated only by the author's name and a shortened title.

1 Sources and translations

C. von Tischendorf, *Evangelia Apocrypha*, Leipzig 2nd edn. 1876, reprint Hildesheim 1966, 1987 (this was for a long time, and remains in some cases, the main means of access to the original texts).

E. Klostermann, *Apocrypha* I (KlT 3), Berlin 3rd edn. 1929; *Apocrypha* II (KlT 8), Berlin 3rd edn. 1929; *Apocrypha* III (KlT 11), Bonn 2nd edn. 1911.

E. Preuschen, *Antilegomena. Die Reste der ausserkanonichen Evangelien und urchristlichen Überlieferungen*, Giessen 2nd edn. 1905.

W. Schneemelcher, *New Testament Apocrypha. Rev. edn.; vol. I: Gospels and Related Writings*, Cambridge 2nd edn. 1991, Eng. trans., ed. R. McL. Wilson, of: *Neutestamentliche Apokryphen*, 5th edn., 1987 (identical with 6th edn. 1990). This is the standard edition in German and English. A new edition is in preparation (see above).

W. Michaelis, *Die apokryphen Schriften zum Neuen Testament* (Sammlung Dieterich 129), Bremen 3rd edn. 1962.

E. Weidinger, *Die Apokryphen. Verborgene Bücher der Bibel*, Aschaffenburg 1985.

J. M. Robinson (ed.), *The Nag Hammadi Library in English*, Leiden 3rd edn. 1988.

K. Dietzfelbinger, *Apokryphe Evangelien aus Nag Hammadi*, Andechs 3rd edn. 1991.

G. Lüdemann and M. Janssen, *Bibel der Häretiker. Die gnostischen Schriften aus Nag Hammadi*, Stuttgart 1997.

A. Schindler, *Apokryphen zum Alten und Neuen Testament* (Manesse Bibliothek der Weltliteratur), Zurich 1998.

K. Berger and C. Nord, *Das Neue Testament und frühchristliche Schriften*, Frankfurt a. M. and Leipzig 1999 (consistently maintains an early dating which I find untenable).

K. Ceming and J. Werlitz, *Die verbotenen Evangelien. Apokryphe Schriften*, Aschaffenburg 1999.

D. Lührmann, *Fragmente apokryph gewordener Evangelien in griechischer und lateinischer Sprache* (MThSt 59), Marburg 2000.

U. K. Plisch, *Verborgene Worte Jesu – verworfene Evangelien. Apokryphe Schriften des frühen Christentums*, Stuttgart 2000.

J. K. Elliott, *Apocryphal New Testament: A Collection of Apocryphal Christian Literature in an English Translation,* Oxford 1993 (most recent edition of a standard work in English).

R. J. Miller, *The Complete Gospels. Annotated Scholars Version,* San Francisco 3rd edn. 1994.

F. Bovon and P. Geoltrain, *Ecrits apocryphes chrétiens* I (Bibliothèque de la Pléïade), Paris 1997 (leading edition in French).

A. de Santos Otero, *Los Evangelios Apócrifos* (BAC 148), Madrid 8th edn. 1993 (important because it often offers the original texts in Greek and Latin as well as translations).

M. Erbetta, *Gli apocrifi del nuovo testamento* I,1: *Scritti affini ai vangeli* ..., Turin 1975; I,2: *Infanzia e passione di Cristo* ..., Turin 1981.

L. Moraldi, *Apocrifi del Nuovo Testamento* I: *Vangeli,* Casale Monferrato 2nd edn. 1996.

H. M. Schenke, H. G. Bethge, U. U. Kaiser (eds.), *Nag Hammadi Deutsch* I: NHC I 1–V 1 (GCS.NF 8), Berlin and New York 2001.

J. R. Porter, *The Lost Bible. Forgotten Scriptures Revealed,* Chicago 2001.

2 Bibliographies

M. Geerard, *Clavis Apocryphorum Novi Testamenti* (CChr.SA), Brepols 1992.

J. H. Charlesworth, *The New Testament Apocrypha and Pseudepigrapha: A Guide to Publications, with Excurses on Apocalypses* (ATLA Bibliography Series 17), Metuchen, N.J. 1987.

3 Scholarly works on the apocrypha

W. Bauer, *Das Leben Jesu im Zeitalter der neutestamentlichen Apokryphen,* Tübingen 1909, reprint Darmstadt 1967.

K. Beyschlag, *Die verborgene Überlieferung von Christus* (GTBS 136), Munich 1969.

R. Cameron, *The Other Gospels: Non-Canonical Gospel Texts,* Philadelphia 1982.

R. Cameron (ed.). *The Apocryphal Jesus and Christian Origins* (= *Semeia* 49), Atlanta, Ga. 1990.

J. D. Crossan, *Four Other Gospels. Shadows on the Contours of Canon,* Minneapolis 1985.

P. Jenkins, *Hidden Gospels: How the Search for Jesus Lost Its Way,* New York 2001.

J. Jeremias, *Unbekannte Jesusworte,* Gütersloh 3rd edn. 1963.

J. D. Kaestli and D. Marguerat (eds.), *Le mystère apocryphe. Introduction à une littérature méconnue* (Essais bibliques 26), Geneva 1995.

A. J. F. Klijn, *Jewish-Christian Gospel Tradition* (SVigChr 17), Leiden 1973.

W. G. Morris, *Hidden Sayings of Jesus. Words Attributed to Jesus Outside the Four Gospels*, London 1997.

F. Neirynck, 'The Apocryphal Gospels and the Gospel of Mark', in: Idem, *Evangelica* II: *1982–1991, Collected Essays* (BEThL 99), Louvain 1991, 715–72.

A. Piñero, *Der geheime Jesus. Sein Leben nach den apokryphen Evangelien*, Düsseldorf 1997.

W. Rebell, *Neutestamentliche Apokryphen und Apostolische Väter*, Munich 1992.

A. Resch, *Agrapha. Ausserkanonische Schriftfragmente* (TU 30), Leipzig 1889, 2nd edn. 1906, reprint Darmstadt 1974.

K. L. Schmidt, *Kanonische und apokryphe Evangelien und Apostelgeschichten* (AThANT 5), Basle 1944.

4 Further secondary literature

S. Byrskog, *Story as History – History as Story. The Gospel Tradition in the Context of Ancient Oral History* (WUNT 123), Tübingen 2000.

S. Döpp and W. Geerlings, *Lexikon der antiken christlichen Literatur*, Freiburg i. Br. 2nd edn. 1999 (brief, informative articles on almost all the texts discussed in the present book).

J. Hartenstein, *Die zweite Lehre. Erscheinungen des Auferstandenen als Rahmenerzählungen früchristlicher Dialoge* (TU 146), Berlin 2000.

H. Koester, *Ancient Christian Gospels: Their History and Development*, Philadelphia 1990.

S. C. Mimouni, *Le judéo-christianisme ancien. Essai historique*, Paris 1998.

S. Petersen, *'Zerstört die Werke der Weiblichkeit!' Maria Magdalena, Salome und andere Jüngerinnen Jesu in christlich-gnostischen Schriften* (NHS 48), Leiden 1999.

P. Vielhauer, *Geschichte der urchristlichen Literatur. Einleitung in das Neue Testament, die Apokryphen und die Apostolischen Väter* (GLB), Berlin 1975.

INDEX OF SELECTED TEXTS

Old Testament

Genesis

1:27f., 58, 116, 172
2:16f., 57
2:25, 58, 117
3:16, 56, 57
19:17, 16
49:11, 29

Leviticus

19:18, 45–46

Numbers

5:21f., 69
15:32–36, 9

Deuteronomy

18:20, 214–15, 219
21:21–23, 84, 94, 217

Psalms

2:7, 52–53, 214
22:2, 85
24:7, 95
118:22f., 118

Isaiah

1:3, 79
11:2, 41
57:19, 13

Jeremiah

8:4, 19

Ezekiel

33:20, 14

Habakkuk

3:2 LXX, 79

Sirach

6:27f., 39–40, 122
24:7, 41

Wisdom

7:27, 41

New Testament

Matthew

2:1–12, 50–51
3:14f., 46, 52
4:8, 40
5:22, 48
6:33, 16
7:7, 39
12:9–14, 47, 49
12:40, 47
18:20, 112
18:21f., 47, 48
19:16–24, 44–46
21:1–3, 49
27:24f., 92
27:52f., 95–97
27:65, 47, 86

Mark

1:40–44, 24, 92
4:1–20, 113
5:25–34, 92, 103, 154, 155
6:4, 118
6:35–44, 154
8:27–30, 114
9:49, 15
10:17f., 35, 45
10:34f., 34
12:1–11, 118
12:13–17, 24

13:21f., 111, 162
14:38, 15
14:51, 34–35
16:9–20, 10, 82, 93
16:14 W, 10–11

Luke

1:35, 101, 128
2:41–52, 73, 137
4:23f., 118
6:5 D, 9–10
12:49, 15
17:20–23, 111, 162–63
18:1, 15
22:15, 51–52
23:34, 49
23:43, 85, 96
23:46, 85, 93
24:39, 155

John

1:47–51, 99, 100, 103
7:53–8:11, 19, 24, 40, 41
10:30–32, 23, 29
14:9, 17, 124
14:22, 110
18:16, 50
19:13, 84
19:25, 129
19:26f., 203
19:34f., 31
20:17f., 30, 162, 164

Acts

14:22, 16
20:33–35, 8

1 Corinthians

2:9, 115
10:23, 10
11:18f., 14
14:34f., 8

2 Corinthians

12:9, 8

Galatians

3:27f., 58, 126

1 Thessalonians

4:15–17, 9
5:21, 17

2 Timothy

2:17f., 130

James

1:12f., 16

2 Peter

1:16–18, 82

1 John

1:1–3, 154, 155

Jewish writings

Syriac Baruch

29:5, 13

Christian apocrypha

Acts of Peter

10, 17

Book of Bartholomew

1:2, 102
2:2, 102
8:1, 102–103
10:3, 103
20:1, 103

Epistula Apostolorum

1, 153
2, 153–54, 159
5, 154–55, 159
11f., 155
14, 155–56, 159
17, 152, 156, 159
21–25, 156
31, 157
33, 157
43, 157–58
51, 159

Gospel of Nicodemus

Prologue, 89–90
1:1–6, 91
2:1–5, 91
9:1–5, 92
11:1–3, 93
13:1–3, 93
15:1–6, 94
16:1–8, 94
17:1f., 95
20:1–3, 95
21:1–3, 95

Gospel of Peter

1:1f., 84
2:3–5, 83, 84
3:7, 84
4:10, 85
4:13f., 85
5:19, 85
7:26, 83, 86
8:30–33, 86
10:39–42, 86
11:44–49, 86–87
12:50–54, 87
14:60, 83, 87

Infancy Gospel of Thomas

2:1–5, 18, 74, 99, 215
4:1, 74, 77
6:4, 74–75
9:1–3, 75
10:2, 75

11:1f., 75
12:1f., 75
13:1f., 75
14:1f., 75–77
15:1–4, 76
16:1f., 76
18:1f., 76
19:4, 76

Protevangelium

4:1f., 67
4:4, 67
6:1–3, 67–68
13:1, 69
14:1f., 69
17:1f., 70, 72
18:2, 70
19:1–3, 70
19:2, 70, 71
22:2, 71
23:3, 71
24:2, 71
25:1, 71

Ps.-Clement

Hom. 2.51.1, 17

Ps.-Matthew

3:2, 79
13:3, 79
14:1, 79

Questions of Bartholomew

2:4, 100
2:15–21, 100–101
4:12–14, 101

Christian papyri

PBerlin 11710, 22

PBerol 22220, 28–32

PCairo 10735, 22

PEg 2, 23–26

PKöln 255, 23

PMerton 51, 22

POxy
1, 107–108, 112, 119
210, 22
654, 38, 107–108, 110,
    111
655, 107–108, 120
840, 7, 26–27
1081, 147
1224, 13, 22
2949, 83
3525, 160, 163
4009, 83
PRyl 463, 160, 166
PVindob G 2325, 22, 83

Apostolic fathers

Barnabas

7:11, 12

1 Clement

13:2, 11

2 Clement

4:5, 49
12:2, 58

Church fathers

Aphrahat

Dem. 4.16, 14

Clement of Alexandria

Ex. Theod.
2.2, 16
78.2, 150
Stromateis
1.158.2, 16
2.45.4, 206
2.45.5, 38
3.45.3, 56
3.63.1, 56

3.66.1f., 57
3.92.2–93.1, 58
5.96.3, 38

Epiphanius of Salamis

Panarion (Adversus haereses)

26.3.1, 207
26.13.2f., 123
30.13.2f., 51–54
30.13.4f., 51
30.13.7f., 52–53
30.22.4f., 51–52
78.23.8, 192

Eusebius

Historia Ecclesiastica

4.22.8, 43
5.10.3, 38
6.12.1–6, 82–83

Hippolytus

Refutatio

5.7.20, 107

Irenaeus of Lyons

Adversus haereses

1.20.1, 74
1.29.1–4, 169
1.31.1, 207
3.11.9, 135
5.33.3f., 12–13

Jerome

Adv. Pelag. 3.2, 36, 46, 47
In Is. 11.2, 41
In Mt. 6.11, 47
In Mt. 12.13, 47
Vir. 3.2, 42

Justin

1st Apology
35.9, 90
Dialogue
35.3, 13–14
47.5, 14

Origen

In Jer. 3.3, 15
In Mt. 15.14 (Latin),
    44–46
In Joh. 2.12, 40

Tertullian

Apol. 21.24, 90
De baptismo 20.2, 15

Nag Hammadi writings

AJ (BG)

19,30–21,6, 170–71
22,10–16, 171
23,19–24,6, 171
51,15–20, 172–73
55,9–13, 173
76,7–15, 174

Dial

1, 185–86
15f., 186
21–23, 186–87
35f., 187–88
37, 188
49–53, 188–89
84f., 189
89–94, 189–90

EvEg

41,7–12, 60
51,5–14, 61
58,23–59,4, 61
63,10–13, 61
64,1–18, 61–62
69,9–22, 61

EvMar

7,1–9, 161
7,10–20, 161–62
7,20–22, 162
8,12–9,5, 162–63
9,5–10,8, 163–64
10,9–16, 164
10,16–22, 164–65
15,1–22, 165
16,1–17,9, 165–66
17,10–18,5, 166–67
18,6–21, 167

EvPhil

1, 124–25
4, 125
6, 125
11, 127
14, 127
17, 125, 128–29, 133
21, 129–30
23, 130–31
26, 130, 133
29, 124
32, 129, 134
43, 131
48, 125–26
49, 126
50, 127–28
51, 126–27
52, 126
53, 124, 133
54, 80, 123, 131
65, 134
67, 127, 132
68, 132
72, 123, 131, 133–34
76, 132–33
82, 132, 133
90, 130
91, 124, 129
92, 129
93, 128
95, 131–32
99, 128

EvThom

1, 109–110
2, 38, 107, 109, 110–11,
    163, 188
3, 111, 162
4, 107
6, 112–113
7, 38, 113, 127
9, 113–14
11, 112
13, 114–15
17, 115
22, 58, 111, 115–16, 120,
    123
23, 112
28, 109, 116–17
30, 112, 119
31, 107, 117–18
37, 58, 109, 117
39, 120
42, 18, 113
50, 109, 117
58, 111
65f., 109, 118
77, 107, 118–19
90, 111
97f., 107, 119
108, 109, 115
113, 111–112
114, 116, 120–21, 190

EvVer

16,31–17,4, 136
16,31–35, 106
18,21–31, 137
19,17–34, 137–38
20,10–28, 138
22,2–15, 138
25,25–26,15, 139
29,8–28, 139–40
30,13–16, 140
31,35–32,22, 140
33,1–9, 140
36,19–34, 141
38,7–17141–42
42,11–38, 142

LibThom

138,1–10, 178
138,39–139,16, 179
139,24–42, 180
140,21–31, 180–81
141,10f., 181
141,41–142,2, 182
142,19–143,5, 182–83
143,11–19, 183

SJC (NHC)

91,10–22, 148
94,5–95,18, 148
97,19–24, 148–49
101,9–16, 149
107,11–25, 149–50
117,8–21, 150–51
119,8–17, 151

**Graeco-Roman
writers**

Diogenes Laertius

Vit. Phil. 6.37, 19

Homeric Hymns

4.45f., 77

Plato

Republic 588B-589B, 106,
    113

Thucydides

2.97.4, 8

INDEX OF MATTERS AND PERSONS

Acts of Apostles, 17, 19, 95, 104, 106, 123, 146, 160, 174, 205, 217
Adam(as), 59, 61, 69, 95, 100, 127, 171–73
Agrapha, 6–21
Amplification, 64
Andrew, 29, 87, 166–67, 196, 205
Anointing, 94, 126, 129, 131–32, 134, 141, 143
Apocalypses, 99, 105–106, 146, 188
Apocrypha/apocryphal, 1–3, 6–7, 18, 40, 64, 78, 82, 106, 157, 159, 175, 192, 204, 211, 219, 221–24
Apostle, 30, 53, 128, 134, 150, 152–54, 156–57, 178, 217
Apostolic fathers, 1, 205
Ascension (of Jesus or others), 29–30, 85, 94, 117, 122, 123, 138, 145, 146, 151, 159, 162, 165–66, 176, 180, 186, 189, 193, 203, 215–17

Baptism of Jesus, 41–42, 46–47, 52–54
Barbelo, 169, 171
Barnabas (Gospel), 205, 208–10, 223
Bartholomew, 38, 99–104, 149, 197, 205, 223
Beatitude, 29, 107, 109, 111, 140, 181, 183
Beloved disciple, 50, 129, 167–68
Bridal chamber, 132–33, 158, 188, 191

Canon/canonical, 2–3, 6, 82, 88, 94, 106, 121–22, 211, 222–24
Choral conclusion, 73, 76
Crucifixion, 31–32, 64, 85, 88, 92–93, 100, 102, 137–38, 143, 155, 158–59, 195, 210

Decretum Gelasianum, 2–5, 99, 194, 205, 210
Descent to hell, 86, 90, 94–96
Dialogue, 10–11, 22, 31, 56–57, 82, 106, 123, 145–91, 223
Docetism, 32, 53, 72, 77, 80, 82, 85, 88, 133, 139, 154

Encratism, 55–58, 63
Eucharist, 8, 31, 101, 103, 104, 130–34, 156

Eve, 66, 69, 102, 128, 173, 207

Farewell discourses, 162, 203
Freer logion, 10–11

Gethsemane, 15–16, 27, 29, 30, 32
Gnosis/gnostic, 10, 16, 29, 32, 39, 42, 54, 58, 74, 77, 105, 108–109, 114, 116–17, 122, 123, 124, 128, 129, 134, 135–36, 138, 139, 143, 145–46, 147, 150, 153–54, 158, 159, 160, 162, 166, 169, 171, 174–75, 178, 184, 188, 190–91, 207, 209, 223–24
Golden Rule, 11
Gospel, 1–3, 59–60, 63, 64, 106, 123, 135, 146, 170, 174–75, 211, 221–22

James, 42–43, 65, 71–72
Jewish Christianity, 36–54, 114, 209, 219, 224
John, apostle and evangelist, 50, 100, 170–71, 193–97, 203, 218, 223
John the Baptist, 46, 51–52, 64, 65, 68, 71, 81, 217, 221, 223
Joseph, father of Jesus, 50–51, 65–70, 74–76, 80–81, 91, 129, 212–214, 223
Joseph of Arimathaea, 50, 84, 88, 93–94, 97, 98, 102, 223
Judas Iscariot, 13, 31, 80, 87, 102, 207–208, 215, 216

Koran, 17–19, 209

Levi, 87, 131, 167–68

Mark, 64, 65, 83, 196–97, 203, 221
Mary Magdalene, 30, 50, 87, 102, 120, 129, 149–51, 160–68, 186–90, 223
Mary, mother of Jesus, 50, 64–72, 76, 78–80, 91, 100–101, 103, 128, 129, 160, 192–204, 212–214, 223
Matthew, 53, 114, 148–49, 178, 186, 190, 197
Miracle, 18, 25, 47, 49, 71, 73–76, 79–80, 91, 92, 98, 118, 154, 198–200, 202, 209, 214–16

Nag Hammadi, 1, 3, 15, 59, 63, 105–106, 123, 135, 145, 160, 223–24

Nathanael, 99, 103, 153–54, 223
Nicodemus, 88–89, 92, 93, 97, 223

Oral dimension, 3, 25, 58, 121–22, 221

Papias, 12–13, 36, 40
Parables, 107, 109, 113–14, 119,
    124–26, 134, 138, 139, 157–58, 179
Paul, 8–9, 14, 115, 156–57, 196–97,
    203, 208, 210, 218
Peter, 83, 87, 100–102, 114, 120,
    161–67, 196, 218
Philip, 124, 129–30, 148, 170, 196, 223
Pilate, 48, 84, 86–87, 88–93, 97–98,
    203, 223
Prophecy/prophet, 9, 14, 107, 117–18,
    209, 214–15

Rest/place of rest, 111, 117, 137–38,
    142, 143, 151, 166, 181, 182, 183,
    185, 186, 189, 191, 224

Sabbath, 9–10, 20, 36, 47, 74, 213
Salome, 34, 56–58, 66, 70, 102, 190
Seeking and finding, 38–40, 109–10,
    111, 122, 137, 143, 181, 185, 186,
    188, 191, 206, 224
Seth, 59–63, 95, 173
Simeon, 71, 94–95, 97
Sophia, 129, 133, 137, 147–150, 172,
    184
Summons to wake up, 109, 117, 138,
    140, 148–49

Thomas, 70, 73, 74, 104, 108, 110,
    114–15, 148, 150, 170, 176–78, 186,
    196–97, 223
To Ioudaïkon, 46, 48–49
Transfiguration, 30, 32, 40, 82

Woe, cry of, 26, 107, 109, 183

INDEX OF MODERN SCHOLARS

Asin y Palacios, M., 6, 18, 21
Attridge, H.W., 136, 143

Baars, W., 78
Bammel, E., 220
Bauer, W., 223, 224, 225, 226
Bell, H.I., 23, 26
Berger, K., 7, 8, 21, 226
Bernabé Pons, L.F., 210
Bertrand, D.A., 27, 54
Bethge, H.D., 121, 191, 226
Beyers, R., 80, 81
Beyschlag, K., 88, 226
Blatz, B., 121, 168, 191, 208
Böhlig, A., 63
Boer, E. De, 168
Bovon, F., 27, 64, 226
Brown, R., 88
Brown, S.G., 35
Byrskog, S., 3, 5, 122, 225, 227

Cameron, R., 227
Carleton Paget, J., 37
Ceming, K., 97, 226
Charlesworth, J.H., 226
Cherix, P., 104
Cirillo, L., 210
Clayton, M., 194, 204
Conick, A.D. de, 122
Crossan, J.D., 2, 84, 87, 88, 227
Cullmann, O., 72, 77, 78, 81

Demandt, A., 98
Dietzfelbinger, K., 107, 225
Di Segni, R., 211, 220
Dobschütz, E. von, 3, 205, 208
Döpp, S., 227
Dormeyer, D., 225
Duensing, H., 153, 160

Elliott, J.K., 97, 98, 99, 104, 204, 208, 226
Emmel, S., 27, 32, 185, 191
Erbetta, M., 226
Esbroeck, M. van, 194, 204

Fieger, M., 121
Fletcher, J.E., 210
Frankemölle, H., 225

Franzmann, M., 107
Frémaux, M., 210
Frey, J., 10, 32, 51
Fuchs, A., 88

Geerard, M., 226
Geerlings, W., 227
Geoltrain, P., 226
Gijsel, J., 78, 81
Gounelle, R., 97
Gronewald, M., 23, 26
Guistolisi, E., 210

Haibach-Reinisch, M., 204
Hartenstein, J., 146, 152, 158, 160, 168, 175, 227
Heckel, T.K., 225
Hedrick, C.W., 32
Heldermann, J., 78, 137, 143
Hengel, M., 225
Hennecke, E., 1
Hills, J.V., 158, 160
Hock, R.F., 64, 72, 78
Hörmann, W., 107
Hofius, O., 7, 21
Hornschuh, M., 160
Howard, G., 54

Isenberg, W.W., 134
Izydorczyk, Z., 97

Janssen, M., 63, 107, 143, 152, 226
Jenkins, 227
Jeremias, J., 7, 21, 23, 25, 27, 227
Jones, 168

Käser, W., 10
Kaestli, J.D., 102, 104, 227
Kaiser, U.U., 226
Karawidopulos, J., 19
King, K.L., 168
Klauck, H.J., 63, 134, 208, 220
Klijn, A.J.F., 37, 42, 43, 49, 50, 51, 54, 227
Klostermann, E., 225
Koester, H., 1, 5, 23, 146, 185, 191, 227
Kollmann, B., 210
Krause, M., 143
Krauss, S., 218, 219

Layton, B., 107, 136, 143
Leirvik, 210
Liebenberg, J., 121
Linges, S.M., 210
Lüdemann, G., 63, 107, 143, 152, 226
Lührmann, D., 2, 5, 23, 25, 27, 35, 37, 40, 43, 54, 59, 83, 88, 121, 152, 168, 206, 208, 226

MacRae, G.W., 143
Manns, F., 204
Mara, M.G., 88
Marguerat, D., 227
Marjanen, A., 191
Markschies, C., 1, 5, 136, 144
Maurer, C., 88
Mayeda, G., 26
McGuire, A., 107
McNamara, M., 225
Merkel, H., 35
Meyer, A., 40
Meyer, M.W., 35
Michaelis, W., 97, 225
Miller, R.J., 2, 5, 226
Mimouni, S.C., 37, 43, 51, 54, 192, 194, 204, 227
Mirecki, P.A., 28, 32
Moraldi, L., 226
Morenz, S., 81
Morris, W.G., 21, 227
Müller, C.D.G., 153, 159

Nagel, 32
Neirynck, F., 227
Nicklas, T., 10, 88
Nord, C., 7, 8, 21, 226

Onuki, T., 175
Oudenrijn, M.A. van den, 98

Parrott, D.M., 152
Pérès, J.N., 160
Perkins, P., 146
Petersen, S., 55, 57, 59, 146, 168, 191, 227
Piñero, A., 227
Plisch, U.K., 28, 32, 63, 134, 168, 184, 191, 226
Porter, J.R., 226
Preuschen, E., 225
Puech, H.C., 168, 208

Ragg, L. and L., 210
Rebell, W., 2, 5, 107, 227

Reinink, G., 37
Resch, A., 6, 7, 8, 14, 21, 54, 227
Rizzardi, G., 210
Robinson, J.M., 107, 225
Rudolph, K., 147

Santos Otero, A. de, 23, 78, 208, 226
Scheidwiler, F., 97, 98, 104
Schenke, H.M., 32, 123–24, 126, 134, 143, 152, 168, 175, 177, 184, 226
Schindler, A., 226
Schirrmacher, C., 210
Schlichting, G., 212, 213, 219
Schmidt, C., 153, 157, 159
Schmidt, K.L., 227
Schmidt, P.L., 37
Schneemelcher, W., 1, 23, 25, 27, 59, 88, 98, 104, 225
Schneider, G., 64, 72, 77, 78, 80, 81
Scholten, C., 184
Schröter, J., 122
Shoemaker, 204
Skeat, T.C., 23, 26
Smid, H.R., 72
Sox, D., 210
Smith, M., 32–33, 35
Strecker, G., 37, 43, 51, 54
Stroker, W.D., 7, 21
Strycker, E. De, 72

Till, W.C., 152, 168, 175
Tischendorf, C. von, 73, 78, 81, 97, 194, 204, 225
Turner, J.D., 107, 177, 184
Turner, M.L., 124, 135

Uro, R., 122

Vaganay, L., 88
Valantasis, R., 121
Vielhauer, P., 37, 43, 51, 54, 59, 77, 78, 227

Waitz, H., 42–43
Wajnberg, I., 153, 159
Waldstein, M., 175
Weidinger, E., 225
Werlitz, J., 97, 226
Williams, M.A., 175
Wisse, F., 63, 175

Yuseff, M.A., 210

Zöckler, T., 122